REVISITING OUR CONSTITUTION

REVISITING OUR CONSTITUTION

Editors

Ram Bahadur Rai

Dr. Mahesh Chandra Sharma

PRABHAT PRAKASHAN

RESEARCH & DEVELOPMENT FOUNDATION FOR INTEGRAL HUMANISM

Published by
PRABHAT PRAKASHAN PVT. LTD.
4/19 Asaf Ali Road,
New Delhi-110 002 (INDIA)
e-mail: prabhatbooks@gmail.com

ISBN 978-93-5322-752-4
REVISITING OUR CONSTITUTION
Ed. Shri Ram Bahadur Rai & Dr. Mahesh Chandra Sharma

Edition
2025

Price
₹ 700.00 (Rupees Seven Hundred only)

Printed at
R-Tech Offset Printers, Delhi

Dedicated to
the holy memory of
Babu Jayaprakash Narayan,
a stalwart of the people's policy and
partyless democracy

Dr. Ambedkar to Sheikh Abdullah on Article 370

"You wish India should protect your borders, she should build roads in your area, she should supply you foodgrains and Kashmir should get equal status in India. But Government of India should have only limited powers and Indian people should have no rights in Kashmir. To give consent to this proposal would be a treacherous thing against the interests of India and I as the Law Minister of India, will never do it. I can not betray the interests of my country."

—Dr. S.N. Busi

Dr. B.R. Ambedkar
Framing of the Indian Constitution
Vol 4 (-6) Page No. 472
Publisher A.V.A. Mumbai 2016

Preface

In India, the concept of an ideal state (Dharma Rajya) is not being envisioned as a theocratic state. In Indian linguistics, the nearest translation to the term 'dharma rajya' in western terminology would be a constitutional state. India has never accepted the concept of wilful monarchies. The Indian hypothesis of a monarch also differs from the western premise of feudalism or the feudal system. There should be a holistic study on the subject. These days, in our academic world, while studying political science, we relate the Indian concept of the monarch with western feudalism.

In India, the canopy covering the concept of dharma (religious duty) is very vast. One of its meanings bears a close relationship with the term 'vidhi' (law). A long Indian tradition of the aeonian interpretations of the Sanatan dharma (eternal religion) is also germane to history; it is imperative that it should also be researched and studied. The black shadows of the middle ages which lie between ancient and modern times shroud our past and our present. It is this darkness which has pushed us onto western path. The decolonisation of our people has become a pre-condition to understanding of affirmative Indianness. Political scientists categorise periods in eras. The challenge of our times is how we can conduct our studies with integrity to our Indianness after we decolonize ourselves.

India has its own character, its own culture and it also has its own distortions. We can only understand our distortions and character under the torchlight of our culture.

It is under this light that we have to create our present times. Our current Constitution ascertains the religion of our state. How Indian or un-Indian is this Constitution, basically? The process of the formation of this constitution should be put to test on the basis of logic and its past and present (history) should be studied. This is why this book – Revisiting Our Constitution.

This book is a collection of well-researched essays published in two volumes that brainstorm about the Constitution. Academic endeavours have been made in this book to examine and perceive the Constitution from the perspective of 'Ram Rajya' (Ideal state). A single-government system emerges from the constitution. Ram Rajya has been considered the supreme ideal of any government system in India. Mahatma Gandhi had also stated that Ram Rajya was the goal of Independent India. On the sesquicentennial year of Gandhi, 'Manthan' has taken up a responsibility and that is a review of the journey of India's Constitution. This effort is not as simple and easy as is believed. In actual fact, it is difficult, complex. If one passes through a blind tunnel and there is no hope for any light for miles on end, then is a review possible? This comparison is not imaginary. The realism of Indian politics can be glimpsed in it. The entire extent of this reality is occasionally somewhat impossible to grasp. Crucial and trivial controversies that have been raised regarding the Constitution have arisen because of this. The belief that the Constitution is a well-considered script for a future vision far exceeds the conviction regarding its relationship with the rise and fall of history. It will be a rare person who will make a claim that he has seen history the way Arjun saw Krishna's divine form in the battle of Kurukshetra. Therefore, how can this book of 'Manthan's' essays claim that readers will get a vast view of the freedom movement in the journey of the Constitution? Making such a claim would be inappropriate. But, what can be more inappropriate than not attempting a review?

The dividing line between apposite and unsuitable is a creation of circumstances. If the atmosphere is positive and there is an environment of acceptance, then that period of history which has been ignored for political reasons can be understood from a fresh angle through a review. Its inception takes place in the year 1937. It will be easy to understand the period through the essays in the book. It will only help in strengthening the Constitution. Those who do not understand this will regard the review as retrogressive. A pertinent change is not regressive. It is a periodic reform. There are several such moments during the arguments in the Constituent Assembly, and statements made by its erudite members that have remained challenging issues. Should they be allowed to remain riddles? Anyone would say 'no'. This is also a reason why a review is necessary. Why had Jawaharlal Nehru called the Government of India Act, 1935 an instrument of slavery? Why was it made the core foundation of the Constitution? There must be a clarification in this regard. This is only possible when those circumstances are relooked, understood and deliberated upon again for a holistic solution. Similarly, why is there such a deep shadow and imprint of colonialism in the Constitution of India? Its profound influence is intact. Why did the advisor of the Constituent Assembly, Sir Benegal Narsing Rau go around the globe to take the 'good points' from other Constitutions in the same way as Kartikeya had once done? But, he remained far from his goal. Dr. Raghubir had earmarked this error in his own fashion quite accurately in the Constituent Assembly. He had asked why he had forgotten the Ganesh circumambulation (Parikrama). This is an independent topic for research. What can be said is that the advisor of the constituent assembly had not even looked towards the Indian system of governance. Was this a mere coincidence?

An endeavour in this direction is necessary. This book is a reminder to this end. Attempts to raise several such unsolved questions have been made in this book so that they help in correcting these errors. This is enough. It strikes the mind that when an individual makes a mistake and ponders over ways to correct it, similarly, a government and society too can do the same. This is the responsibility of an alert society. Where, when and how many mistakes were made? It is not our job to put forward examples in this regard. Our work is to recognise the symptoms. Because of its comparison to Ram Rajya, there is a context that also affects the Constitution of India. It is related to the Ramayana. Bali's killing was extremely necessary in the search of Sita. It was the first condition for a positive attempt in the search for Sita. Bali had received a boon. He was successful in absorbing half the strength of anyone who faced him. There is a Bali sitting over India's Constitution, too– which is a symbol of the colonial system. The sad part is that the Constitution has given it a secure place within its casing. Until it is recognised and killed, there can neither be a search for the symbol of India's soul, Sita and nor can Ram Rajya be established once again.

This book differs in its attempt from legal experts. It has

freshness. There has been an effort to introduce all those conundrums which are hitherto untouched or unsolved. There has been a question mark on the Constitution of India from day one. This has its own history. Are these questions there because of an ignorance of the Constitution? If so, then this book opens the windows and doors of a Constitution which has satirically been described a 'paradise for lawyers'. It creates the possibility for vital air. From my experience, I can say that even big lawyers are ignorant about the Constitution because it is extremely complex. How can it become comprehensible? Anyone desirous of solving this question will find more than sufficient material in this book. The complexity of the Constitution is another reason why it could not become a beloved text for the ordinary citizen. The way a citizen believes in his religious book, the Constitution should be the religious text of the system of governance. Until this does not happen, deliberations should continue. Any discussion is only germane and successful when it addresses the core question which is how can the fundamental issue regarding the Constitution of India be recognised for discussions? The answer to this is extremely simple. The goal of freedom was clear when the Constitution was being envisioned. The rebuilding of freedom and the nation are two goals that are inherent in the Indian Constitution. Have these been achieved? This is the basic question.

It has a history. It can be found in the labyrinths of Constitutionalism. Nobody can enter and stay in this maze without deep astonishment. What is surprising is how much the attachment for the Constitution has fooled our national actors. Did they ever experience this? The British viewed the Constitution and used it as a beneficial instrument for colonialism. What has not been contextualised here is how successful they have been. The Congress leadership regarded the Constitution as a beacon of freedom and understood the path of freedom from subservience. Mahatma Gandhi, in his long essay in 1939, said that Constitution was only one of the paths. Constitutionalism also gave Jinnah an approach and helped him give shape to his dream of Pakistan. The period of the Indian freedom struggle is full of the magic of Constitutionalism. We will call it the miracle of Constitutionalism that our national players took the risk of partition and yet did not abandon the path of the Constitution. They kept advancing. In the end they made the Constitution. It exists today and is waiting to be developed, although it has been amended several times. The Constitution is waiting to be refined just the way Ahilya waited after she turned to stone. Another name for refinement is sophistication. Pandit Deendayal Upadhyaya advised that the Constitution should be accepted when there was a dilemma regarding what should be done. He gave the mantra – a prize for refinement. The principles of democracy, fundamental rights and equal opportunity in the Indian Constitution were born on Indian soil. That is why, they have become fruit-bearing trees. Even then, they must be pruned and wherever the ruins of colonialism are found, they must be swept away.

Aiming at a single goal, while underscoring the difference of opinion, the basic texts of five speeches in the Constituent Assembly have been compiled in this book. Pandit Jawaharlal Nehru plays the greatest role in giving final shape to the current Constitution. His speech, in this context, is the most important. Babu Rajendra Prasad was not only the Chairman of the Constituent assembly. He was a political leader dedicated to Gandhian thought. His speech is educational from this perspective. Rajendra Babu and Jawaharlalji are among the biggest leaders of the Congress of that period.

Dr. Radhakrishnan is mainly a philosopher and academic talent and Acharya Raghubir is also an expert in Indology and a linguist. Both these speeches break the compulsions and boundaries of colonialism. The fifth speech is very important because he was never a Congress supporter, but was, in fact, a staunch opponent of the party. It is indicative of the intelligence and liberalism of the leadership of the time in India that Wise Man (Pragyapurush) Dr. Bhimrao Ramji Ambedkar was chosen as the Chairman of the drafting committee of the Constituent Assembly. Because of this role of his, he is also known as the creator of the Constitution.

But this statement is hyperbolic and does not even do justice to Dr. Ambedkar. Here his historic speech is especially worth delineating.

This was a difficult period for the Rashtriya Swayamsevak Sangh. The bi-nationalist partition of India had wounded the leadership and volunteers of the Sangh. Rescuing supporters of undivided India (Akhand Bharat) from bi-nationalist, secessionist and violent communal attacks had become its priority. We had not even emerged from the tragedy of partition when a mad man killed

Mahatma Gandhi. The Sangh fell prey to malefic politics and was banned. We have nevertheless presented Guruji (M.S. Golwalkar) and Mr. Deendayal Upadhyaya's thoughts during contemporary discussions at the time in the form of an essay in this book. The Sangh is a fierce opponent of the colonial background of the Constitution.

An intelligent lesson has been received from this book. In it, the collected essays narrate an interesting tale of the journey to release the imprisoned Constitution from the clutches of the Constitutional and legal experts posing as its priests and worshippers, from which anyone can glean two things – first that the Constitution itself has become a problem. We can also say that the main source of the problems that we face today is the Constitution. When, instead of being a solution, the Constitution becomes something else, then it is called an incomprehensible riddle. Such situations occur more often when certain things are accepted. Even if they are without head or tail and have no basis, whatever becomes sacrificed in the fire of its foundation cannot possibly be gold, whatever else it may be. This is why acceptance is advised against. Whoever adopts a method of knowing before accepting, examining before knowing, accepts only what he understands. This method which seems simple enough while being heard calls out each moment to stay alert. Whoever hears this call with his heart and examines it with his mind will become an objective citizen, that is someone who can see things holistically. It is the presentation of this voice and objective understanding that has been attempted here. It can be successful with your active support. The beginning is taking place with this, not the end. This beginning will give birth to infinite possibilities. Most of the essays in this book have adopted the seeds from these possibilities. The day Indian society understands its Constitution will be the day that a Constitution will dawn which will drive away the darkness and extend an invitation to prosperity. This book is an advance invitation for that hour. Whoever accepts this will find a union with religion, money, work and salvation in this life itself. This is a big invitation, is it not?

—Ram Bahadur Rai

—Dr. Mahesh Chandra Sharma

Contents

Constitution of India: The Inside Story

—Ram Bahadur Rai

What exists today as the 'Constitution of India' has come to us through an interesting journey, full of roller-coaster rides. A look at it can fill anybody with curious amazement and intriguing questions. It was December of 1946. Delhi was almost frozen with bone-chilling cold. The dark clouds of Partition were hovering in the Indian sky. Many months had passed since the elections for the Constituent Assembly were held. It was supposed to frame the Constitution for a unified, 'unpartitioned' India. Viceroy Lord Wavell invited the freedom fighters and they presented themselves in Delhi in spite of the adverse weather conditions. They were brimming with a strong sense of responsibility as they were there to write the destiny of India. They gave shape to the Constituent Assembly. They became the creators of our Constitution. The challenge was humongous. Jawaharlal Nehru was in a state of near trance. All he could mutter was: "The day may be overcast with clouds, but it is the last day after all; hence, it has to burst out of the clouds."[1]

Everything was so badly placed at that time, and came an unexpected turn. What was taken as a historic opportunity by the Congress leadership was actually full of intricacies. Congress had, in fact, got entangled in the web it had woven itself. It could not pull its steps back from the Constituent Assembly. To know how it got entrapped in the complexities that emerged is an exercise to get acquainted with the history of that time.

In the drive to frame the Constitution lies that history. Congress kept claiming that it has concrete historical evidence to back its campaign. It rested in the premises that Britishers are engaged in dividing and diffusing the rising national consciousness in India, to remain in power. The British government is working on a three-pronged strategy. Firstly, it is encouraging Muslim separatists which may lead to Partition. Secondly, it is trying to scare and create a sense of insecurity amongst the princely states so that they fear for their existence. And lastly, the British are interpreting the diversities in the Hindu society as their differences so that it can break away communities, especially Dalits, from mainstream Hindus.

While confronting the Britishers, Congress admitted that the Constitution campaign has logically culminated in formation of the Constituent Assembly. The party took it as a sacred responsibility granted by history. But there were some different views as well. One was that constitutionalism in India is a contribution of British imperialism. Britishers introduced it to slow down the process of de-colonisation and Congress fell into the trap. Another opinion was that the demand for a Constitution facilitated the attainment of freedom. The campaign for the Constitution was of great help to tread the path of freedom and ultimately reach the goal. Today, a third point of view asserts itself with force that the Constitution has got overwhelming imperialist influences.

The Constitutionalism has its roots in our past. When did Congress get formally associated with it? We have to understand this. Prof. Devendra Swaroop hits the nail on the head when he says, "To contain the expanding influence of the national movement and to appear addressing the expectations of the people, the British government constituted Simon Commission in 1927 CE." As there was no Indian member in the commission, all political parties including Congress opposed it. One of the results of the Simon Commission was that our national leaders decided to develop a framework for the Indian Constitution. The idea sprang up in the Madras convention of Congress in 1927.[2] A committee with Motilal Nehru as head was constituted that submitted its report in August 1928. The report was based on the recommendations of the all-party convention held in Lucknow. It was accepted by the Congress, but, the Muslim League of Muhammad Ali Jinnah rejected it in the December convention. The report had given a framework for the principles of the Constitution. It was a milestone in the journey that our Constitution went through. The Motilal Nehru Committee report demanded just the Dominion Status. When that report was tabled in the Calcutta convention, a debate ensued on whether Congress should choose dominion status or Purna Swaraj (complete self-governance). Serious differences emerged. The year was 1928 CE. Youth leaders like Subhash Chandra Bose and Jawaharlal Nehru stood for self-governance, but the frontline leaders favoured dominion status. Mahatma Gandhi intervened and brought about a rapprochement. A resolution for dominion status was passed but the British government was given one year to comply with. Congress warned that if the government does not declare the dominion status, it would go on an agitation. When the government rejected the demand, Congress passed a resolution in the Lahore Convention of 1929, demanding complete self-governance. In this very convention, it was decided that 26 January will be celebrated as the Independence Day. Thus began the practice of celebrating the day as Independence Day. Republic Day is just a transformation of this day.

Talks for the Constituent Assembly between the British government, Congress and Muslim League were on. Then Congress said that India cannot accept but a Constitution framed by its own people, a Constitution without any interference from the foreign authority. Some people forcibly associate framing of the Constitution with a statement Gandhiji made on January 5, 1922. He had written that, "Swaraj (self-governance) won't be a gift from the British Parliament, but a declaration of the acceptance of the demands of the people of India, which will be granted to us after the British Parliament passes a law regarding it. This declaration will be only an amiable settlement of Indians' long-standing demands in the form of a treaty or an agreement in which Britain will be a party. When this agreement will come in force, the British Parliament will accept the demands of the people expressed through their elected representatives."[3]

Gandhiji was against the imperialist concept of the Constitution. So, he remained neutral about the demand made by Congress. He, in his own way, always tried to explain and interpret the basic concept of self-governance to Congress so that they could digest it. But after the failure of the Round-Table Conferences,[4]

Congress came to the conclusion that it had to tread the path of Constitution. The political current had taken an altogether new turn and Gandhiji also felt that the goal of freedom could be reached through the path of Constitution as well. He changed his thoughts. It was 1937 CE. He felt that Congress had become a moribund party. It showed no enthusiasm over the future. It has a fatigued and disappointed leadership. To save Congress from these negativities, he changed his path, thinking and strategy. A new wisdom sprang up within him—taking the Constitution campaign forward. This was a decisive moment when Gandhiji was preparing to take the nation on a new path of history. He took Congress on the same path of Parliamentary politics that he ruled out with vehemence. The long-term plans he had presented in Hind Swaraj were postponed. This churning took two years. This process makes it clear that the diplomatic battle that began after 1931 was effective enough to enable the British government to persuade Gandhiji to take the path of electoral politics, which was totally against his wishes and to which, as per his principles, he never agreed.[5]

At last, on 19 November 1939, he wrote in 'Harijan': "Besides many other things, Jawaharlal Nehru compelled me to study the inherent meaning behind the Constituent Assembly. When he included it in the resolutions of Congress, I gave my acceptance on the basis that he understands the nuances of democracy more than me. But I myself was not without my doubts. But now, confronted with hard facts, I am a more enthusiastic supporter of the concept of the Constituent Assembly than Jawaharlal, as perhaps he does not feel like me that besides being a medium of political and other types of education, the Constituent Assembly could be the solution for our communal and other problems as well. Only the Constituent Assembly can create a Constitution that represents the indigenous sensibilities and the aspirations of the people of the country in the truest sense."[6] In this way, Gandhiji ensured three criteria for framing the Constitution – power to eliminate communal problem, indigenous nature and aspirations of the people. In 1936 CE, Nehru as Congress president had put forth a well thought-out framework for the demand of the Constituent Assembly.[7] He had made it clear that Congress wanted it to be set up to attain democracy and freedom and it will be elected through adult franchise. The Congress Working Committee got the green signal from Gandhiji and Nehru, and passed the resolution for the Constituent Assembly for the second time in 1939.

The Constituent Assembly was elected through indirect election. The members of the Constituent Assembly were chosen by the provincial assemblies elected through restricted franchise.[8] Gandhiji could, in no way, be a part of that Constituent Assembly. It was on his suggestion that journalist B. Shivaram was granted the membership of the Constituent Assembly. Same was the case with Dr. Bhimrao Ambedkar. When the elections for the Constituent Assembly were held, Ambedkar got elected as a candidate of Scheduled Caste Federation with the support of Muslim League from Bengal as in Mumbai Provincial Assembly, his federation did not get even a single seat. After the partition of India, his membership was no longer valid. Gandhiji intervened to persuade Dr. Rajendra Prasad and Sardar Patel to write to the Chief Minister of Mumbai, B.G. Kher that he had to ensure that Ambedkar gets elected to the seat gone vacant with the resignation of Dr. M.R. Jayakar. In this way, he got elected to the Constituent Assembly for the second time on 22 July 1947. But the question remains that did the Constituent Assembly act in the way Gandhiji wanted to. When it came into existence, did the Congress leaders heed to his suggestions? Did not the British government have any alternative but to agree to the conditions laid down for the Constituent Assembly?

Everybody knows that the Constituent Assembly came into existence under a plan of the Cabinet Mission. But a Constitution comes into existence when people decide for it; people snatch it from the rulers. But the contrary was happening here and Gandhiji suggested that the invitation of the Viceroy should be rejected.[9] This was the most appropriate suggestion under the circumstances. It is essential to consider some facts to understand this. A deadlock existed over the Constituent Assembly. The Muslim League had already boycotted it. Lord Wavell could not bring a compromise. Then Nehru, Jinnah and Sardar Baldev Singh travelled to London with a compromise and unity deal, but nothing positive came forth. Gandhiji realised that under the circumstances, the Constituent Assembly can't be constituted or function properly, nor it should be. Congress was going back on its promises about the Constituent Assembly. Its members were not elected through adult franchise, but inducted by the invitation of the Viceroy. So, it was clear that the Assembly was being set under the plans of the British government. The boycott from the Muslim League and the hesitation of the representatives of the provinces had made the whole thing lopsided. Such a Constitution could never be universal in nature. But the Congress leadership was not in a mood to listen to Gandhiji's arguments.

It was 4 December 1946. Mahatma Gandhi was in Noakhali. He penned down a note in Shrirampur expressing his views about the Constituent Assembly. He clarified that the Constituent Assembly was, in fact, the creation of the British Government[10]. Anyway, absence of Muslim League and provincial representatives violated the conditions the government had put for it. Hence, Gandhiji wrote to Patel in the note that if the government still wants the Constituent Assembly to meet, it should go for a new pact with Congress. He also underlined that if the government does not want to go for a new pact, Congress should stay away from the Constituent Assembly. On 26 November 1946, Gandhiji had written a letter to Ghanshyamdas Birla emphasising the point that if the Constituent Assembly has to sit under the shadow of bayonets, it is better that it does not sit at all.[11] It's clear from this that the shape the Constituent Assembly was taking was unacceptable to Gandhiji. History is the witness to the fact that the Congress leadership did not care a hoot about Gandhiji's suggestions. They did what the British government wanted them to do.

That was the time when India was under two types of governance—British India and Provincial India. In the Constituent Assembly, 296 seats were allotted to British India and the provinces got 93 seats. So, 389 seats were going to constitute the Constituent Assembly, for which indirect voting was organised in July-August 1946. Congress got a vast majority of about 60% of seats. It was obvious that they had a significant mass following. They were working as national representatives. It fielded those who were actively involved in the national movement. There were some exceptions too The Constituent Assembly had no authorised representative from communist and socialist parties and none from Hindu Mahasabha also. So, all of them were chosen by Congress only. So, it will not be off-key to conclude that the traditional, prevalent and modern ideologies were absent in what was referred to as the Constituent Assembly. The elected members of the Muslim League were lesser than those from Congress.

The first meeting of the Constituent Assembly was held on 9 May 1946; it was a Monday. The meeting elected elderly member Dr. Sachchidanand Sinha as the interim president. His name was proposed by Acharya J.B. Kripalani who emphasised two points for his aptness for the post – he was an old Congress hand and was the eldest member. Accepting the responsibility, Sinha read out the greetings sent by the governments of US, China and Australia. The guiding principles for the Constituent Assembly were laid down in his inaugural address. The essence of his address was that nowhere in this world we need logical provisions and wise agreements more than we need these to frame the Constitution of the country such as India. He accepted that "today we have assembled here as per the British Cabinet Mission Plan."

Sinha simplified the oath-taking process of the members and saved time. Of the 296 members elected, 207 took oath on the first day and signed the register. Muslim League had 73 members. Ambedkar was among the members who took oath on the first day. After two days, on 11 December, Rajendra Prasad was chosen as the president of the Constituent Assembly. On 24 January 1947, the responsibility of the vice president was given to Dr. H.C. Mookerjee. Benegal Narasimha Rao had already been appointed as the 'Constitutional Advisor' to the Constituent Assembly. His office had been active for many months before the meeting. The resolution to grant that office a legal validity was moved by Nehru on 10th December. He told the Assembly about these facts.[12]

It is clear that this office was the source and Rao in his capacity of Constitutional Advisor was the brain behind all the moves. After Wavell declared creation of the Constituent Assembly on 19 September 1945, the first step he took was to appoint Rao in the reforms department. On his instructions only, Rao had a long conversation with Nehru on 21 November 1945. The conversation paved the way for acceptance of Rao as the Constitutional Advisor.

Rao had studied the Constitutions of Britain, Canada, America, Australia, South Africa and Ireland and provided the examples from these in three volumes to the members of the Constituent Assembly. He also gave his advice in writing to Rajendra Prasad and Nehru.

In addition to this, a questionnaire was circulated among the members. Rao's office made the primary draft which then reached the Draft Committee, from where it reached the Constituent Assembly to get chiselled and refined. It was this draft that the committee headed by Ambedkar used to discuss and after that, the proposals of the committee were discussed by the Constituent Assembly. When Rao passed away, Rajendra Prasad paid tributes to him saying it was Rao who had planned the Constitution and laid its foundation. Lok Sabha Speaker Ganesh Vasudev Mavalankar said that Rao gave us an invaluable work in the form of the Constitution.

The Preamble to the Constitution was created afterwards. But the indications of the aims and objectives of the Constitution can be found in the Objectives resolution of Nehru that he moved in the Constituent Assembly on 13 December 1946. The resolution was seconded by Purushottam Das Tandon. While moving the resolution, Nehru accepted that the Constituent Assembly was not at all of the kind that they wanted it to be. It came into existence under special circumstances and the British government had its hand in its creation. In these words of Nehru is hidden the history of those times. His sense of regret about not heeding to the suggestions of Gandhiji is also clear. In his typical suggestive style, he conveyed that "it would have been better to wait for some more time."

The political environment of the country was vibrant with an unprecedented enthusiasm, firm commitment and the indomitable spirit of rebuilding the country, but the sky was not without its share of dark clouds of uncertainty, doubt and confusion. It was under such circumstances that Nehru said that the resolution he was moving explained the aims and the objectives we as a country were going to pursue. The framework of the plan was also explained in the resolution. Nehru added that the resolution makes it clear that which path we are going to tread. It is a firmly held belief that Nehru drafted the Objectives resolution himself. He had included in the resolution the goals like fundamental rights, federalism, republic, etc. By 1946, these concepts had become part and parcel of the action programme of Congress. But what is amazing is that there was no mention of 'socialism' in the Objectives resolution. Why? Was Nehru a socialist just to show off? Nehru's biographer Michael Braker has raised this question and concluded that perhaps Patel did not allow it to happen.[13]

Translating the spirit of those historical moments into words, Nehru said, "We have assembled here on an extraordinary historical moment. In these times of change, I feel somewhat amazed. It is the kind of amazement we feel when a night changes into a day." An amazed Nehru said that in one way, it is just like an agreement deed. This agreement was being done by those who despite being the members of the Constituent Assembly were not a party to a unified decision. These were the people of the Muslim League. It is clear that Nehru was apprehensive about partition of India. The Objectives resolution was discussed for seven days. Jayakar suggested an amendment on 16 December 1946 in which he appealed to the Assembly to postpone the discussions on the Objectives resolution till the members from the Muslim League and the representatives of the provinces attend its meeting. On 21 December 1946, the discussions were postponed till further orders. This gave Muslim League a month's time, but it did not change its decision. At last, on 22 January 1947, the members stood up to adopt the Objectives resolution.

The Constituent Assembly had almost finished its job. In its 10th session on 17 October 1949, the Preamble was adopted after a short discussion. Making the Preamble clear, Ambedkar said that it is divided into three parts.[14] The first one is declarative, second one descriptive and the third one is objective. He suggested that the first part should begin with the phrase "We the people of India." Mahavir Tyagi interrupted saying, "How come 'people' got into it? We have only the members of the Constituent Assembly." Tyagi was known for his ability to tell the truth through his piercing sarcasm. That day also he touched the same chord. Ambedkar got the point and said in unequivocal terms, "My friend Tyagi says that the elections to the Constituent Assembly were held through a limited franchise. This is absolutely true." He accepted the fact and said that "the subject in front of us is in no way associated with this truth." Giving examples from the Constitution of America, he silenced any counter-arguments. So, just like the American Constitution, the Preamble began with "We the people of India."

The Preamble is the soul of a Constitution. The philosophy of a Constitution is reflected in its Preamble. Since the practice of framing Constitution for countries came into existence, the indications of the faith, the fundamental values and the vision of the future of a country have been included in the Preambles. In the notorious times of Emergency, Indira Gandhi effected a controversial change in the Preamble of our Constitution. Two words—socialism and secularism—were added. Thus began the political misuse of the Constitution. Constitutional experts are of the view that this kind of tampering with the Constitution is very 'original' in nature. The creators of the Constitution did not want to associate it with any ideology, any 'ism' or any particular economic principle. They took the Constitution as a flowing river that could carve its path wherever it found necessary. But when Indira Gandhi established her autocracy through the murder of democracy, she set aside the wisdom of the creators of the Constitution, ignored the Constitutional philosophy and added some unwanted words. When democracy was re-established under the rule of Janata Party, much morbidity were removed through a Constitutional amendment. But the tampering with the Preamble was left intact.

To understand the Constitution, it is essential to know what sort of an institution the Constituent Assembly was, what processes were involved in its creation and how were the decisions made. It is essential to know this for the reason that the Constitution was framed under adverse circumstances. That is why, the process of framing of the Constitution attains extraordinary importance. Writing about the Constituent Assembly in his book 'The Indian Constitution: Cornerstone of a Nation', American historian Granville Austin has said, "The Constituent Assembly was primarily a one-party assembly that was being run by Indian National Congress that enjoyed massive public support. But the party represented the whole of India. Its internal processes too were democratic."[15]

The Constituent Assembly was considered synonymous with Congress and Congress was taken as analogous to India. Congress had the power of numbers and a long line of leaders. Despite that, the Congress Working Committee ensured that such representatives are elected to the Constituent Assembly who had administrative, legal and constitutional expertise. Dr. Sinha, Dr. Ambedkar, K.M. Munshi, A.K. Ayyar and Dr. Syama Prasad Mookerjee were such experts.

The Constituent Assembly worked in three phases. In the first phase, it was tied up with the conditions laid down by the British government. Its hands were tied. This phase was from 9 December to 2 June 1947. The second phase from 3 June to 14 August 1947 was the phase of declaration of Partition of India, marked with unprecedented turbulences, massacres and bloodshed. In the third phase, India stands divided and the war of Independence proves to be partially successful. It began on 15 August 1947. The Constituent Assembly became the sovereign authority. It continued its work till 26 November 1949.

The Constitution was framed. But the beginning some months caused utter confusion to the Constituent Assembly. For six months since its inception, it was just waiting and watching. Within the Assembly and outside in the social arena, Congress kept feeling the pressures of the circumstances and changing its policies, postponing its plans. Congress kept waiting in the hope that, at last, the Muslim League will come to the Constituent Assembly. But, none from the League turned up. Giving an account of this hoping-against-hope by Congress, Austin writes that for the whole month of December, Nehru and other leaders in the Assembly kept on hoping that perhaps the League will tell its leaders to participate. For this reason, they kept changing or postponing their policies in the Assembly and outside it. But the hope taken as a good breakfast proved to be a bad supper. All efforts to get the Muslim League to the Constituent Assembly failed. When the second session of the Constituent Assembly was held in the last days of January 1947, it had become amply clear that the League was never going to join the Constituent Assembly. Despite this, the Assembly kept working. It kept on involving itself in the foundational jobs of setting up the committees to hold talks with the provinces, to decide about the fundamental rights and federal structure of the country. Austin adds that when in the last days of the month of April, the third session of the Constituent Assembly was held, the issue of Partition was in the air. So, the discussion about the federal provisions was postponed. For the whole month of May, different committees of the Constituent Assembly kept postponing all work decided under the Cabinet Mission Plan.

We need to understand that why did the Muslim League boycott the Constituent Assembly even when it participated in the elections held to choose its members. Dr. Subhash Kashyap writes: "Two things happened in the meanwhile which had a deep impact on the point of view of the Muslim League. One was that the elections for 296 seats of British Indian Provinces were completed in July 1946. Out of these seats, 205 were taken by Congress when the League got just 73. Witnessing Congress sweeping the polls with such massive majority did not just disappoint Jinnah, but filled him to the brim with apprehensions. This fire got more fuel from a press conference on 10 July 1946 when Jawaharlal Nehru, the then president of Congress, gave the unfortunate statement that 'the provinces can decide to join or not to join any federation or a group', which means the classification was optional and not essential. A possibility was there that no classification may have occurred. But Nehru's this statement proved disastrous. The Muslim League got an opportunity to comment that Congress, in fact, had not accepted the Cabinet Mission Plan in its totality."[16]

Maulana Abul Kalam Azad has also accepted that the statement given by Nehru on 10 July was such an unfortunate step that it changed the course of history. In short, disagreement about the 'classification of the provincial groups' occurred between Congress and the Muslim League. This was a Cabinet Mission Resolution. On 6 December 1946, the British government granted support to the point of view of the Muslim League. The patronage of the British government to the Muslim League was clear. The initial framework of the Partition of India was inherent in this patronage. The Muslim League saw its old demand being met and boycotted the session of the Constituent Assembly that began from 9 December 1946. So, the members elected from Bengal, Punjab, Sindh, frontier provinces, Balochistan and Silhet in Assam ceased to be the members of the Constituent Assembly of India. New elections were held. On 26 November 1949, when the Constitution was adopted, 284 members signed the original copy of the Constitution.

After it was finally decided to split the country, the members of the Muslim League attended the Constituent Assembly just for one day. It was 14 July 1947. When President Dr. Rajendra Prasad called the name of Haji Abdul Sattar Seth to present his identity card and to give his signature, freedom fighter Deshbandhu Gupta raised a question—whether Haji believes in two-nation theory or not? The President declared the question null and void. The Constituent Assembly became a sovereign authority on 15 August 1947. After the Partition, the majority of Congress in the Constituent Assembly jumped to 82%. A remarkable ideological diversity marked the structure of the Constituent Assembly. Nehru favoured parliamentary democracy and Euro-American policy of governance. He had a central role in the framing of the Constitution. Ambedkar was the voice of the most oppressed social group called 'Dalits'. His role was significant in turning the Constitution into an instrument of social change. Those who followed Gandhi, to be very fair, were very less and their voice was not heard. These Gandhians were trying to achieve a decentralised democracy based on village self-governance and panchayatiraj system. K.T. Shah stood for equality of all states when India establishes itself as a country with its Constitution. Tandon and Mookerjee were nationalists. Their role was reduced to almost nothing. The Constitution that was framed was Euro-American in its basic character. This is the greatest irony inherent in the structure of our Constitution. The Constituent Assembly was primarily led by Nehru, Patel, Rajendra Prasad and Abul Kalam Azad. Austin says that these four leaders had constituted an oligarchy in the Constituent Assembly. These four leaders exercised their power and influence to the hilt to maintain their oligarchy in the Constituent Assembly. In addition to these, Ambedkar, Alladi Krishnaswami Iyar, T. Krishnamachari, Sharat Chandra Bose, K.M. Munshi, Ananthasayanam Ayyangar, N. Gopalaswami Ayyangar, Jairamdas Daulatram, Shankar Rao Dev, G. Durgabai Deshmukh, H.C. Mookerjee, Pandit Govind Vallabh Pant, N. Madhav Rao and

Dr. Satya Narayan Sinha were the most influential leaders of the Constituent Assembly. All these had a significant influence on the creative process of Pattabhi Sitaramayyah and Benegal Narasimha Rao. Though Narasimha Rao was not a member of the Constituent Assembly, yet as the Constitutional Advisor, he was the axis on which everything moved. He presented himself in every committee whenever required. He was a scholar of Constitutional history who had done a deep study of Euro-American Constitutional practices. He had exceptional grip on drafting. It was he who, with the consent of the oligarchy,[17] led by Nehru, gave a Euro-American character to our Constitution.

The discussions between the members of the Constituent Assembly were most of the time informal in nature. The time of these discussions was almost fixed. When the Constituent Assembly used to be in session, the members would sit in the Constitution House and open their hearts to each other. Sometimes clashes too occurred. The Constitution House used to be in the complex of Diwan Shri Apartments (Firozeshah Road) of today. The issues over which serious differences existed were individual freedom and property rights, federal provisions and language. Over these issues, deep divisions existed within Congress. The Constituent Assembly was faced with a genuinely tedious problem—they had to determine the nature of government for the country. One way was to adopt the Euro-American constitutional tradition and establish a government based on it. This was accepted by the Constitutional Committee. Taking the Euro-American constitutional tradition as the ideal was in essence to take the same path[18] on which India was being driven during the imperialist rule. This was done in the Constituent Assembly in April 1948. This led to the adoption of such a Constitution and such a system of government based on it, which was nothing but the extension and a new edition of the imperialist rule. The Constituent Assembly did not feel the necessity to delve deep into the glorious legacy of India to explore the ancient indigenous institutions which could go a long way to ensure the fulfilment of the needs of our country. On 19 November 1949, Dr. Raghuvir raised this question in the Constituent Assembly. He said that when the advisors, the mentors of our Constitution, such as Rao and other gentlemen could go to Ireland, when they could go to Switzerland and America, just to see how other countries ran their governments, then, was not there a single learned scholar in this country, who could suggest that this country too has got some experience, this country also has got its wisdom and ideas internalised by its people and we should benefit from such wisdom and ideas.[19] It was certain that democracy is to be adopted. But the discussion about the polity was very serious. Mahatma Gandhi put up two resolutions in front of the Constitutional Committee of Congress—The first one in 1946[20] and the second one in 1948.[21] The second one that he had written in the last night of his life was more explicit. That only is the treasure he has left not only for the country and the society, but for the whole world. But that resolution was rejected by Congress. After Gandhiji passed away, Shriman Narayan Aggarwal also made an attempt. He presented a draft of the Constitution based on Gandhian thoughts. That too was rejected. In this way, the Constituent Assembly chose one out of two alternatives. At that time and even today, the question stands that what kind of government should we adopt to eliminate the vices such as inequality, that keep plaguing the social structure of India since the days of imperialist dominace? Can we bring about a social revolution through the continuation of the discriminatory, disruptive policies of the imperialist era? This is the haunting question that the 'oligarchy' hegemonising the Constituent Assembly did not want to listen to.

Austin observes that the credit to motivate India towards the present Constitution goes to the Expert Committee[22] of Congress with Nehru as its chairman. This committee was constituted by the Congress Working Committee. Its aim was to create working material for the Constituent Assembly. It needs to be mentioned that eight members of the working committee had been recently elected to the Constituent Assembly. Though Patel was not a member of the Committee, yet he had participated in several meetings organised by it. These meetings began in mid-July 1946 and continued for four days during the session of the Assembly. The series of meetings began afresh after a month and continued again for four days. The members of the Committee, working under the Cabinet Mission Plan, gave general suggestions regarding autonomous areas, provincial governments and the powers of the Centre along with the amendments required to regulate various powers. These members had prepared the draft for a resolution that was almost similar to the Objectives resolution issued in the coming month of December. This resolution besides clarifying the social aims of the Constitution explained power as a phenomenon emanating from the people. Though Cabinet Mission had moved ahead on the assumption that India will get its motivation for the Constitution from the Government of India Act of 1935, but enough room was allowed for the Expert Committee to suggest to the Constituent Assembly to make arrangements for indirect and Panchayat governments as well. But the committee did not give any importance to Gandhian point of view and took into consideration the institutions of a parliamentary system only to come up with an uncertain type of recommendation that the Constitution should be a loose structure.[23] This makes it evident that the point of view of the Constituent Assembly was contrary to the Gandhian thought. In the fifth session of the Constituent Assembly, Ramnarayan Singh suggested that the primary units of the government should be established in villages. He was for the village self-governance-based government. He too was ignored and the parliamentary system was adopted. The drafting of the Constitution was entrusted to the drafting committee and the Constitutional Advisor Benegal Narasimha Rao. The draft that was made had no mention of family, village or Panchayat. It immediately attracted the attention of the members. They had got enough time to go through the draft. Dr. Rajendra Prasad, the President of the Assembly, was the first to point out this folly.[24] He wrote to B.N. Rao on 10 May 1948,[25] emphasising that the draft of the Constitution needs amendments. In his letter, he writes in plain words that the Constitution should begin from villages and then reach the Centre. The basic units of this country have always been the villages and will always remain so. Those who followed the Gandhian line of thought wanted the Panchayats to be elected through adult franchise and the legislators and parliamentarians through indirect election. This was strongly advocated by Rajendra Prasad in his letter. What is both amazing and interesting is that this suggestion from the President of the Constituent Assembly was rejected by Rao. Was this his own decision? This exchange of correspondence occurred when the Constituent Assembly was not in session. When the Assembly was in session again after eight months, the Panchayat issue dominated it. On 4 November 1948, Ambedkar presented the draft Constitution. He was fully aware that the draft that had been released for consultations was the centre of discourse, inviting various arguments and counter-arguments. Serious discussions were going on all over the country over two main questions. These discussions echoed in the Constituent Assembly. The members could not digest the arguments given while presenting the draft. They fired a volley of sharp arguments on Ambedkar. The written accounts of the proceedings of the Constituent Assembly testify to this.[26] There were two questions. These very questions are regarded as the touchstone of effectiveness of a Constitution – "what should be the nature of the government?" and "what sort of Constitutional arrangements have been made to establish such kind of government?" The members raised questions on the draft presented in the Assembly that showed a clear tilt towards centralisation. The members wanted to expand the sphere of democracy. So, they wanted village self-governance and they stood up one after the other to shower the Assembly with the arguments in favour of Panchayat system-based government. One major reason behind this bitter criticism of centralisation was that the members felt that the leadership was unwilling to fulfil its promise to go for a federal government. They wanted the promise to be fulfilled. They were well aware of the dangers a government armed with too much of power may pose. But the draft of the Constitution was leaning towards a unitary government because the Partition of India had put the unity and integrity of the country at the forefront.[27] It was in face of this challenge that the leadership had back-pedalled on the issue of federal government. Most of the members had expressed deep reservations over that part of his lecture in which he had said that do we really have villages? He had referred to villages as the abodes of 'a frog in the well' syndrome and the dungeons of ignorance, narrow-mindedness and communalism. He had expressed his happiness over the draft in which 'village' had been thrown aside and 'individual' recognised as the part of the nation.[28] This caused a furore in the Constituent Assembly. A heated debate ensued. Nehru had to intervene, though he did not give direct answers to the questions raised by the members. After all, he was a daydreamer. But through his long speech on 8 November 1948, he gave many messages. His personality had a compelling charm and his words had a mesmerising sway. The effect of both is recorded in the proceedings of the Assembly.[29] With his alluring persona, when he stood up to speak, the whole Assembly burst into an overwhelming applause. This happened more than once. A part of his speech is quoted very often but in a half-baked and sketchy form. The relevant portion, in fact, goes like this, "...while we, who are assembled in this House, undoubtedly represent the people of India. Nevertheless, I think it can be said, and truthfully, that when a new House, by whatever name it goes, is elected in terms of this Constitution, and every adult in India has the right to vote—man and woman—the House that emerges then will certainly be fully representative of every section of the Indian people. It is right that the House so elected—under the Constitution, of course, will have the right to do anything—should have an easy opportunity to make such changes as it wants easily. But in any event, we should not, as some other great countries have done, make a Constitution so rigid, that it cannot be easily adapted to changing conditions. Today especially, when the world is in turmoil, and we are passing through a period of very swift transition, what we do today may not be wholly applicable tomorrow. Therefore, when we make a Constitution which is sound and as basic as we can make it, it should also be flexible and, for a period, we should be in a position to change it with relative facility."[30] These words of Nehru reflect a sense of specific direction. Every Lok Sabha has been drawing inspiration from this. These words are still relevant. Two prominent members of the Constituent Assembly brought balance to this debate about Panchayats and prevented it from going lopsided. The second point in the draft Constitution that invited criticism was that a large part of the Government of India Act, 1935 was incorporated into it without any change. The Constitution is not original. Dr. Ambedkar's reply to this is noteworthy. He said that he does not need to be apologetic for the allegation that a large portion of the

Government of India Act, 1935 had been incorporated into the draft. As Ambedkar was making this statement, it did not occur to even a single Congressman that the Government of India Act, 1935 was rejected by the party in the Conference of the Representatives elected in 1937 elections. Even a resolution was passed to observe "Anti-Constitution Day." In this resolution it was declared that the conference reiterates the opinion of the people of India that the nature of Government of India Act, 1935 is such that it nourishes the roots of exploitation and slavery of India. It only reinforces the foundations of British Imperialism in India.[31] There was consensus in the Assembly regarding adoption of democracy. But serious disagreements existed over the structure and form of government that could facilitate it. In his long speech, Ambedkar had made it clear that the Constitution of India establishes a "parliamentary democracy." Those who wanted a government based on Gandhian thought suggested elections for Village Panchayats through adult franchise and the elections for the provinces and the Centre through indirect elections. Bihar member, Ramnarayan Singh made a statement about this that appears to be so accurately predictive. Underlining the appreciation shown by Ambedkar for a parliamentary democracy, he expressed his clear-cut view that this was going to give rise to a party system that has failed in the West. K. Santhanam and M. Ananthasayanam suggested similar kind of amendments. To the amazement of the Assembly, Ambedkar immediately and unhesitatingly accepted the amendments, and the inclusion of Panchayat in the Constitution was facilitated. This shows how generous Ambedkar was. He set aside his own ideas to incorporate the amendment and showed utmost reverence for the spirit of the Constituent Assembly. The need to invite voting for the question did not arise. This was on 22 November 1948. The Constituent Assembly was filled with a sense of utmost satisfaction for which T. Prakasam became the spokesman. Thus, a middle path was achieved in the Constituent Assembly that enabled the inclusion of Panchayats in Article 40. This Article says that the provincial governments will take steps to establish Village Panchayats. The Panchayats will be granted such powers and authority that they are able to function as autonomous administrative units. However, the Nehru government at the

Centre and the Congress governments in the States remained indifferent to the Panchayat issue for a long time. For some reason, Jai Prakash Narayan did not attend the Constituent Assembly. But, from a distance, he kept a watchful eye on the process while the Constitution was being framed. He studied the Constitution thoroughly and it did not take much time to a man of his experience to conclude that the state governments were reluctant to implement the Panchayati Raj system. To achieve self-governance, he called a Rashtriya Gramdan Conference. Many Chief Ministers and political leaders attended it. He wrote a path-breaking article giving suggestions about the reconstruction of the Indian polity.[32] He made two points in the article. The first one was that freedom and democracy are integral to the spirit of the Constitution. But it stands on a reversed pyramid which means that self-governance is being instilled top down. His second suggestion was that we need to evaluate our democratic experience of the last 10 years. This evaluation must be done in the background of the experiences of other counties of Asia, Africa and profound democracies of the West. This is the essence of his thought. He wanted proper amendments in the Constitution so that the concept of village self-governance becomes a reality. This happened around 1959 CE. Jaiprakash Narayan's article had stirred the whole nation. A serious debate ensued. Balwant Rai Mehta Committee was set up by Prime Minister Nehru. Many more committees followed, each suggesting ways to establish the Panchayat system. But the administration and the political leadership were under the firm grasp of the imperialist mindset and it was but natural that the suggestions were ignored. The recommendations of these committees lay in the cellar of the Ministry of Rural Development. When Prime Minister Rajiv Gandhi got entangled in the Bofors scam, he sent an honest officer on punishment transfer as Secretary in the Ministry of Rural Development. The officer was Vinod Pandey. One day, the officer went into the cellar and found the documents. He studied the report given by Balwant Rai Mehta Committee and suggested to Rajiv Gandhi that if the Constitution is amended to establish the Panchayat system in villages and autonomous bodies in cities, the people may most probably forget the allegations of corruption and ensure a victory for Congress in the elections. This was the reason behind the amendment Bill initiated by the Rajiv government.[33] But Gandhi's advisors had other plans. They suggested that the Bill should be passed in Lok Sabha and then it should never come out from Rajya Sabha, the blame for which should be slapped on the Opposition, which will ensure the victory for us. People will vent all anger on the Opposition as they did not allow the implementation of the historic decision of decentralisation of power. At any rate, the government of P.V. Narasimha Rao gave the same Bill the form of 73rd and 74th amendments. The 73rd amendment granted Constitutional validity to Panchayats. The power to make laws for Panchayats was granted to the states. In this way, on 24 March 1993, Panchayats on district, intermediate and village levels were established in every state except Jammu and Kashmir, Delhi and Arunachal Pradesh. The number of representatives elected to the Panchayats were 34 lakhs. The Panchayat system has three levels of representations—Gram Panchayat at the village level, Zilla Panchayat at the district level and the states with more than 20 lakh population have the system of intermediary-level Panchayats. The 74th amendment of the Constitution has given depth and expansion to the democratic system in the cities. Autonomous bodies have been established.

Have these amendments brought about village self-governance? Has the Panchayat system been established in villages or not? Have the decentralised bodies been established in cities or not? Such questions still stand unanswered because in Articles 40 and 243(G), power and responsibilities have been assigned to Panchayats in the form of 'self-government'. This is easier said than done because the stumbling block still remains as it was always and that 'self-government' has still not been defined even in the General Clauses Act, Black's Dictionary or the Legal Lexicon. It very badly needs a definition. One more amendment for the Constitution is essential to make it obligatory for the states to give more power and responsibility to the Panchayats. Similarly, the Eleventh Schedule that covers Panchayat-related subjects should be added as the fourth list to the Seventh Schedule of the Constitution mentioning 'self-government'. These are the two most important things. To define 'self-government' is the need of the hour.

Chandrashekhar Pran, who has been running study and research programmes and a campaign for the 'Third Government' for many years now says that if it happens, the whole perspective will change. It will be a big step in the direction village self-governance. Many such administrative measures and constitutional amendments will set everything in motion. When it happens at the level of the Central government, only its countrywide implementation will be possible. It is clear that the 'Ganga' of village self-governance still stands entangled with the twisted hair locks of the Constitution, waiting for salvation. A 'Bhagirath' can only get her onto the earth. It is beyond doubt that the inclusion of Article 40 in the Constitution was a realistic decision. But it still remains a mere signpost. Even today, people stand deprived of their participation in self-governance, development and the local economy. The people want these powers and responsibilities. Had Congress been a Gandhian party, this right could have been given to people in 1948 itself. Austin, too, is of the view that Congress did not hold the basic ideals of Gandhiji in any esteem.[34] It took the Constituent Assembly two years 11 months and 18 days to frame and write the Constitution. It was adopted on 26 November 1949. On 26 January 1950, it became totally effective. Before that, on 24 January, the Constituent Assembly held its last meeting. On this day, the members put their signatures on the Constitution. The original Constitution had one Preamble, 22 parts, 395 Articles and 8 Schedules. Till now, 102 amendments have been made and 22 amendments are proposed. The Constitution we have today has even its Preamble amended. The parts have increased to 25 and with that, the number of Articles has grown to 465 and the Schedules have gone up to 12. It is the longest written Constitution in the world. The American Constitution is the oldest and the smallest written Constitution that has undergone very less number of amendments. The great sage Kabir would certainly comment that the long bedspread of the Constitution has got in it numerous holes which have been covered with patchwork. Better to weave a brand new bedspread now.

References

1. *The official report of the discussions in the Constituent Assembly, Issue-1, No. 5, Hindi Edition, Nehru's Lecture on Objectives Report, p.7.*
2. *The members of the Simon Commission were Clement Atlee, Edward Cadogan, George Lane-Fox, Vernon Hartshorn, Donald Howard, Harry Levy-Lawson, Sir John Allsebrook Simon. In the Joint Parliamentary Commission, four members were from the Conservative Party, two from the labour and one from the Liberal Party. No Indian member was included.*
3. *Young India, 1919-1922, (Collection) pp 111-117, the interim President of the Constituent Assembly Dr. Sachchidanand Sinha, in his inaugural address, had referred to this statement of Mahatma Gandhi. Vaad Vivad, Issue-1, pp. 9-10.*
4. *On the recommendations of Simon Commission, three Round-Table Conferences were held in 1930-32. To understand the full context, please refer to Samaj Vigyan Vishwakosh, Ed. Abhay Kumar Dubey, Vol. 4, pp. 1254-55. Bharat Ka Samvaidhanik Vikas aur Samvidhan, Dr. Subhash Kashyap, pp 125-134. Yeh Samvidhan: Hamara Ya Angrezon Ka, Devendra Swaroop, pp. 143-144.*
5. *Bharatiya Samvidhan Ki Aupaniveshik Prishthbhumi, Devendra Swaroop, p. 200.*
6. *Sampoorna Gandhi Vangmaya, Vol. 70, pp 407-410, Publications Division, 1978, July 16 to November 30, 1939.*
7. *The framing of Indian Constitution: Select Documents, Ed. B. Shivarao, Vol. 1, Part. 1, p. 81.*
8. *Ibid, P. 214, point no. 18, of the statement of the Viceroy in the Constituent Assembly on May 16, 1946.*
9. *Sampoorna Gandhi Vangmaya, Vol. 86, pp. 208-209, 1998.*
10. *Ibid, p. 216.*
11. *Ibid, p. 181.*
12. *The Constituent Assembly of India Debates (Proceedings), Hindi Edition, Loksabha Secretariat, Vol. 1, Book-2, p. 12.*
13. *Nehru: A Political Biography, Michael Braker, p. 330.*
14. *The official report of the Constituent Assembly of India, Hindi Edition, Loksabha Secretariat, Vol. 10, Book-9, October 17, 1949, p. 3445.*
15. *The Indian Constitution: Cornerstone of a Nation, Granville Austin, (Hindi translation by Naresh Goswami), p. 30.*
16. *The statement of Jawaharlal Nehru in a Mumbai press conference, See R.A.I-1946, pp. 145-147.*
17. *Granville Austin has referred to the group of Jawaharlal Nehru, Dr. Rajendra Prasad, Sardar Vallabhbhai Patel and Maulana Abul Kalam Azad as 'Oligarchy' within the sphere of the Constituent Assembly. See 'The Indian Constitution: Cornerstone of a Nation',*

list of references in the first chapter, ref. no. 72, p. 61 (Hindi Translation).

18. *The Indian Constitution: Cornerstone of a Nation, Granville Austin, (Hindi translation by Naresh Goswami), Chapter-2, p. 65.*
19. *The Constituent Assembly of India Debates (Proceedings)-(Hindi Edition Vol. 11) Book-10, Dr. Raghuvir's address, November 19, 1949, p. 3848.*
20. *The details of both plans put up by Mahatma Gandhi are available in Development of the Congress Constitution, by N.V. Rajkumar.*
21. *Ibid.*
22. *The Congress Working Committee constituted the Expert Committee on July 8, 1946 with Jawaharlal Nehru as its head. Other members were Kanhaya Lal Manik Lal Munshi, N. Gopalaswami Ayangar, K.T. Shah, Kasturiranga Santhanam, Humayun Kabir and D. Gadgil.*
23. *The Indian Constitution: Cornerstone of a Nation, Granville Austin, pp. 71-72.*
24. *One Venkatramani had written an article in Swatantra journal about the drastic mistakes in the draft of the Constitution. On the basis of this article, Dr. Rajendra Prasad wrote to B.N. Rao, the Constitutional Advisor to the Constituent Assembly.*
25. *Correspondence and Select Documents, Dr. Rajendra Prasad, Vol. 9, pp. 51-53, Ed. Valmiki Choudhary.*
26. *For a vivid account of this, see The Constituent Assembly of India Debates (Proceedings), November 4, 1948 and November 17-26, 1949. The prevailing mood in the Constituent Assembly is reflected in the comments of perturbed and agitated members.*
27. *The Making and Working of the Indian Constitution, Shibani Kinkar Chaube, (Hindi Anuwad Sangh) Chapter-7, p. 58, Para-3.*
28. *The Constituent Assembly of India Debates (Proceedings), November 4, 1948 and November 17-26, 1949, Vol. 7, Book-3, p. 77.*
29. *Ibid, November 8, 1948, pp. 303-316.*
30. *Ibid, p. 314.*
31. *The resolution is available in Jawaharlal Nehru Vangmaya, Vol. 8, p. 63.*
32. *This article is published in book form by Sarva Seva Sangh Prakashan, Rajghat, Varanasi. The Book is titled Bhaarateeya Raajya Vyavastha kee Punarrachanaa: Eka Sujhaava (The Reconstruction of Indian Polity: A suggestion). There are seven chapters in the book.*
33. *That is why the Constitution Amendment Bill was initiated on May 19, 1989. It was passed by the Lok Sabha but Rajiv Gandhi ensured that it gets stuck in Rajya Sabha.*
34. *The Indian Constitution: Cornerstone of a Nation, Granville Austin, (Hindi translation by Naresh Goswami), p. 78.* □

Politico-Ideological Foundations of Constitutionalising India

—Prof. Bidyut Chakraborty

A 'Constitution' is not merely a statement of provisions; it is equally reflective of the conceptual foundation in which it unfolds as a mechanism of governance. In case of India, the story is multifaceted since India is perhaps one of those decolonised polities in which the past influence did not seem to have been less significant even after the attainment of political freedom from the British rule in 1947. Reasons are plenty, prominent among them was definitely the consensus that the nationalists developed over the acceptance of the ideological-cum-institutional fabric that the colonisers had created and also consolidated in the wake of colonial rule. How was it possible? Explanations need to be couched in terms of the ideational compatibility that the nationalists had shared with their bête noire, the rulers.

It happened presumably because the former was nurtured in an environment in which liberal constitutionalism was privileged in a socio-political milieu in which ideas supportive of the prevalent system were generally encouraged. Primarily, it was an ideational appreciation by the nationalists which, inter alia, created an environment where the Westminster form of constitutional democracy seems to have gained precedence. The outcome was inevitable: despite attempts by some of those nationalists who were opposed to imitating what they experienced during colonialism, constitutional liberalism became an acceptable option for Independent India.

Implicit here is the argument that the design that emerged in India during the British rule did not seem to have been imposed, but had evolved spontaneously since a majority of those who opposed colonialism upheld the system in view of its utility even after decolonisation. The argument is a reinforcement of the point that largely due to an ideational endorsement, it was possible for the Westminster mode of governance to take roots in India.

The British Liberal Inputs

A threadbare analysis of the ideas of a select group of British thinkers shows that the civilising zeal of the rulers appears to have governed their priorities in India as soon as India became a British colony. The serious differences notwithstanding among those who shaped the cognitive understanding of colonialism, there was hardly a formidable opposition to the continuity of colonial rule till when the British paramountcy was severely challenged by the nationalists. Besides the obvious economic gain, India as a colony was also a laboratory for testing some of the interesting ideas which were considered to be integrally connected with the fundamental civilising mission of the colonisers.

This was never seriously questioned and the leading thinkers, despite their concern for liberty, fraternity and compassion, appeared to have endorsed the colonial practices as being needed to elevate the colonies to an improved state of being civilised. As is known, it was James Mill who endorsed colonialism as it was a panacea for the natives to avoid despotic rule justifying priestcraft. Despite being hailed as an important treatise on British India, Mill's views in the *History of British India* are "so simplistic and so unremittingly dark, often so pathetically foolish in their lack of nuance" that they are criticised, rightly so, for being rooted in self-obsessed racial prejudices. Nonetheless, Mill's ideas did play a critical role in shaping the attitude of the colonisers at the dawn of colonialism in India, as evidence demonstrates.

For the colonisers, the British colonialism was a panacea for the 'barbarian' Indians because it would help them become civilised and enlightened by being introduced to the philosophy of Enlightenment espousing liberty, equality and fraternity. It is, therefore, not surprising that even for Edmund Burke, who initiated the impeachment motion in parliament against the first Governor-General of Bengal Warren Hastings in 1788 for his misconduct, never questioned the British endeavours towards colonising

India. They were keen to warp governance in India in the format of liberal constitutionalism, of course, at the behest of the British 'patriarchs'. Such a concern led to the unfolding of two important processes: on the one hand, efforts were undertaken to gradually install the institutional fabric of constitutional democracy in India which gained strength, as history has shown, in the wake of colonial rule; the structure of constitutional governance upholding colonialism derived its sustenance by drawing, and, on the other, the ideological resources that the colonisers shared with the colonised while administering India.

Conceptually, it was an innovative design which had its root perhaps in the ignominious defeat of the British colonisers in the American War of Independence (1775-83). By being vanquished, the rulers had evolved a strategy to accommodate the dissenting voices in India by creating a structure of governance in which Indians were also allowed to participate. Justifying the design as an extension of the philosophy of Enlightenment, the British rulers seem to have put in place, rather perfunctly, a system which the colonised appear to have accepted as days passed by. This segment is, thus, of critical importance to the principal argument since it helps us understand how the Enlightenment ideas which led to the consolidation of colonialism in India became a source of empowerment to the colonised in course of time.

An uncritical look at the selective, but major, landmark constitutional initiatives during the colonial rule may lead one to conclude that these were initiated by the British for the Indians. Hence, the spirit of nationalism is underrated. If one goes beyond the surface, what is evident is that the inclusion of Indians in administration was but an outcome of the British effort to defuse popular discontent. Hence, the argument that every constitutional drive was initiated by the Raj does not seem to be persuasive. History reveals that there were situations which forced the British authority to adopt measures to control agitation. For instance, the Congress campaign in the 1880s contributed a lot to the introduction of the 1893 reforms. Behind the 1909 Morley-Minto Reforms lay the *Swadeshi* movement and revolutionary terrorism. Similarly, the 1919 Montague-Chelmsford Reforms were attempts at resolving crises that began with the Home Rule

League and climaxed with the 1919 Rowlatt Satyagraha and the Non-Cooperation Movement of 1920-22. To a large extent, the Gandhian Civil Disobedience Movement (1930-32) accounted for the introduction of constitutional measures seeking to involve Indian politicians in public administration.

Furthermore, the interpretation of these constitutional designs remains partial unless linked with the broader socio-economic and political processes in which they were conceptualised. An attempt to analyse the structure and dynamics of constitutional politics without reference to the broader social matrix and economic nexus is futile because the politic-constitutional structure reflects economic and social networks, religio-cultural beliefs and even the nationalist ideology which impinged on the organised world of administrative and constitutional structure. So, an urgent and unavoidable task for an analyst is not to completely ignore the broader socio-economic context, but to ascertain its relative importance in shaping a particular constitutional initiative. For instance, the 1932 Communal Award was believed to have been initiated by the British to expand political activity among the Muslims in Bengal and Punjab. But, as studies have shown, it was also a concession the British was forced to grant in order to make the maintenance of the Empire easier.[1] The sharing of power with the native elites was, thus, prompted by considerations other than merely British initiatives.

The constitutional landmarks were a clear testimony to those imperial efforts that defused opposition rather easily on most occasions. What was distinct about British colonialism was its success in welding a significant section of population to the system of governance that the British introduced. It was possible due perhaps to its triumph in ideologically moulding people towards liberal political values and ethos. Barring the militant nationalists, most of the nationalists were content with the method of three Ps – petition, prayer and protest – until the rise of Gandhi who radically transformed the complexion of anti-British confrontation. The scene was not the same with the ascendancy of the 'extremist' nationalists who pledged to fight for India's independence even by deploying coercive means. They were gradually exterminated by following a due process of law which was, however, managed by the British authority so efficiently that an image of the Empire being true to its commitment to the subjects was built and consolidated. It was, therefore, not surprising that the nationalists took to legal means to save their colleagues from gaol which also confirms that these constitutionally recognised institutions of governance gained credibility among them despite being staunch opponents of the British rule.

Here, too, the argument that the nationalists upheld liberal values which, they felt, were protected by these complementary political institutions is reinforced. Fundamental here is the point that the legal stipulations and the institutions that they brought about led to the consolidation of British imperialism by most effectively managing (and also defusing) the nationalist counter-attacks before they became threatening to the Empire. In the process, these institutions also evolved as integrally connected with the evolution of India as a constitutional democracy which was rooted in the British endeavour towards constitutional India, an effort which also received adequate support from the nationalists notwithstanding being opposed to the alien rule.

The Nationalist Inputs

The 1950 Constitution of India was the culmination of a process in which contrasting ideas converged to evolve an acceptable set of principles for a socio-culturally and economically diverse population. The account is historical too because the ideas that became pre-eminent in the Constituent Assembly had their roots in the tumultuous days of India's freedom struggle in which various waves of thought were also discernible. By arguing that our Constitution was the outcome of a complex ideational battle in different phases of India's struggle for freedom, one challenges the conventional notion that it is merely a mindless, if not haphazard, borrowing of constitutional provisions and practices prevalent elsewhere.

The argument supporting the contention that the Indian Constitution is a borrowed doctrine seems vacuous given the fact that it is also a break with the past. One of the most significant brakes was to constitutionally recognise the principle of representative government in its unalloyed form through universal adult suffrage, an ambition that the nationalist had been nurturing since the adoption of the 1928 Motilal Nehru Report. Besides the emergent need of tackling contingent circumstances following Partition which created a strong demand for the continuity of the available colonial administrative machinery, the founding fathers also felt the need of a strong administration to translate into reality their ambitious plan of transformation. It has, thus, been persuasively argued that "while continuity was sought in the service of the break in this way, the claim of break itself was called upon to justify certain continuities." A careful study of the arguments that were marshalled in favour of incorporating mechanisms and institutions from the colonial era confirms the point.

The aim here is also to comprehend how British constitutionalism, which consolidated colonialism in India, gradually became a source of empowerment to those opposed to alien rule. Colonialism for the colonised was nothing but a mode of exploitation, and yet, it created an ambience in which the demand for freedom was also couched in a language which was derivative of the philosophy of Enlightenment. It is possible to argue that it gained precedence presumably because it conforms to some of the fundamental ideas that had indigenous roots. There is hardly a disagreement that the ideas of liberty, equality and fraternity are not alien to Indian psyche, presumably because of the well-nurtured tradition of *Vasudhaiva Kutumbakam* (the world is a family) since time immemorial.

This does not seem to be an over-stretched argument because the idea was not only hinted, but forcefully argued in the public domain and also in the three-year proceedings of the Constituent Assembly. In view of India's well-entrenched diversity, the idea of world being a family appears to have emerged instinctively though there were aberrations and fierce, and also sordid, battles were fought among the communities; the most revealing example being the creation of Pakistan on the basis of widely publicised 'two-nation theory'. Nonetheless, it is fair to argue that liberal constitutionalism had evolved organic roots in India during colonialism which gained resilience in its aftermath largely because it remained an effective mode of bringing together disparate Indians for a cause amidst chaos and uncertainty.

A cursory look at the processes that influenced constitutionalism in India reveals that there are three critical areas – social justice, liberal constitutionalism and group representation – in which an ideational battle took place involving those who were responsible for charting out a specific course for India's constitutionalism to follow. A careful analysis of the past in which the nationalists endeavoured to constitutionalise India reveals how Enlightenment values were privileged presumably because they conformed to what they derived by being nurtured in and appreciative of well-entrenched indigenous intellectual legacies. It was further confirmed in the debates in the Constituent Assembly when the founding fathers upheld the ideas and also forms of governance which they derived out of their encounter with colonialism; their heartfelt concern for constitutionalising India was articulated in a series of efforts which culminated in the Constituent Assembly when the founding fathers sat together to make a Constitution for independent India in a historical perspective which is both derivative and context-driven: derivative because it was drawn on liberalism that had no parallel in India, and context-driven since Indian socio-economic and ideational reality did not seem to favour liberal socio-economic and political practices.

The Constituent Assembly and the making of the Constitution

The making of free India's Constitution by the Constituent Assembly over a period of little more than three years is reflective of the efforts that the founding fathers undertook to translate into reality the nationalist and democratic aspirations of an independent polity following decolonisation. Furthermore, while the Constitution is a continuity at least in structural and procedural terms, it was also a clear break with the past since the 1950 Constitution drew on an ideology that sought to establish a liberal democratic polity following the withdrawal of colonialism. There can be no greater evidence of the commitment to constitutionalism and rule of law on the part of the founding fathers than the Constitution that they framed despite serious difficulties due to Partition. The commitment to liberal democratic values, as the

Constituent Assembly proceedings suggest, remained paramount in the making of the Constitution.

Set up as a result of negotiations between the nationalist leaders and the members of the Cabinet Mission over the possible constitutional arrangement in the post-war India, the Constituent Assembly was not, it is argued, convened "by any national provisional government, but by the British government to bring together the delegates of the major political parties."[2] The task of the Constituent Assembly was to draft a Constitution for India. The objective resolution that Jawaharlal Nehru moved was, according to Dr. B.R. Ambedkar, "an expression of the pent-up emotions of the millions of this country."[3] While defending the objective resolution, Nehru argued strongly for democracy and socialism: he strongly defended 'democracy' as the most appropriate system of government that "fits in with the temper of our people and be accountable to them."[4] Similarly, socialism, he firmly believed, would bring about economic democracy to India. For him, political independence was futile unless it was supported by democratic governance and socialistic vision. Hence, he was critical of the princely states that were reluctant to relinquish monarchy for democracy. As a true democrat, who had no doubt that socialism was the ultimate solution for India's stark poverty, Nehru set the tenor of the discussion in the Assembly by providing a philosophical lay-out for free India's Constitution.

Nonetheless, the political context in which the Constitution was being deliberated was full of uncertainty because of (a) Hindu-Muslim rivalry, and (b) reluctance of most of the princely states to join independent India. While the former led to the dismemberment of India following the British withdrawal in 1947, the latter necessitated threat or application of coercion, on occasions, to geographically unify India by bypassing the claim of the existing rulers of the princely states. By staying away from the Assembly, the Muslim members clearly stated their preference for Pakistan that gained momentum especially after the adoption of the 1940 Lahore resolution. The 1946 Calcutta and later Noakhali riots confirmed the Congress apprehension that it was possibly strategically correct to accept Partition to avoid further bloodbath. What was clear when the Constituent Assembly met for drafting the Constitution was that Pakistan was inevitable and a strong state was required to fulfill its socio-economic goals.

The Outcome

Comprising 395 provisions, the 1950 Constitution of India is perhaps the bulkiest of the Constitutions. It was made so, as Ambedkar explained, because the founding fathers did not want to leave any space for their whimsical interpretations in future. Whatever revision is required to be incorporated has to be done in accordance with the procedure established by law (Article 21). This is a testimony to the concern of the framers of the Constitution for liberal values that undoubtedly had a clear imprint in the discussion in the Assembly and also in the articulation of the provisions of the Constitution. While being committed to liberal constitutionalism, which was not exactly derivative of other traditions, the framers of the Constitution were equally respectful to what they learnt from their existential experiences as Indians. The offshoot was the 1950 Constitution which, while being drawn to liberal constitutionalism, had also space for Gandhian notion of *Gram Swaraj* (village self-rule) in the chapter on the Directive Principles of State Policy.

A perusal of the constitutional trajectory since the inauguration of the 1950 Constitution reveals that what the founding fathers upheld while contributing to the making of the Constitution continues to be as effective as it was then. It is true that given the fact that India's Constitution is neither extremely right nor whimsically flexible, it cannot be compared with the established liberal Constitutions around the world. Here, the cautionary note of Ambedkar appears to be instructive. Babasaheb was not in favour of a rigid Constitution simply because it needed to be adapted to the rapidly changing socio-economic and political milieu. Unless this is admissible, a Constitution ceases to be organic to the society, and it becomes a mere lifeless document comprising provisions without being effective. That it should be flexible should also be understood with reference to whether the amendment is absolutely necessary under the circumstances; and, it should be kept in mind that change is allowed so long as it does not adversely affect the basic character of the Constitution.

So, Ambedkar's caution helps us comprehend why India's Constitution is so distinctive among other functional Constitutions in contemporary world.

There is a final word. A careful perusal of the processes leading to constitutionalising India reveals that it was a creative blending of influences, both indigenous and exogenous: the latter gained ground because (a) they were obviously privileged and (b) they seem to have resonated with the former. That these ideas were not exactly foreign is clearly evident when Swami Vivekananda in his 1893 speech before the Parliament of World Religions in Chicago exhorted that he was "proud to belong to a religion that has taught the world both tolerance and universal acceptance" and furthermore, he also believed "not only in universal toleration" but also accepted "all religion as true." This is perhaps the clearest articulation of the widely accepted claim for *Vasudhaiva Kutumbakam* (the world is a family) which is ideologically akin to the fundamental Enlightenment principles of liberty, equality and fraternity; unless this is appreciated, one cannot immerse oneself with others as part of the same family. So, perhaps the rootedness of the Enlightenment values in indigenous traditions automatically, if not naturally, created a definite opportunity for the derivative ideas to strike roots.

References

1. *I have shown this in my 'The communal award of 1932 and its implications in Bengal', Modern Asian Studies, Cambridge, February 23, 1989.*
2. *Shibanikinkar Chaube, Constituent Assembly of India: springboard of revolution, Manohar, New Delhi, 2000, p. 49.*
3. *Constitutional Assembly Debates, Vol. I, p. 104.*
4. *Constitutional Assembly Debates, Vol. I, p. 62.*

□

Constitutional Democracy and Basic Structure Doctrine

—Ravi Shankar Prasad

(Supervising a rights-oriented jurisprudence through the basic structure doctrine)

"The institutions under which we live are being changed continually by the Parliament because we are never satisfied with them. Sometimes they are scrapped for new ones; sometimes they are altered; sometimes they are done away with as nuisances."[1]

— George Bernard Shaw

Introduction

The amendment of the Constitution sometimes becomes necessary to adapt to the changing needs of national development and to overcome the difficulties which may encounter in future and to realise any popular demand for changing the political system. Our Constitution is the supreme political document of this country which governs the political administration and rule of law in our society. As the need of society keeps changing because of its organic nature, our supreme political text has also been made capable enough to evolve organically. The provisions of amendment in our Constitution under Article 368 give very wide power to the Parliament "in exercise of its Constituent power to amend by way of addition, variation or repeal any provision of the Constitution" inserted by the Constitution (24th Amendment) Act, 1971.

This power raises a question that whether in a Constitution which makes no separate provision of total revision but simply prescribes the machinery to amend the Constitution, such power of amendment would include the power to make total revision of the Constitution that is to substitute by another. In India today, by virtue of power of judicial review, the Supreme Court has imported the concept of 'unamendability of the basic structures' by way of interpretation and held that there are certain essential parts of our Constitution which are so basic that its amendment will change the character of the Constitution itself and, hence, cannot be amended and Parliament doesn't enjoy absolute Constituent Power under Article 368 for this purpose.

Historical Evolution of Amendability of Fundamental Rights

Perhaps the most essential doctrine that emanates from the principles enshrined in the Constitution of India is the "basic structure doctrine" which was enunciated by the majority in the case of Keshavananda Bharati v. State of Kerala.[2] The same would be discussed in detail below.

Pre-Keshavananda Position

The Parliament's authority to amend the Constitution, especially the chapter on the Fundamental Rights of Citizens was challenged in 1951. In the case of Shankari Prasad v. Union of India,[3] the validity of the Constitution (First Amendment) Act, 1951, which sought to curtail right to property guaranteed by the then Article 31 was challenged. The main argument contested against the validity of the First Amendment was that Article 13 prohibits enactment of a law infringing or abrogating the fundamental rights, and that the word 'law' under Article 13 would include any law, even a law amending the Constitution, and the validity of such a law could be judged and scrutinised with reference to the fundamental rights which it could not infringe. Approaching literal interpretation of the Constitution, the Supreme Court upheld the validity of the Constitution (First Amendment) Act, 1951. The court rejected the contention and limited the scope of Article 13 by ruling that the word 'law' in Article 13 would not include a constitutional amendment passed under Article 368.

The same question was once again raised in the case of Sajjan Singh v. State of Rajasthan[4] wherein the validity of the Constitution

(Seventeenth Amendment) Act 1964, was challenged. The impugned amendment adversely affected the right to property yet again. The court rejected the argument by a majority of 3:2 by ruling that the 'pith and substance' of the amendment was only to the extent to aid the state legislature to efficiently effectuate the policy of an agrarian reform, ergo upholding the ratio in Shankari Prasad's case.

With the position as regards to amendability of fundamental rights being set as the ratio decided in Shankari Prasad and Sajjan Singh's case, the question as to the validity of the First Constitution Amendment Act, 1951, Fourth Amendment Act, 1955, and Seventeenth Amendment Act, 1964 was challenged in the case of I.C. Golak Nath v. State of Punjab.[5] Constituting an 11-judge Bench, and a majority of 6:5, the cases of Shankari Prasad and Sajjan Singh were overruled on the ground that the Fundamental Rights were non-amendable through the constitutional amending procedure set out in Article 368 while the minority upheld the line of reasoning adopted by the court in the two earlier cases. The majority now took the position that the Fundamental Rights occupy a 'transcendental' position in the Constitution, so that no authority functioning under the Constitution, including Parliament exercising the amending power under Article 368 would be competent to amend the Fundamental Rights. It was also observed that Article 368 merely laid down the procedure and it did not confer on Parliament the power to amend the Constitution.

To counterbalance the effect of Golak Nath case, a Bill was introduced on 7 April 1967 in the Lok Sabha to restore the Parliament's power to amend the Fundamental Rights. The primary object of this bill was to restore the original power of the Parliament to amend the Constitution, thereby following the procedure under Article 368.

Post Golak Nath case, the following amendments were brought in, which set the stage for Keshavananda Bharati's case.

- *The Twenty-fourth Amendment Act in 1971 was passed and introduced certain modifications in Articles 13 and 368 to assert the Parliament's power to amend.*
- *The Twenty-fifth Amendment Act introduced Article 31C (Saving of laws giving effect to certain directive principles).*

- *The Twenty-ninth Amendment Act included the Kerala Land Reforms (Amendment) Act 1969 and 1971 into the scheme of the Ninth Schedule.*

The case of Keshavananda Bharati is a landmark decision in the history of constitutional law and philosophy which has culminated the entire question of amendability of fundamental rights and has once and for all settled the position of law on the same.

In this case, the petitioner had challenged the Kerala Land Reforms Act, 1963, and contested that the same was unconstitutional. It was further contended that the rights contained and guaranteed under Articles 14, 19(f), 25, 26, and 31 were violated by way of the impugned Act. While this case was pending before the Supreme Court, the Parliament had passed the Twenty-fourth Amendment Act, 1971, the Twenty-fifth Amendment Act, 1971, and the Twenty-ninth Amendment Act, 1972. These Amendment Acts, too, were challenged before the Court. A bench comprising 13 judges delivered separate judgements. The main issues that were to be decided were:

i. *Whether the parliament possesses unlimited power of amendment under Article 368;*
ii. *Whether basic features of the Constitution can be amended;*
iii. *What is the content of basic features in other words what constitutes basic features of the Constitution.*

Majority of the seven judges upheld the constitutionality of the challenged Amendments and overruled the decision of Golak Nath case and laid down that the power of amendment contained therein under Article 368 is unlimited. The Parliament can amend any part of the Constitution which includes the Preamble. However, this amending power should not affect the basic features of the Constitution. The court did not however define what basic structure was. However, it can be seen through some instances. By way of the 42nd Amendment to the Constitution, clauses (4) and (5) were included in Article 368 which postulated that any amendment to the Constitution under Article 368 shall not be called in question in any court on any ground and that there shall be no limitation whatsoever on the power of the Parliament to amend. Consequently, the 42nd Amendment amended Article 31C to provide primacy to all directive principles over the fundamental rights. This was challenged in Minerva Mills v. Union of India[6] where the Supreme Court struck down these provisions and held the same to be unconstitutional on the ground that they destroyed the essential features of the Constitution.

Doctrine of Basic Structure

The keystone and the dominant characteristic of the Indian political structure is that the Parliament has the right to make or unmake or amend any law. But there are certain safeguards and restrictions placed upon the same as conferring unfettered powers is antithetical to the principles of the Indian Constitution. By Article 245(1) of the Constitution, the legislative power of Parliament has been specifically made 'subject to the provisions of the Constitution'.[7] Thus, the Parliament has, therefore, to function within the constraints of the Constitution from which its legislative powers emanate. Now the question arises that can the union legislature remove such constraints or hindrances from their way of bringing into amendments so as to enable them to exercise their power under the Constitution without any system of checks and balances? The answer to this is the judicial promulgation of the basic structure doctrine.

The judicial development of the notion 'basic structure' brought new contours in the realm of constitutionalism in India. It changed the perspective of amendability of the Constitution in reference to Fundamental Rights enshrined under Part III of the Constitution. There are different modes of bringing into effect an amendment to the Constitution. Article 368 of the Constitution contemplates the procedure for bringing into effect certain constitutional amendments, which equally applies to amending of fundamental rights. The power of the Union Legislature to effect amendments cannot be stalled or taken away by means of judicial pronouncements.[8]

It is necessary to identify the basic features of the Constitution which are not amenable under Article 368 of the Constitution. In Keshavananda Bharathi[9] case, the Supreme Court termed supremacy of the Constitution, separation of powers, secular and federal structure of the Constitution, etc., to be as basic feature of the Constitution. The court further held that though the same is not an exhaustive list and can be strengthened further through judicial pronouncements.

In the case of Indira Gandhi v. Raj Narain,[10] the Supreme Court made certain important observations as to what constitutes basic feature: "...To be a basic structure, it must be a terrestrial concept having its habitat within the four corners of the Constitution. What constitutes the basic structure is not like a 'twinkling star' up above the Constitution. It does not consist of any abstract ideals to be found outside the provisions of the Constitution..."

Considering the scope of fundamental rights, the court, in the case of Ashoka Kumar Thakur v. Union of India,[11] observed to the effect that fundamental rights as enshrined in Part III of the Constitution are part and parcel of the basic feature of the Constitution. Further, the concept of equality which is basic to the rule of law and that which is regarded as the most fundamental postulate of republicanism is embedded in Article 14 and that the doctrine of equality enshrined in Article 14 of the Constitution, which is the basis to the rule of law, is the basic feature of the Constitution.[12]

One of the remarkable features of the doctrine is its expansive nature as it has been observed in various judicial pronouncements, wherein, the judiciary has denied to foreclose the list of the basic features of the Constitution. The said approach is based upon the rationale that the Constitution is a living document and not a static piece of document and grows with the course of time.

Amendability of Fundamental Rights: An Enigma

The Constitution (Forty-second) Amendment Act, 1976 is the most controversial and debatable piece of constitutional amendment ever taken in the Indian constitutional history. The fundamental objection against this amendment was that it disturbed the balance of power between the executive and the judiciary as the amendment limited the power of the latter and was more inclined towards the former. Furthermore, it also conferred the constitutional amendments immunity from judicial review altogether, whether on procedural or substantive ground. It can be easily submitted that the same was in sheer violation of the basic principles of the Constitution and became the sole ground for being declared as void by the Constitution Bench decision in the Minerva Mills case.[13]

The Constitution makers gave the power to amend it in the hands of the Parliament by making it neither too rigid nor too flexible with a purpose that the Parliament will amend it as to cope up with the changing needs and demands of 'WE THE PEOPLE OF INDIA'. The Parliament in exercise of its Constituent power under Article 368 can amend any of the provisions of the Constitution and this power empowers the Parliament to amend even Article 368 itself. The 'Doctrine of Basic Structure' is a judge-made doctrine to put a limitation on the amending powers of the Parliament so that the 'basic structure of the basic law of the land' cannot be amended in exercise of its 'Constituent power' under the Constitution. So, the question arises, is not there any limitation on the amending powers of the Parliament? If the answer to this question is not in affirmative with a reason that the Constitution makers did not intend for such limitation otherwise, they would have provided for such limitation in the Constitution, then another question arises, to what extent can the Parliament amend the basic law of the land? And, if there will be no limitation on the amending power of the Parliament, are there no chances that this power of amendment in the name of 'Constituent power' can be abused, as happened during the period of Emergency as typified by the 42nd amendment.

That there is some implied inherent limitation on the amending power of the Parliament originates in the German constitutional theory. The said argument which Mr. Nani Palkhivala successfully pleaded in the Keshavananda case was the same that Mr. M.K. Nambiyar tried in Golakh Nath case unsuccessfully.

A Critical Analysis of the Basic Structure Doctrine as Laid Down in Keshavananda Bharathi Case by the Supreme Court

A 13-judge Bench of the Supreme Court laid down or rather 'created' a law more than 45 years ago. This Bench in the Keshavananda Bharati v. State of Kerala (1973) 4 SCC 225 ruled that Parliament can amend any part of the Constitution, including the fundamental rights enshrined in Part III of the Constitution subject that such amendment should not violate the 'basic features of the Indian Constitution'. This decision of the court had overturned a settled position which had laid down by the same court speaking through its eleven judges, where the court in I.C. Golaknath v. State of Punjab had held that the Parliament can amend any part of the Constitution but cannot take away any of the fundamental rights mentioned in Part III. Keshavananda case held a contrasting position where it said that even a fundamental right can be taken away, condition being such abrogation of the fundamental right does not offend the basic structure of the Constitution.

No doubt as Sikri, C.J. has held in Keshavananda case that "the doctrine of basic structure will act as a safety valve against the arbitrary use of amending power by Parliament" will serve a great purpose in safeguarding the freedom and liberty of the citizen in a case of totalitarian regimen like Emergency during Indira Gandhi government. But the question which is in front of us today is that what if the courts start applying the principle of doctrine of basic structure in every case against the popular will of the country and start intervening with the power of legislature, contrary to the doctrine of separation of power.

Interestingly, what the court in Keshavananda case evolved as the 'basic structure doctrine' – does not find any discussion or slightest of mention in the constitutional text. Next, when the court was faced with the question as to what constituted the basic structure of the Constitution, the court (through the seven of their judges, writing for the majority) was quick to rule that the basic structure consists of values, such as democracy, secularism, etc., but the same shall be determined by this court as and when the need will arise. Article 368 of this Constitution provides the Parliament with the Constituent powers, i.e., the powers to amend the Constitution. Articles 245 and other subsequent articles provide the Parliament with the legislative powers under which the Parliament enacts different statutes (which must pass the scrutiny of Article 13(2) – that the "Parliament shall not enact any law which violates any provision of Part III").

If we read the original Article 368, i.e., as it stood before the 24th Constitutional Amendment Act.

368. Power of Parliament to amend the Constitution and procedure therefore

1. *Notwithstanding anything in this Constitution, Parliament may in exercise of its Constituent poweramend by way of addition, variation or repeal any provision of this Constitution in accordance with the procedure laid down in this Article.*
2. *An amendment of this Constitution may be initiated only by the introduction of a Bill for the purpose in either House of Parliament, and when the Bill is passed in each House by a majority of the total membership of that House and by a majority of not less than two-thirds of the members of that House present and voting, it shall be presented to the President for his assent and upon such assent being given to the Bill, it shall be presented to the President who shall give his assent to the Bill and, thereupon, the Constitution shall stand amended in accordance with the terms of the Bill...*
3. *Nothing in Article 13 shall apply to any amendment made under this Article.*

The marginal note for the Article under consideration defines the Article providing for the power with the Parliament to amend the Constitution. The dispute amid the 13 judges is not the contention that needs to be discussed here. However, what is of importance is the fact that post Keshavananda verdict, the Supreme Court imbued itself with excessive powers. The court went beyond the mandate of the Constitution to read into the text what was not provided by the drafters of the Constitution itself.

One thing which is of extreme importance we should not forget while we subsequently segue into the parameters of the usage of this doctrine by the apex court is the fact that the doctrine was aimed to test only an amendment to the Constitution and not any legislation or enactment of the Parliament, for they are already subjected to the scrutiny of Part III. For that purpose, there must lie something which cannot be deleted or abridged, as the court held, which would be used to test the validity of such amendment to the Constitution. Basic Structure of the Constitution is that answer.

Time and again in a plethora of judgements such as in Indira Nehru Gandhi v. Raj Narain, Kihoto Hollohon, S.R. Bommai v. Union of India and Poudyal v. Union of India cases, the SC ruled at different times such as in Bommai case, the court held that 'secularism' is a part of the basic structure of the Constitution or, in Raj Narain case, the court held that 'democracy' is a part of the basic structure. However, there has been very limited scrutiny of the said pronouncements, the Bommai case of upholding dismissal of elected state governments, having no connection to any breakdown of constitutional machinery, only on ground of 'secularism' and basic structure, is a case in point.

As this country witnessed in the fourth judges' case, famously known as the National Judicial Appointments Commission case of 2015, where the Supreme Court held that 'primacy and independence of judiciary' are a part of the basic structure of the Constitution. The court, while striking down the NJAC Act, held that it is unconstitutional on the part of the Parliament to, therefore, do away with the collegium system, and introduce a commission system, which, according to the court, hampered the independence of the judiciary.

Such trends are very much worrying, especially with the kind of usage of the 'basic structure doctrine' by the court. While it is not correct to say that the judiciary is a counter-majoritarian institution and rules against what the popular sentiment is, because in a constitutional democracy like ours, the role of judiciary is extremely crucial. They are tasked with the job to check the functioning of other organs of the state, but is it legitimate on their part to transgress the boundaries which are set and laid down by the Constitution under the garb of the basic structure? The duty of the Parliament is to represent the popular sentiment of the people as they are the elected representatives of the people. Therefore, an enactment of the Parliament is representation of the popular sentiment.

It is, therefore, a running concern as to what is the role of the judiciary to term any amendment to the Constitution as violative of the (undefined) basic structure. In many parts of the NJAC judgement, the majority is found to say that the "hidden and silent inferences of Article 141 will lead this court to the conclusion that the Act of the Parliament is violative of the primacy of judiciary as a basic feature." The court placed its reliance on the word 'consultation' as mentioned in Article 124 of the Constitution to rule that 'primacy and independence' are basic features of the Constitution.

The most significant problem with this kind of jurisprudence as laid down by the court is twofold – When the court decides that a particular amendment is violative of such element of basic structure, which is not yet a part of the basic structure, but would henceforth constitute one. This, in the most academic sense, would amount to 'a retrospective application of laws' as the Parliament was never made aware that their action would end up in being violative of some feature, which the court 'might' hold to be a part of the basic structure. Secondly, this extrapolation of the basic structure doctrine through Minerva Mills case, where the court had held that the "limited amending powers of the Parliament is in itself a part of the basic structure", gives unforeseen power to the judiciary.

When the court deflects from an already established principle that it is only the constitutional abstract values, such as equality, freedom, democracy, etc., which shall become a part of the basic structure, it opens the floodgates through judgements like in Minerva Mills case to read remote and ancillary of meanings that could be inferred from the Constitution is fit enough to become an essential element of the basic structure.

The defence of the doctrine is given that the Parliament is absolutist and is prying over the rights of the citizens so that the same can be abrogated the moment it has a chance. It is simply a stretch and a logical fallacy of 'appeal to fear'. If the Parliament has the power to take away the rights of the people, the elected leaders will also have to face their electorate in the elections and will have to be answerable for their actions once the elections come. This is not the case with the judges.

The Doctrine of Basic Structure in the Light of Various Judicial Pronouncements

Hence, with the narrow margin of 7:6, it was held in the Keshavananda case that there are certain basic features of the

Constitution which are unamendable and Parliament can't exercise its power under Article 368 on similar line as of Constituent Assembly to amend the 'basic structures of the Constitution' and it can only be done by replacing the existing Constitution.

As one can read into the Constituent Assembly debates, there is neither any such scheme provided by our forefathers nor it has been found any place in our Constitution for any classification of Constitutional provisions which are beyond the scope of Article 368. But, after Keshavananda case, the scope of parliamentary power to amend the Constitution under Article 368 has been curtailed and came under the purview of judicial scrutiny that whether it is violative of basic structure of the Constitution or not.

According to Sikri C.J., the 'basic structure' was built on the basic foundation, i.e. the freedom and dignity of individual. He observed in:

Para 292: ...The true position is that every provision of the Constitution can be amended provided in the result the basic foundation and structure of the Constitution remains the same. The basic structure may be said to consist of the following features:

1. *Supremacy of the Constitution;*
2. *Republican and democratic form of government;*
3. *Secular character of the Constitution;*
4. *Separation of powers between the legislature, the executive and the judiciary;*
5. *Federal character of the Constitution.*

As per Shelat & Grover JJ, Para 582: ...If the historical background, the Preamble, the entire scheme of the Constitution, relevant provisions thereof including Article 368 are kept in mind, there can be no difficulty in discerning that the following can be regarded as the basic elements of the constitutional structure. (These cannot be catalogued but only be illustrated):

1. *The supremacy of the Constitution.*
2. *Republican and democratic form of government and sovereignty of the country.*
3. *Secular and federal character of the Constitution.*
4. *Demarcation of power between the legislature, the executive and the judiciary.*

5. *The dignity of the individual secured by the various freedoms and basic rights in Part III and the mandate to build a welfare state contained in Part IV.*
6. *The unity and the integrity of the nation.*

So, after Golak Nath case, no fundamental right could be taken away or abridged and, after Keshavananda case, it is for the court to decide whether a fundamental right or other provisions contained in the Constitution is a basic structure or not. If it is so, then it cannot be amended or abrogated.

In Indira Gandhi V. Raj Narain (AIR 1975 SC 2299), the Supreme Court added the following features as 'basic structure' to the list of basic features laid down in Keshavananda case:

i. *Rule of law;*
ii. *Judicial review;*
iii. *Democracy, which implies free and fair elections;*
iv. *Jurisdiction of Supreme Court under Article 32.*

Further in Minerva Mills case, the Supreme Court by 4:1 majority struck down clauses (4) & (5) of Article 368 on the ground that these clauses destroyed the essential feature of the basic structure of the Constitution. The court held that the following are the basic features of the Constitution:

i. *Limited power of Parliament to amend the Constitution;*
ii. *Harmony and balance between fundamental rights and directive principles;*
iii. *Fundamental rights in certain cases;*
iv. *Power of judicial review in certain cases.*

The judgement, thus, makes it clear that the Parliament is the creature of the Constitution and derives its power from the Constitution, including the power to amend under Article 368 and it is the constitutional interpretation of the Supreme Court for any amendment to the Constitution which will prevail in India and not the Parliament. Each amendment by the Parliament has to satisfy the judges of the Supreme Court that it does not violate the Constitution. The court, however, held that doctrine of basic structure is to be applied only in judging the validity of amendments to the Constitution and it does not apply for judging the validity of ordinary laws made by legislatures.

Doctrine of Basic Structure as it Stands Today

After the re-affirmation and extension of the applicability of the doctrine of basic structure in the Minerva Mill case, it is now evident that so long as the decision in Keshavananda case is not overturned by another full Bench of the Supreme Court, any amendment of the Constitution is liable to be interfered with by the court on the ground that it affects one or other of the basic features of the Constitution.

Thereafter, by way of judicial interpretation, the list of features of the Constitution which has been held as basic and essential, that cannot be amended by the Parliament, is ever increasing by the Supreme Court. One major post-Keshavananda development of the doctrine is that the court has declined to foreclose the list of basic features as suggested by the different judges in the Keshavananda case.

In Indira Gandhi case, it has been observed that the claim of any particular feature of the Constitution to be a 'basic feature' would be determined by the court in each case that comes before it.

So far, quite a multitude of features have been acknowledged as a 'basic structure' by different judges, individually in different case, though there is no consensus as regards each of them, in particular.

a. *Secularism [I. R. Coelho V. State of Tamil Nadu (AIR 2007 SC 861), Valsamma Paul (Mrs.) V. Cochin University (1996) 3 SCC 545]*
b. *The 'essence' of other fundamental rights in Part III [Waman V. Union of India (AIT 1981 SC 271)]*
c. *Power of Supreme Court under Articles 32, 136, 141 and 142 [Delhi Judicial Services Assn. V. State of Gujarat (1991) 4 SCC 406]*
d. *Parliamentary Democracy and Multiparty system [Kuldip Nayar V. UOI [(2006) 7 SCC 1]]*
e. *Right of equality in public employment [State of Karnataka V. Uma Devi (2006) 4 SCC 1]*
f. *Part IV in toto, Directive Principles of State Policy [Bhim V. Union of India (AIR 1981 SC 234 (Krishna Aiyar J. in para 18))]*

g. *The balance between Fundamental Rights and Directive Principles [Minerva Mills & I. R Coelho Case (Supra)]*

h. *Independence of the Judiciary [Gupta V. UOI (AIR 1982 SC 149), Supreme Court AOR Assn. V. UOI ((1993) 4 SCC 441)]*

In a recent case challenging the Constitutional validity of 99th amendment to the Constitution, which paved the way for NJAC, Supreme Court Advocates-on-Record Assn. v. Union of India, (2016) 5 SCC 1, the Supreme Court has struck down the amendment by majority of 4:1, brought after overwhelming political consensus to bring transparency in judicial appointments as an alternative to collegium system adopted by the court on the basis of violation of basic structure of the Constitution. It has held indirectly that collegium system is a basic feature of our Constitution. It is hereby pertinent to notice that such system has no existence either in Constituent Assembly debates or in our written Constitution and was not even in practice till 90s.

It is very important to note that if basic structure theory is a doctrine evolved by 13 judges of the Supreme Court in the Keshavananda case and reaffirmed in other judgements, then it is equally binding on the judiciary as well. Independence of judiciary is important and rightly a basic structure, but so is democratic and republican form of government and separation of powers as well. This also means that governance must be undertaken by those elected to govern by the people of India and law-making by those elected to make laws by the people of India. There has to be rightful balance among various basic structures *inter se*.

Critique to the Doctrine of Basic Features:

The court has taken upon itself the task of differentiating between the essential and non-essential features of the Constitution, though according to the canons of interpretation all parts of the written Constitution, in absence of any specific provision to the contrary, are to be given equal importance. To find out essential or non-essential features is an exercise in imponderables. Again, the question arises who will make such a distinction [D.D. Basu Comparative Constitutional Law, 2nd edition, p. 318].

According to H.M. Seervai, the dichotomy between unessential parts of the Constitution and the fundamental structure of the

Constitution is not correct. Between 'unessential' provisions and the fundamentals, there are varying degrees of importance which no one can call unessential [Constitutional Law of India, 4th Edn. Vol III at p. 3159]. In the light of the above discussion it can be said that the basic feature doctrine is itself subject to serious debate among jurists.

Conclusion

There cannot be an ever-evolving doctrine that can be open to judicial interpretation. Doctrines like that of 'basic structure' require consistency on judicial measurable standards. The apparent conflict between the judiciary and legislature should be avoided. The reconciliation between the 'Basic Structure Doctrine' and 'Doctrine of Separation of Powers' can only be achieved if the different organs of the state adopt the 'Doctrine of Self Restraint' or wisdom when to exercise such power.

Both the Parliament and judiciary are partners in the progress of Indian state and its vibrant democracy, and, therefore, it would be apt to conclude this paper with this famous quote of Lord Byron: "A thousand years scarce serve to form a state; an hour may lay it in the dust."

References

1. *Sir George Bernard Shaw*
2. *Keshavananda Bharati v. State of Kerala, AIR 1973 SC 1461*
3. *Shankari Prasad v. Union of India, AIR 1951 SC 459.*
4. *Sajjan Singh v. State of Rajasthan, AIR 1965 SC 845*
5. *I. C. Golak Nath v. State of Punjab, AIR 1967 SC 1643*
6. *Minerva Mills v. Union of India, AIR 1980 SC 1789.*
7. *Article 245 of the Constitution of India, 1950*
8. *Keshavananda Bharati v. State of Kerala, AIR 1973 SC 1461*
9. *Ibid*
10. *Indira Gandhi v. Raj Narain, AIR 1975 SC 2299*
11. *Ashoka Kumar Thakur v. Union of India (2008) 6 SCC 1*
12. *Nachane Ashwini Shivram v. State of Maharashtra, AIR 1998 Bom 1*
13. *Minerva Mills v. Union of India, (1980) 3 SCC 625*

□

Indian Constitution and Federalism

—Prof. Rekha Saxena

Throughout almost 200 years of British rule, clashes between Indian kingdoms in the peninsula were curbed by a robust colonial power at the Centre. The federal scheme was thought essential near the time of the transfer of power in 1947 both by the British rulers and Independent Indian bests. Federal roots in the Indian Constitution can be traced from pre-Independence days, when British parliament enacted Government of India Act, 1935. This Act has provisioned several federal features like establishment of federal system of governments in Indian provincial units. Also, the framers of the Indian Constitution had opted for the federal model of governance along with British parliamentary system. The parliamentary form of government persists on legislative supremacy. The amalgamation of both federal structure and parliamentary system was considered to be essential by the constitutional experts in order to accommodate the interests of all sections of the society and also to satisfy the expectations of all regions by reconciling the centripetal and centrifugal forces.

The Constituent Assembly debates reflect two strands of arguments on federalism. The Objectives Resolution moved by Jawaharlal Nehru on 13th December 1946 envisioned a confederation with autonomous federating units.[1] In the context of impending Partition, the Union Constitution Committee, in its second meeting, recommended federal structure with a strong Centre.[2] While presenting the draft Constitution, Dr. B.R. Ambedkar emphasised the need to reconcile federation and unity by ensuring uniformity in basic matters.[3] Thus, the dominant view in the Constituent Assembly favoured a federal structure with strong Centre. However, there were some members such as Brajeshwar Prasad and K.M. Pannikar who favoured a unitary state. Pannikar opined that a federation will result in economic inequality between the provinces and also weaken the nation on all fronts.[4] On the other hand, there were members such as Lokanath Mishra, Mahboob Ali Baig, Mohammad Ismail Sahib and B.M. Gupte who favoured the 'confederal' model with strong federating units as envisaged in the Objectives Resolution.[5] Gupte spoke against the economic dependence of federating units on the Centre.[6]

Federalism is based on the principle of Unity in Diversity. This implies forging of unity while affirming diversity. However, some of the thinkers and leaders like Deendayal Upadhyaya propounded the ideology of one nation, one culture and one nationality. Upadhyaya opposed linguistic reorganisation of states. He said, "...Even today, fresh attacks are made on our culture. Language-based state demarcation is just a sample. To distort the nation is a conspiracy of the British and the Communists... To say that every state has a different language and culture is an ideological mistake. Spread of such malice is really not required. Therefore, it is our ideology that this is one nation, one culture and one nationality."[7]

Article 1 of the Constitution describes India as 'Union of states' which, Dr. Ambedkar said, means states are indestructible part of the Union. Though the term 'federal' is not mentioned anywhere in the Constitution, it was often used in the Constituent Assembly debates. The reason behind this was that the Constitution framers wanted a strong Centre because of various historical reasons. Therefore, K.C. Wheare described India and Canada as 'quasi-federacy', but he made an interesting distinction that Canadian Constitution was quasi-federal, but since 1960s-70s, Canada had become more federal despite its Constitution, whereas Indian Constitution as well as in practice, it is 'quasi-federacy'.[8]

India started as a centralised federation under the one-party dominance of the Indian National Congress, but since 1989, the Indian political system has been gradually moving towards greater federalisation. Douglas Verney has gone to the extent of arguing that transformation of the Indian party system to a regionalised multi-partisan conformation has fostered the evolution of the Indian political system from 'quasi-federation' to 'quasi-confederacy'.[9]

The reasons for greater federalisation are social mobilisation, rise of identity politics, decline of national parties to muster majority on their own, rise of regional/state-based parties, advent of coalition politics, judicial interpretations favouring the cause of state autonomy, liberalisation, privatisation and globalisation (LPG) that created pressure to link the national economy with global economy and its spin-off effect created pressure within the nation to decentralise power to the grassroots level. Singh and Saxena perceptively observe that the occurrence of federalism in India has grown historically and is in the course of fruition. Its historical trail has passed through the imperial 'revenue and law and order model' to a 'planned development model' to a 'cooperative' federalism model to a federal 'bargaining' model to a 'collaborative model'.[10]

Post-Independence, India has witnessed the demands from various corners to create new states on linguistic basis. Under compulsion, the Union government created multi-lingual states to accommodate regional interests. Based on the report of the first State Reorganisation Commission, which has detailed study on demands of new states, the Union government has redrawn the boundaries for new states. In this regard, Article 3 of the Constitution gives a unilateral power to the Parliament to regroup the states of the Union by the procedure of legislation which is different from constitutional amendment. This has repeatedly been seen as a blatantly 'unfederal' feature as the only obligation on part of the Union is to 'consult' the state(s) concerned, where consultation doesn't mean concurrence. Though, more or less, there is a consensus on this issue, it became a controversial issue in the case of creation of a separate state of Telangana as the 29th state of India because the parent state, Andhra Pradesh, was not in favour of it.[11]

The Federal Scheme

The most important feature of a federal Constitution is the distribution of legislative powers between the Union and the states. The distribution of powers and the scheme of federal system reflect in our Constitution under the Seventh Schedule. The Constitution has set up a parliamentary federal government. The Parliament has two Houses – the 'council of states' known as Rajya Sabha and 'house of the people' known as Lok Sabha. The federal state has bi-cameral legislative houses, but a few states chose to have unicameral legislative house, i.e., legislative assembly.

The President of India is the constitutional head of the Union. The Union government appoints Governor as the constitutional head of the states. Both the President and the Governor are formal heads who safeguard the constitutional norms. The Prime Minister and the Chief Ministers of the states are the executive heads of their respective government.

The Constitution has provisioned uniformity in all basic matters which are essential to maintain the unity of the nation. It provides single citizenship for the whole nation. There is a single judiciary and with uniformity in fundamental, civil and criminal laws. Judiciary, as guardian of the Constitution, also plays a significant role in balancing the relations between the Union and the states. The Constitution empowered judiciary to review legislature and executive actions of the Union and the states.

Another uniform feature of our Constitution is All India Service, which includes IAS, IPS and IFS. The recruitment of these services is done by UPSC and the candidates are allotted to states and they briefly serve in the Union government.

To ensure proper coordination and to resolve matters between the Union and the states, the Constitution, under Article 262, empowers the President to establish an Interstate Council with the Prime Minister as chairman and the Chief Ministers as members. In 1990, the then PM an V.P. Singh formed, Interstate Council based on the recommendations of Sarkaria Commission. The council had provided a platform for states to discuss policies and issues of common interest.

Similarly, in 1952, the National Development Council was set up by a Union Cabinet resolution. This council is the highest deliberative body in the field of planning and policy-making. The Prime Minister is the chairman and the members of the Planning Commission, and the Chief Ministers are its members. The council reviews the key aspects of the economic policies and recommends measures to implement the national plans.

Asymmetrical Provisions of Power Sharing in the Constitution

In the Indian context, federalism accommodates the Indian diversity. The Constitution deals with the peripheries of the states in ambit of the Constitution. This practice is called 'asymmetrical federalism'. In comparative political theory,[12] Ronald Watts makes an interesting distinction between political asymmetry and constitutional asymmetry. He argues that political asymmetry exists in each federation in terms of geographical and demographic size of the units, whereas by constitutional asymmetry, he means specifically "differences in the status or legislative and executive powers assigned by the Constitution to the different regional units." He classifies India as an illustration of both these types of asymmetry.[13]

Example of political asymmetry is Rajya Sabha, known as 'council of states' and its members of the House represents the federal states. The Rajya Sabha is a continuing body and it cannot be dissolved. The Fourth Schedule of the Indian Constitution mentions about the allocation of seats to the states and Union territories in Rajya Sabha. The reservation of seats is made on the basis of the population strength of each state. As a result of the reorganisation of states and formation of new states, since 1952 the number of elected seats in the Rajya Sabha allotted to states and Union territories has changed from time to time. The states are represented in Rajya Sabha not on the footing of formal equality like in USA. Here, in India, states are represented according to their population strength which is termed as 'weightage proportional representation'. Uttar Pradesh has 31 seats in Rajya Sabha, whereas smaller states like Meghalaya, Mizoram, Manipur, Puducherry and Goa have one seat each in Rajya Sabha.[14]

The constitutional asymmetry can be found in specific provisions made for states like Maharashtra, Gujarat, Assam, Andhra Pradesh, Sikkim, Manipur and Arunachal Pradesh in the subjects related to the law and order, administering tribal areas and in dealing with inter-state regional disparities. For example, Article 371 provides that the Governor of Maharashtra or Gujarat would have a 'special responsibility' for the establishment of separate development boards for certain backward regions with equitable allocation of development funds and provision of facilities for technical education, vocational training and employment opportunities.

In the same way, Article 371-A provides special provision for the state of Nagaland. The Parliament passed the 13th Amendment Act, 1962, and inserted Article 371-A in 1963 and in the same year, the Nagaland state was formed. This provision was incorporated after a 16-points agreement was signed between the Centre and the Naga People's Convention in 1960. According to Article 371-A, if the Parliament passes any Bill related to the religious or social practices of the Nagas or Naga customary law and procedure or administration of civil and criminal justice involving decisions according to Naga customary law or the ownership and transfer of land and its resources, then the concurrence of the state legislature is mandatory. This Article also provides 'special responsibility' to the Governor of Nagaland with respect to law and order in the state with regard to internal disturbances occurring in the state, especially in the Tuensang district.

Besides, Articles 371-B and C empower the President to ensure the setting up of a committee of the Legislative Assembly in the states of Assam and Manipur, consisting of members elected from tribal/hill areas to look after the welfare of those communities. Furthermore, Articles 371-D and E enjoin the President to ensure 'equitable opportunities and facilities' for the people in different regions of Andhra Pradesh in respect of public employment and education and the establishment of a Central university in the state. Articles 371-F and I guarantee that the Legislative Assembly of Sikkim and Goa "shall consist of not less than 30 members." The former Article also places on the Governor of the state certain "special responsibility for peace and for an equitable arrangement for ensuring the social and economic advancement of different sections of population" of the state. Article 371-H gives "special responsibility with respect to law and order" in Arunachal Pradesh and empowers the incumbent, i.e., the Governor, to act in his 'individual judgement' after consulting the council of ministers.

Further, the most significant among these is Article 370 of Indian Constitution which gives autonomous status to the state of

Jammu and Kashmir. This Article is termed as the greatest degree of asymmetry in our Constitution which provides 'temporary, transitional and special provisions' to J&K. The Article provides scope for self-governance to the people of J&K in order to preserve their identity and security to their future. It may be recalled that during the time of integration of Jammu and Kashmir into the Indian Union, then princely ruler of Kashmir, Maharaja Hari Singh has signed 'Instrument of Accession' with India like others.

Furthermore, another important example of constitutional asymmetry relates to special status to the states of North-East under Fifth and Sixth Schedules. This special status has been granted due to historical peculiarities. The Fifth Schedule allocates some areas inside the present states for distinct action. On the assistance of the state Cabinet, the Governor of the state can announce that no laws of the Parliament or the state shall apply to the scheduled areas in interrogation. It has enormous legislative power that comprises the power to alter or repeal acts of the Parliament and the state legislature. Further, they can establish Tribal Advisory Council for the scheduled area concerned, if the President so pronounces. The Sixth Schedule is more intricate and relates to tribal areas of Assam, Meghalaya, Tripura and Mizoram. They have carved out autonomous districts and regions to be administered by district and regional councils of their own. They can make laws on subjects pertinent to their district or region, and also constitute village courts. However, these Schedules together can be modified by a simple Act of Parliament. There are many more provisions in the Constitution to satisfy sub-state autonomy demands. "This rewrites federal governance to cater to the politics of collective identity without necessarily putting the federation at risk under pressure from turmoil and threats of secession."[15]

Under the Indian Constitution, there is financial asymmetry as well that is discussed subsequently

Yet another example of constitutional asymmetry is a special unit in the Indian federation referred to as Union territories (UTs). At the moment, there are 7 UTs in India, which are created by the Union government over a period of time. The UTs are geographically small and unviable to function as a state unit.

The Union government appoints Lieutenant Governors as the administrative head of the UTs. Unlike other UTs, Puducherry and Delhi are distinct. Both have unicameral legislature. The Parliament passed respectively the Constitution (Fourteenth Amendment) Act, 1962, and the Constitution (Sixty-ninth Amendment) Act, 1991, to create legislative bodies in Puducherry and Delhi. The Chief Minister and the council of ministers of both the states are directly elected by the people. Both Delhi and Puducherry have Lieutenant Governors who formally perform the executive functions of the UT government. The power over land, police and law and order in Delhi is entrusted to the Union. Despite being a UT, Puducherry enjoys control over these subjects. This unique status of both Delhi and Puducherry has been the major bone of contention between the Union and the UT governments of Delhi and Puducherry.[16]

Administrative Relations

The executive controls of the Union government as well as State governments are co-terminus with the legislative dominion. Article 256 stipulates that the State shall exercise its executive power in a way that it safeguards "compliance with the laws made by the Parliament." Additionally, "the executive power of the Union shall extend to the giving of such directions to a State as may appear to the government of India to be necessary for that purpose."

An important bone of contention relates to the executive power of the Union to sign international treaties or conventions under Article 253 of the Constitution that requires a Parliamentary legislation for actualisation of these agreements. This provision became contentious in the context of globalisation especially when India signed the WTO treaty in 1995 as it involved obligations for the federating States even in areas that fell in their exclusive jurisdiction like agriculture. Exactly on this issue, the States of Punjab, Rajasthan, Odisha and Tamil Nadu filed petitions in the Supreme Court that they were not consulted. However, later, they withdrew the objections seemingly on assurances from the Union government that in future, they will be consulted. Article 253 also became controversial at the time of the signing of Indo-US nuclear civilian deal in the Parliament in 2007 when the Opposition, especially the Left allies of the Congress-led coalition government in New Delhi and State units of the Left parties, withdrew support from the ruling UPA-I government. This issue also ignited on the debate on the role of FDI in multi-brand retail.[17]

Another tension area between the Union and the States is the role of the Governor. He plays a dual role. Firstly, he is the constitutional head of the provincial State where he acts as the guardian of the Constitution to confirm that the Ministry of the State is accountable to the legislature. Secondly, he is the agent of the Union in the State as eyes and ears of the President to safeguard that the administration of the State is carried out in harmony with the larger provisions of the Indian Constitution.

However, the office of the Governor has become a controversial issue in Union-State relations with regard to biased appointment of Governors by the ruling party at the Centre and blatantly political role played by the incumbent to appease the Union government. The office of governorship has been habitually presented to political stalwarts and bureaucrats as a kind of post-retirement employment. Further, another matter of concern is the habit of dismissing Governors with the change of guard at the Centre replacing the Governors appointed by the preceding government by the Prime Minister for political reasons, and without giving any reason under President's 'pleasure' under Article 156 (1) of the Constitution.

Certain parties and State governments, in the memorandums submitted to the Sarkaria Commission, demanded the abolition of the office of Governor and maintained that the Chief Minister of the State concerned must be consulted in advance before appointment of a Governor. The Sarkaria Commission was not in favour of the idea to abolish the office of Governor but suggested to follow the custom to appoint persons who have not been lately active in the politics of the concerned State and also consult the Chief Minister. Further, the commission proposed that the Governors should usually allow the test of a majority claim on the floor of the House and not in Raj Bhawan.

In this context, it is essential to mention Article 356 that discusses emergency power of the Union government to take over the government of a State on the advice of the Governor. This provision has been most abused by parties at the Centre as a political revenge to remove Opposition parties ruling in States. Therefore, many parties and State governments, in their memorandum to Sarkaria Commission, insisted to revoke this provision or take along it under more constitutional restrictions.

The Sarkaria Commission did not accept such extreme suggestions, but powerfully advised the federal officials to use this power with check. Besides, it specified rules for the Governor, and by insinuation for the President and the Union Cabinet. But it was only when one-party dominant system was transformed into a multi-party system that there was a check on this power. Also, another reason that curbed the misuse of Article 356 was that the Supreme Court departed from practice and, in its landmark judgement in S.R. Bommai & Others v. Union of India (1994), made President's Rule subject to judicial review. Further, the oppositional majority in the Rajya Sabha also acted as a deterrent.[18]

Financial Competencies Between the Union and the States

As far as financial relations are concerned, there are two main components related to financial arrangements. First is the distribution of taxation heads and second relates to the distribution of revenues and sharing the resources between the Union and the States. The Seventh Schedule of the Constitution has List I and List II with separate heads of taxation. In the Union List, there are 13 taxation heads like income tax, corporate tax, customs and excise duties, etc. In the State List, there are 19 taxation heads, such as land revenue, taxes on agricultural income, sales tax, entertainment tax, stamps and registration. However, the statutory provisions in the Constitution related to taxation and revenues have several short-comings in the practical functioning. The States have pointed out imbalances in the taxation structure and also inadequacies in the revenue sharing. The tax base of the State government is relatively small in comparison to the Union government. Moreover, the States have more responsibility in building the social infrastructure and more spending on socio-economic development. The State government carries more burden in particularly the development of public institutions, like schools, hospitals and also maintaining law and order. Due to existing taxation structure, which has significant gaps, the States are bound to depend on the Union government for more financial aid and other fiscal resources.

Since 1990s, there has been a paradigmatic change in economic policies and Union-State relations as economic liberalisation has not only increased the autonomy of both the private sector, but made the State governments more autonomous. Singh and Saxena argue that "federalisation has accentuated the tendency towards political as well as economic regionalism. While a more decentralised planning is still in place, the public investment in the economy has considerably gone down. This has opened up opportunities for economically more developed States to chart out their own strategies of development in collaboration with the private sector, both national and multinational. As Rudolphs observe, a 'new federal market economy' has emerged." However, on the other hand, adds Singh and Saxena, "backward States have been put to disadvantage on account of lack of their own resources and declining public investment on the part of the federal government. Private capital has been reluctant to invest in backward States and regions. Since the early 1990s, when economic liberalisation and globalisation accelerated, there has been a tremendous increase in regional economic disparities among states."[19]

With the initiation of neo-liberal economic reforms in 1991, many tax reforms have been implemented. The most important was the replacement of States' sales tax by State value-added tax (SVAT) and its replacement by a Goods and Services Tax (GST), an indirect tax imposed on the supply of goods and services, by merging a number of Central and State taxes. Originally proposed and presented by the Congress-led UPA, the proposal failed when the term of the 15th Lok Sabha was over. Subsequently, the BJP-led NDA government initiated the 122nd Constitutional Amendment Bill in 2014, but it was finally passed in the Parliament on 29th March 2017. However, the Act came into effect on 1st July 2017.

Further, the Constitution provides certain institutional mechanisms for fiscal transfers. According to Article 280, the President constitutes Finance Commission, which is a constitutional body. Such a commission oversees the institutional framework of revenue sharing between the Union and the States. It is a semi-judicial expert body which enjoys greater trust and legitimacy among the State governments. The Sarkaria Commission has recommended for better coordination between the Finance Commission and Planning Commission so that an integrated view on the flow of Central assistance to the States becomes durable. On the contrary, the Union government in 2014 headed by Prime Minister Narendra Modi abolished Planning Commission and replaced it with NITI Aayog (National Institution for Transforming India) as a policy think-tank. It consists of a civil servant who is its chief executive, two full-time experts – one economist and other a defence research and development expert, six Union minsters – three of whom are ex-officio and remaining are special invitees, free-market economist Arvind Panagariya as the deputy chair and PM Modi as the chairman. The function of NITI Aayog is to cultivate a 'national agenda' for the Prime Minister and the Chief Ministers to promote 'cooperative federalism'. Further, its Governing Council encompasses Chief Ministers of the States and Lieutenant Governors of Union territories, besides the Prime Minister as chairperson. Furthermore, a substantial way of federal fiscal transfers to States is done via Centrally sponsored schemes as part of five-year plans started by many Union ministries in the three competencies, namely Central, State and Concurrent.[20]

Conclusion

To conclude, I would argue that Indian federalism has been an evolutionary process. It has been rewritten all the time through constitutional amendments, statutory changes and the reconsideration of the executive power (RD_RS). Indian federalism that started as a centralised federation has been moving towards greater federalisation of its polity. The reasons behind this federalisation have already been discussed above. However, the effects of federalisation can be seen in the working of the constitutional functionaries like the Election Commission, the President, the Governors, etc., who have acquired greater discretionary manoeuverability in their functioning. Another impression can be seen in the strengthening of the third tier of the federal structure that got constitutional footing by 73rd and 74th Constitutional Amendment Acts. Further, influence can be seen in the setting up of more independent regulatory bodies with quasi-judicial nature in sectors of economy. Furthermore, an upshot of this federalisation can be witnessed in the growing importance of inter-governmental relations both at the vertical and horizontal levels. In the era of privatisation and globalisation, such interactions have multiplied and there are new actors that have come in picture, i.e., market and civil society. There are many challenges like terrorism, pandemics, epidemics, climate change, etc., that need concerted inter-governmental action, deliberation, policy-making. This cannot be tackled by one order of government. It has to be a concerted multilateral effort involving all governments, civil society institutions and the market forces.

References

1. *Constituent Assembly Debates, Book 2, Vol. VII, November 4, 1948 to January 8, 1949, pp. 36-7.*
2. *Constituent Assembly Debates, Book 2, Vol. VII, November 4, 1948 to January 8, 1949, p. 372.*
3. *Constituent Assembly Debates, Book 2, Vol. VII, November 4, 1948 to January 8, 1949, p. 241.*
4. *Constituent Assembly Debates, Book 2, Vol. VII, November 4, 1948 to January 8, 1949, pp. 330.*
5. *Constituent Assembly Debates, Book 5, Vol. X-XII, October 6, 1949 to January 24, 1950, p.844.*
6. *Constituent Assembly Debates, Book 5, Vol. X-XII, October 6, 1949 to January 24, 1950, pp. 613.*
7. *Deendayak Upadhyaya, 'Bharatvarsha ki Rashtriyata aur Uska Aadhar', Panchjanya, July 19, 1953, p.8*
8. *K.C. Wheare, Federal Government, Oxford University Press, New York, 1964, Fourth edition.*
9. *Douglas Verney, 'From Quasi-Federation to Quasi-Confederacy? The Transformation of India's Party System,' Publius, Vol. 33, No. 4, Fall 2003, p. 171. Also see Lawrence Saez, Federalism Without a Centre: The Impact of Political and Economic Reform on India's Federal System, Sage, New Delhi, 2002.*
10. *M.P. Singh and Rekha Saxena. Indian Politics: Constitutional Foundations and Institutional Functioning, New Delhi: Prentice Hall, 2011, Second edition, Chapter 7.*
11. *Rekha Saxena. 'The Problems of Statehood in Indian Federalism:*

A Case for Territorial Pluralism in Harihar Bhattacharyya and Lion Koenig (eds.). Globalisation and Governance in India: New Challenges to Society and Institution, London and New York, Routledge, 2015.

12. *There is an interesting debate on this, See Rekha Saxena. 'Is India a case of Asymmetrical Federalism?' Economic and Political Weekly, January 14, 2012.*
13. *Ronald L. Watts. Comparing Federal Systems. Montreal and Kingston: Institute of Inter-governmental Relations, Third edition, p.127.*
14. *Rekha Saxena 'Role of Rajya Sabha: the federal Second or Secondary Chamber?' Indian Journal of Federal Studies, 2007.*
15. *Rajeev Dhavan and Rekha Saxena. 'Republic of India'. A Global Dialogue on Federalism: Legislative, Executive, and Judicial Governance in Federal Countries, Vol.3, edited by Katy Le Roy and Cheryl Saunders, Quebec: McGill – Queen's University Press, 2006.*
16. *Rekha Saxena. 'Multilayered Governance in Delhi'. State Politics in India. Edited by Himanshu Roy and MP Singh, Delhi, Primus, 2017.*
17. *Rekha Saxena, "Treaty-Making Power: A Case for 'Federalisation' and 'Parliamentarisation', Economic and Political Weekly, Vol. XLII, No. 1, January 6, 2007.*
18. *S.R. Bommai & Others v. Union of India, Supreme Court Cases, Judgements Today, 1994.*
19. *M.P. Singh and Rekha Saxena. Op.cit. chapter 7.*
20. *For a detailed discussion, see Wilfried Swenden and Rekha Saxena. 'Rethinking Central planning: a federal critique of the Planning Commission, India Review, 2017.*

□

Parliamentary Democracy: Our Constitution and its Implementation

—Sumitra Mahajan

For the last seven decades, a parliamentary system and a government based on democratic values is running smoothly and successfully in India. Our glorious democracy is a reflection of political, social and cultural essence along with the philosophy of our glorious nation. In India, democratic system had begun in Vedic era itself. Since Vedic times up to the republic of Lichchhavis, the democratic system has been integral to the basic consciousness of our country. Republic is synonymous with Sanskrit word 'Ganatantra' that has been used several times in Rigveda, Atharvaveda and Brahman granthas or scriptures.

When our coutry became independent, it was after much thinking and elaborate deliberations that we adopted a democratic system of government and a Constituent Assembly was set up to frame the Constitution. An excellent Constitution was created that became effective on 26th January 1950. The highest ideals inherent in the Constitution are the guiding lights to lead our nation on the path of glory it deserves. Our Constitution has made its place in the greatest Constitutions of the world.

The ideals and principles incorporated in the Preamble determine the basic nature of our Constitution. The Preamble begins with "We the People of India." This Preamble declares that we adopted, enacted and gave to ourselves this Constitution to constitute India into a sovereign, socialist, secular, democratic republic and it secures the principle of justice, liberty, equality and fraternity for every citizen of the country.

After an in-depth contemplation, the creators of our Constitution chose parliamentary democracy as the system of government because in a democratic system, the responsibilities of the executive are evaluated on daily as well as periodical bases. Daily evaluation is done by the parliamentarians through debates over questions, resolutions, no confidence motions, adjournment motions and speeches. Periodical evaluation is done by the voters at the time of elections.

India is known all over the world as the largest and and a lively democracy because our parliamentary system has the majority of public, the masses at its centre, who in 16 general elections have used their wisdom and intelligence to exercise their franchise to ensure smooth transfer of power and have changed governments eight times. This, beyond doubt, shows our commitment towards the successful implementation of a democratic Constitution, democratic government and democratic way of life.

We have got a generous polity where collective welfare is considered as important as the individual rights and freedom. Though we are a multicultural nation, our way of thinking and our tradition, that aim at taking everybody along, is reflected crystal clear in our political system. There is hardly any parliament anywhere in this world that incorporates so much of diversity and variety into a unified whole. I am certain that behind the success of a democracy, commitment, energy and fixity of purpose of the people governed by the system are always at work.

In our democratic system, Parliament has been granted the highest place because it is the highest representative and legislativde entity. Our Parliament has got the constitutional power and authority to make laws, regulate the responsibilities of the executive, regulate the expenses of the nation and amend the Constitution. Despite all this, the legislature has to work within the sphere of the Constitution.

The President of India, Lok Sabha and Rajya Sabha are the integral parts of the Parliament. The Constitution is very clear about their powers, sphere of influence, responsibilities, relationship with each other and people. The harmony of the sovereignty of the Parliament and judicial review is a unique characteristic of our Constitution. The legislature, the judiciary and the executive, all execute their responsibilities thoroughly and methodically, within the sphere of the Constitution. They show adequate respect for each other's boundaries and it is expected that they keep doing so.

The key responsibilities of our Parliament are to enact laws, supervise the administration, pass the budget, solve the problems of the people, debate on the national policies, etc. As per the Constitution, the Council of Ministers is collectively answerable to Lok Sabha. After debating and voting on the demands of grants sought by various ministries, the Parliament approves the budget for the country. Lok Sabha has the authority to accept or reject any demand from the government and even lessen the amount of any grant demanded by it. These financial powers of the Parliament help ensure the accountability of the executive. Various procedural instruments are available to the members of the Parliament. These are Question Hour, Call-Attention Motion, No-Confidence Motion, etc., through which they get adequate opportunities to evaluate and influence the policies of the government and ensure the answerability of the Cabinet towards redressal of the grievances of the people.

Our Parliament, through various legislations, has brought about many changes in various fields. Privy purse and special privileges for ex-monarchs have been abolished, land reforms act, reducing the voting age to 18 from 21, provisions to establish separate commissions for Scheduled Castes and Scheduled Tribes, transfer of power to Panchayats and local bodies and at least one third reservation in local bodies for women are some significant legislations laid down by the Parliament. These legislations are important from the point of view of social change and through unanimity on some noteworthy legislations, the Parliament has really set an example of maturity and wisdom.

Our Parliament is working to evolve new strategies to tackle the contingencies which emerge from time to time. It has developed various methods and processes to increase its effectiveness. Half-an hour discussion, short-duration discussion, Call-Attention Motion, Rule 377 in Lok Sabha and special mention in Rajya Sabha to raise issues, the Business Advisory Committee, Committee on Government Assurances and the Committee on Papers Laid on the Table are some completely Indian innovations. The Speakers of Lok Sabha also have tried their best to uphold the privileges and special privileges of the parliamentarians and played an important role in strengthening the democracy.

Recently, in the eleventh session of the sixteenth Lok Sabha, the date fixed for presentation of the Central budget was 28th February, which has now been postponed to 1st Ferbruary. The main aim of this postponement is to pass just one appropriation Bill in a year and to avoid the passing of vote-on-account in the Parliament, so that the time consumed in the acceptance of the budget, especially during monsoons, the execution of projects and the works by the State and the associated governments does not get delayed in any way. Another important development was that a 49-year-old tradition ended and the Rail budget was merged back in the general budget.

In 1993, inception of Standing Committees on various subjects was a major procedural initiative to strengthen the accountability system of the Parliament. This enables monitoring of the activities of all aspects of the government by one or many committees. To achieve a comprehensive point of view in policy-making and a long-term national outlook for the executive, these committees make available necessary guidance, information and instructions. The details of the action taken by respective ministries regarding the recommendations of the committee are provided to the Parliament.

The Opposition and the media play a very important role in a parliamentary democracy. They weigh the pros and cons of a policy framed by the government and play a positive role through appreciation or criticism of the policy. They bring clarity on various issues involved in a policy resolution and stimulate people to debate and have a point of view about the policies. Thus, they have a dual role to play. This is an active and two-way interaction that contributes towards a significantly profound democratic framework. Keen and strict monitoring of the work done by a government is the sign of a healthy democracy. But what remains above all is the welfare of the people and the country. Views may differ, but when it comes to our national interest, we must be unanimous in word and deed.

Democratic values, principles and ideals of India are not just an example for the world, but a source of inspiration. People all over the world watch our parliamentary proceedings and observe them keenly. If somebody tries to stall the parliamentary proceedings or indulges in undignified behaviour, the reputation of our vibrant democracy gets dented. But if constant debates, arguments and counter-arguments are allowed to continue, a significant decision can be arrived at leading not only to the strengthening of democracy, but adding to its glory and reputation as well. But this debate, this difference of opinion and disagreement must be executed according to the acceptable limits of modesty, within the limits of decency so that the people have an unwavering faith in democracy. We, the representatives of the people, must set new standards of conduct and good behaviour. A verse from Shrimad Bhagwad Gita is very relevant and timely:

Yadyadacharati shreshthastat tadevetaro janah.
Sa yat pramanam kurute lokastadanuvartate.

(Whatsoever an accomplished man does, other people take the example and follow that, whatever path he follows is taken as the proof of appropriateness by his followers and they take that proof as the standard action for life.)

It is a matter of pride that our democracy is an active, vibrant, energetic and profound entity. Various political parties in power or in Opposition put forth their ideas with complete consciousness, power and intensity, and on the issues of public interest, express their views as per their political thinking, principles and interests, trying their best to persuade others to subscribe. But whenever national or people's interest is the issue, all parties irrespective of thier party affiliations and political differences give top priority to that. In Atharva Veda, there is the prayer of a king who invokes the divinity to grant that all his courtiers speak in one voice — *"Ye te ke cha Sabhasadaste me santu Savachasa."*

I remember the first winter session of the present Lok Sabha, the whole of which was completely stalled by the Opposition. But on the last day of the seesion, the Rights of the Persons with Disabilities Bill, 2014 was passed with a unanimous vote. Similarly, the 100th Constitutional Amendment regarding Land Boundary Agreement to exchange conclaves and simplify the international border between India and Bangladesh was passed with a unanimous vote in both the Houses.

The time we live in has provided exceptional ways and means through information and communication technology, which ensure better interaction of the Parliament with the people, and the distance between them has lessened. Technology has made it possible for the people to witness the proceedings of both Houses where they can see their representatives at work. Today, we have Lok Sabha and Rajya Sabha TV channels working 24×7, enabling direct telecast of the proceedings of Lok Sabha and Rajya Sabha, respectively. This adds to information of the people and strengthens the foundations of parliamentary democracy. The Parliament has developed its own website, www.parliamentofindia.nic.in. This bilingual website supplies detailed information regarding the initiatives and activities of Parliament. The mobile application of Lok Sabha TV is very popular among the masses. Taking another step forward in the direction of e-Parliament and paperless secretariat, we have developed an e-portal for our members.

For some time, I have been thinking about a platform on which the members can freely interact with specialists over the important issues confronting us, and understand the complex and technical aspects of policy-making. This is important because the members of Parliament are busy most of the time in their constituencies, party work and other social responsibilities. For this purpose, a Speaker's Research Initiative (SRI) has been established in Parliament. Till now, SRI has organised workshops and mutual interaction sessions on subjects like Sustainable Development Goals, the Constitution of India, Unorganised Sector, Goods and Services Tax, Draught, Drinking Water Management, Interlinking of Rivers, Challenges in Education and Health Sector. SRI also organises a fellowship programme for senior fellows and an internship programme for young students. Just in three years, it has attracted the attention of people all over the world. Various countries have admired the experiment and expressed the desire to work with this programme. Besides, in a one and the only initiative of its kind in the parliamentary history of India, a National Conference of Women Legislators has also been organised.

Through its elected members, our Parliament becomes the best representation of the diversity and multiplicity of our nation. It gives expression to the difficulties, problems and grievances present in the society and the administration, and through debate and discussion, finds solutions to these problems. In this way, our Parliament plays its role in strengthening the unity and integrity of our country.

As an institution, let the Parliament establish an ideal and be true to the expectations of all countrymen, so that the country moves forward on the path of development. Here the representative who is elected to the Parliament has a major role to play. I think the public interest must be above everything for the ruling class and the representatives of the people. As Kautilya says in his Arthashastra:

Praja sukhe Sukham Ragnyaha Prajm anam tu hite hitam.

Natmapriyam HitamRagnyaha Prajanam ty priyam Hitam.

(In the happiness of the subjects lies the happiness of the king. He should see his welfare in the welfare of the people. His interest is not in what he likes, but in what his subjects like.)

India does not only meet the test of democracy, but has been successful to a great extent in providing equal opportunities to all citizens, along with an inclusive form of administration and society as well. The elections held from time to time for the various representative bodies ranging from Panchayats to Parliament have strengthened our participatory democratic system. To lend further strength to our parliamentary democracy and to keep unity and integrity of our country intact, every citizen has to contribute as much as he or she can.

□

Parliamentary System and Gram Swarajya

—Dr. Chandrashekhar Pran

Presently, the Indian state machinery is working under the structure of parliamentary democracy wherein Parliament is the primary body. The Cabinet is formed out of its members. Western democracy is primarily of two types – Parliamentary and Presidential. While writing the Constitution of India, Dr. Bhimrao Ambedkar, chairman of the Drafting Committee of the Constitution of India, argued that the Presidential Cabinet of the American Constitution is less answerable to the public as compared to the Parliamentary Cabinet of the British Constitution which is depended upon their votes. That answerability to the public is a more desirable quality than political stability. This is the thought which led to the recommendation of parliamentary system in India.[1]

On the other hand, Mahatma Gandhi had criticised parliamentary democracy harshly in his book 'Hind Swaraj' in 1909. He called the British Parliament 'sterile' and a 'prostitute'. Sterile in the sense that it had not done a single good job and prostitute in the sense that it devoted itself to the party which won. Based on his own experience, he said that even while big debates were going on in the British Parliament, its members would nod off to sleep.[2]

Gandhiji preferred Gram Swarajya over both of these systems (Parliamentary and Presidential). The idea of Gram Swarajya has come from the long tradition of self-dependence in Indian villages. Gandhiji has stressed from the beginning that our political system should be conducive to the nature of our people because the political systems of Britain and America are similarly based upon the nature of their own people.[3]

Panchayat was the foundation of his idea of institutional self-dependence. According to him, in order to govern the villages, every year a Panchayat of five people will be elected. This Panchayat will have all kinds of necessary rights and powers.[4]

The tradition of parliamentary system in the Indian Constitution has a long background. After the acquisition of power by the British Crown, the provision of provincial local government by the Indian Council Act of 1861, 1892 and 1909 and representation to the public in the legislative councils was evolutionary process of the parliamentary system. Various important changes have been made in this direction from the enactment of the Government of India Act, 1919. The most important change was the establishment of bi-cameral Vidhan Mandal instead of Vidhan Parishad (Legislative Council).

The Indian Government Act of 1935 was the next step in this direction which prepared to implement the parliamentary system in a federal structure. In this Act, a Cabinet system consisting of ministers was recommended to help and advise the Governor-General. In this way, it took almost a hundred years for the British Parliamentary system to take shape in India. It is on these foundations that the constitutional structure of India stands upon now.

K.M. Munshi argued in the Drafting Committee that for the past hundred years, the constitutional traditions of Britain have kept inspiring the Indian political life. In such a condition, there is no reason to look elsewhere for a new system.[5]

An agreement on the parliamentary structure to be adopted had already been reached in the Special Committee of the Congress Party even before the Drafting Committee came to exist. In the four meetings that took place after July 1946, the main discussion was about the institutions of the parliamentary government. The Gandhian thought was given no place in this discussion. The two primary members of the Drafting Committee, Pandit Nehru and Sardar Patel openly supported the parliamentary system. While Nehru thought that this system was according to the ancient tradition of India,[6] Patel thought that it was expedient in the given circumstances.[7]

The first meeting to discuss the goals and structure of the Constitution was held on 9th December 1946. But no important discussion could take place due to the boycott of the Muslim League. The discussion was focussed on the goals of the Constitution. The boycott of Muslim League continued and the Drafting Committee was not able to hold a meeting. However, discussion about the fundamental principles of the Constitution kept going on in two important committees. These committees too supported the parliamentary system.[8]

The Gram Swarajya that Gandhiji recommended was based upon the centuries-old structures that continued to exist in the Indian villages. This system was based on hard work, equality, decentralisation, satyagraha, secularism and on concepts like 'trusteeship' and 'placing man on the highest pedestal'. The society was to be governed by Panchayats working on these principles. According to this suggestion, the representatives of the Panchayat elected through exercise of adult franchise would then choose the higher government both in the states and at the Centre.[9]

Many senior Congress leaders during the independence movement supported this thought. At the suggestion of Gandhiji, the most basic unit of the Congress party was constituted in the image of a Panchayat. The higher structure of Gram Swarajya was also used in the party structure. It was the practical face of the Gram Swarajya system. Gandhiji believed that the political structure of India after independence would be based on a system like this. This is why when the writing of the Indian Constitution began, this system based on the Gandhian thought was also presented as an alternative shadow.[10]

At the time of second reading of the Draft Committee, when Dr. Ambedkar strongly condemned the village society and Panchayat system of India in his address, this led to widespread resentment among the members of the Constituent Assembly. Dr. Ambedkar had said in very sharp words that he is surprised to know that those who are against provincialism and sectarianism are advocating about the village itself. "The village is a sink of stinking narrowness. What is there except of the dark den of ignorance, superstition, narrow-mindedness and communalism?"[11]

Many objections were raised in the Constituent Assembly in protest of this statement of Dr. Ambedkar and in the support of the villages. Dr. H.V. Kamath conveyed complete disagreement with Dr. Ambedkar's statement and citing his urban mindset, raised the question whether he has read "The Spirit and the Form of Indian Politics" by Sri Arvind Ghosh, besides Metcalf, in which the political system of the village and the city's self-government is considered to be the greatest period of Indian civilisation. He gave the argument that if in the present times, not only India but whole world wants to achieve peace, security and prosperity, then we will have to accept decentralisation along with 'village republic' and 'town republic'.[12]

A member from West Bengal, Arun Chandra Guha, opposed Ambedkar's statements in a logical manner with great detail. He believed that the structure of the Constitution should not be of inverse pyramid but should be actual pyramid, and its base should be Panchayat. He said that we accept a strong Centre but not with weak feet.[13]

Damodar Swarup Seth, a prominent member of the Constituent Assembly, referred to Gandhiji and suggested to make self-government the very foundation of the Constitution of Independent India. He said that a Constitution which stands on its feet needs to be formed rather than one which is standing on its head.[14]

A member from Madras, T. Prakasham, giving reference of the freedom fighters of the last 30 years, referred to Dr. Ambedkar as a person standing in isolation of them and this being the basis of his negative attitude towards Panchayat system. He raised the question whether this draft would make the Constitution of the common man or of a few people.[15]

A second key member from Madras, K. Santhanam, disagreed with Ambedkar's statement in which he had held the Gram Panchayat responsible for the national calamity. In view of the different sizes and types of Panchayat in different provinces of India, he suggested making village, the very foundation of the future of this country's independence with necessary caution and proper provisions.[16]

Prof. N.G. Ranga, a respected member of Madras, expressing great displeasure over Ambedkar's statement said that if he only knew about the achievements of Panchayat in South India, then surely he would not have said these things. Prof. Ranga clearly suggested that a provision should be made in the Constitution, making states responsible for the establishment of the Panchayat in the form of self-government in every village. Along with this, autonomy should be given to the Panchayat on the social, economic and political issues of the village so that they could become the basis of the upper structure of our Constitution.[17]

Another senior member of Madras, M.A. Iyengar, said that making the autonomous village republic the basis of the Constitution is our prime choice. In the 150 years of the British rule, our basic freedom, decentralised economy and structures of village republic have been destroyed. But in view of the present situation of the village, he also suggested that a section should be added to the policy directive that all the governments should establish the Gram Panchayat in the future and give them political autonomy and economic independence so that they can organise their work according to their own preferences.[18]

In addition to the above members, a lot of other members also gave suggestions and supported the institution of Gram Panchayat as the basis of the state system in the Constitution and to develop the structure of governance accordingly.

Second reading of the Constitution draft was, thus, marked by long debate on the various aspects of the Village Republic as a result of the indignation and dissatisfaction among the members due to the adverse comments made about village society and Panchayat of India. In this regard a proposal was presented by Santhanam.

On 22nd November 1948, Santhanam placed the proposal of a new Article 31-A which is present today as Article 40 of the Directive Principles in the Constitution. The format of the proposed new Article was as follows: "The state will take steps to organise the Gram Panchayat and will give them powers and authority that are necessary for them to be functional as units of self-government."[19]

Dr. Ambedkar announced the acceptance of it in a simple manner without any debate in the House and, finally, it was incorporated in the directive principles of the Constitution.

After this, when there was a general debate on the third reading of the Constitution from 17th to 26th November 1946, many members again filed their objections on Article 31-A with the view that village and Panchayat did not find the importance which they should have been given, that is, it has still not been able to become the base of the Indian Constitution. But, at the same time, they agreed to this amendment, with the hope that it will be possible to complete this gap with the help of Article 31-A in the future.

K. Hanumanthaiah, the member from Mysore, raised questions about the members of the Constituent Assembly itself. According to him, the type of members, as were required, are not present in the Constituent Assembly. By giving an example, he said, "We want to listen to the music of the Sitar and the Veena, but here the music of the English band is playing." However, with full confidence, he expressed his hope that human-will and human-power is a big factor and when the time comes, things will be repaired in a fitting manner.[20]

With great sympathy, T. Prakasam said, "This is not the Constitution which I was expecting for the people of my country. It is also not as per the expectations of those who worked hard during the freedom movement." According to him, "Panchayat is the very target which we planned for the nation." Expressing happiness on the inclusion of the Panchayat in the Directive Principles, he said that its implementation or compensation is dependent on the members and all who will take charge of this nation and its government. If it is implemented properly, then the time is not far away when golden period of India will be back again.[21]

Arun Chandra Guha also, in his address, described this Constitution as a 'failure' in reference to the ideology of freedom movement and the expectation of the people. He urged to make Gram Panchayat, based on economic decentralisation, the base of the new nation. With this, he, however, expressed the hope that this Constitution will be corrected in future by the revolutionary motivation of the people.[22]

In the third reading of the Constitution, in addition to the above-mentioned members, many other members also expressed similar views.

The Constitution came into force on 26th January 1950. This, however, did not change the position of different Panchayat Acts of provinces made in the English period, which continued to be implemented in the states of independent India with slight modifications. The Parliamentary system and Panchayati Raj system started operating in the country simultaneously. For community development, a very comprehensive and ambitious programme was conducted to encourage public participation. When the then Prime Minister Jawaharlal Nehru reviewed the situation in 1956, it was found that it was far behind the target and its biggest reason was lack of public participation.[23] After this, Balwant Rai Mehta Committee was formed which suggested to give a new look to the Panchayat system for its effective implementation.

After Gandhiji, his dream of Gram Swarajya was pursued with complete loyalty and understanding by personalities like Jai Prakash Narayan (JP) and Acharya Vinoba Bhave. While Vinoba was pushing on the social and cultural side, JP was centred on the political and community aspect of Gram Swarajya. Dr. Ram Manohar Lohia and Deendayal Upadhyay also always advocated for Panchayati Raj.

In this way, within two decades of its journey, the anomalies and weaknesses of the Constitution began to appear. This prompted national leaders of that period once again to raise the issues related to decentralisation of power and village Swarajya.

Nehru had moved the Panchayat system from the village to the block and the district levels, but the state governments failed to give it the importance which it actually deserves. JP also became very disappointed with this situation. In 1964, he expressed his concern in the seminar on the basic problems of Panchayat in Rajasthan.[24] After this, the condition of Panchayat worsened even more. For improvement, committees were formed from time to time by the governments. In this regard, Ashok Mehta Committee (December 1977), J.K.V. Rao Committee (March 1985), L.M.

Singhvi Committee (November 1986) and P.K. Thungan Committee (1988) have played an important role. In the recommendations of all these committees, the Panchayat system has been suggested as the basis of democratic decentralisation guaranteed by constitutional protection. This protection was sought from the special meaning of the 'Self-Government' as outlined in Article 40 of the Constitution. Singhvi Committee had gone to the extent of preparing a draft Constitutional Amendment in this regard.

After 40 years of implementation of the Constitution, a meaningful initiative was taken in 1992 in the form of 73rd Constitution Amendment. As we know, the background of this amendment was prepared by the efforts of Prime Minister Rajiv Gandhi.

Addressing the Chief Ministers of all the states on 5th May 1989, he said, "We have learned from experience that at the constitutional provision for the grassroots level, democracy is as mandatory as it is for the state legislatures and Indian Parliament." He said this while pointing out that under Article 40 of the Constitution, there is equal responsibility and equal commitment of the Centre and the states. This responsibility is also in conformity to the ancient village republic system of our country, which was very dear to Gandhiji. Naming it a revolution, he revived the debates of the Constituent Assembly, in which the concerns of the village republic were expressed.[25]

With such thoughts and expressions, he presented 64th Constitution Amendment Bill in the Parliament to bring Panchayat in the mainstream of the Constitution. His speech in Parliament in favour of this Bill on 15th May 1989 is a very significant moment in the course of Gram Ganatantra or Gram Swarajya in India. Describing the constitutional provisions of Panchayat system as a historic step, Gandhi referred to it as an attempt to bring the democracy to the masses by handing over the power to govern itself.[26]

As we all know, the 64th Constitution Amendment Bill for the new Panchayat was passed in 1989 in Lok Sabha but could not be passed in Rajya Sabha. After the Lok Sabha elections held in 1989, the National Front government also tried to pass the Bill in 1990, but due to mid-term elections, it could not become a reality. When the Congress came to power in 1991, Parliament passed this Bill on 22nd December 1992 as 73rd amendment.

With the passage of this amendment, Panchayat got constitutional status as self-government. In Part 9 of the Constitution, some provisions were made compulsory for the State's Acts, but some provisions were left at the discretion of the state legislatures in accordance with the direction of the Constitution. In compulsory provisions, the formation of Gram Sabha, the formation of Panchayat, reservation, period, State Finance Commission and the formation of the State Election Commission are included. However, provisions related to different levels of Panchayat along with their names, powers and authority of the chairpersons were made voluntary. Being a part of the compulsory provisions, Panchayat elections for the last 25 years are being held regularly in every five years. However, a great deal of negligence and carelessness has been observed in the field of finance, accounting and actual powers of governance because they have been left to the discretion of state legislature. As a result, Panchayat in most of the states has been relegated as an implementing agency of the state governments instead of being a unit of self-government.

While speaking in the Constituent Assembly about the relevance of including Panchayat in Directive Principles, Santhanam had said that the size and type of Gram Panchayat are different. Therefore, no strict and quick instructions can be incorporated in the Constitution in this regard. It will be better if the matter is left to the discretion of provincial legislature. Even in the 73rd constitutional amendment, this spirit is reflected. Unfortunately, when it comes to the handing over of the powers, rights and finances to the Panchayat, most of the states are refusing to take into account the spirit of the Constitution and the need of the common man.

All the works related to 29 subjects of the Eleventh Schedule prescribed in the Constitution have not been entrusted to Panchayat in most of the states. The talk of giving necessary manpower and financial resources is still a far cry.

Members of the Constituent Assembly had expressed their will and the desire firmly in the favour of Gram Swarajya.

Furthermore, the Prime Minister presented a resolution in the Parliament regarding 64th Constitution amendment while handing over power to the people. Today, all this has become redundant and meaningless.

Even after 70 years of Independence and 25 years of the 73rd amendment to the Constitution, the campaign of National Rural Self-Government is still crawling at the initial level. In the past 20 years, in order to set up Panchayat system as a self-government in accordance with the spirit of the Constitution, many commissions and committees have been formed and many MoUs have been signed between the Central and the state governments. However, all of this failed to produce anything of substance at grass roots level. The Gram Panchayat Development Plan, prepared by the 14th Finance Commission of India with the allocation of nearly 2 lakh crore rupees to Gram Panchayats, is an attempt to decentralise power in the right sense and fulfil the dream of Gandhiji's village self-government. However, the whole plan is staggering extremely badly for the last four years. There is no sign of public participation in the identification of the problem, the formation of the plan and its implementation at village level.

Famous Constitutionalist Grenville Austen praised the principle of reconciliation of Constitution of India. He expressed the opinion that a better reconciliation between the Central government, provincial governments and the Panchayats (in spite of their contradictory powers) can be established in due course of time. However, today this optimism is under serious doubt.

Members of the Constituent Assembly passed the Constitution with the hope that in due course of time, the Constitution will be amended in accordance with the instructions of Article 40 and, thus, people will get the true self-rule, i.e., swarajya, based on the concept of Gandhiji's Gram Swarajya and the national tradition of 'village republic'. However, all these hopes appear to be blurred.

That is why, the reconciliation between the current parliamentary system and the Gram Swarajya has to be ensured with renewed vigour and determination. For this, we have to explore new solutions in the framework of our Constitution, going beyond the 73rd amendment. On the other hand, the new cultural consciousness of the Indian society needs to be revived, which helps us to achieve national as well as human upliftment relying on the foundation of equality and fraternity in the present context.

References

1. *Dr. B.R. Ambedkar, Constituent Assembly Debates, Volume 7, p-31-33*
2. *Mahatma Gandhi, Hind Swaraj, p-13*
3. *Mahatma Gandhi, Gram Swarajya, p-3*
4. *Mahatma Gandhi Gram Swarajya, p-42-43*
5. *Munshi K. M., Constituent Assembly Debates, Volume 7, p-984*
6. *Nehru, Jawaharlal's Speech, Section 111, Publication Division, Indian Government, p-11*
7. *Patel, BallabhBhai, Constituent Assembly Debates, Volume 7, p-3-4*
8. *Constituent Assembly, Reports of Committees, First Series*
9. *Mahatma Gandhi, Gram Swarajya, p-43*
10. *Constitution of Indian, National Congress, 1948, p-1*
11. *Dr.Ambedkar, B.R., Constituent Assembly Debates, Volume 7, p-213*
12. *Dr.Kamath, H. V., Section 7*
13. *GuhaArun Chandra, Constituent Assembly Debates, Volume 7*
14. *Seth, Arun Chandra, Constituent Assembly Debate, Volume 7*
15. *Prakasham, T, Constituent Assembly Debates, Volume 7*
16. *Santhanam, K. Constituent Assembly Debates, Volume 7*
17. *Prof. Ranga, N.G. Constituent Assembly Debates, Volume 7*
18. *Iyengar, M. A. Constituent Assembly Debates, Volume 7*
19. *Panchayat Raj as the Basis of Indian Polity, Dharmapal works, p-44*
20. *Panchayat Raj as the Basis of Indian Polity, Dharmapal works, p-56*
21. *Panchayat Raj as the Basis of Indian Polity, Dharmapal works, p-59*
22. *Panchayat Raj as the Basis of Indian Polity, Dharmapal works, p-61*
23. *Community Development, Sasta Sahitya Mandal, p-24*
24. *Chandrashekhar Parmanand Mishikar, Pt. Deen Dayal Upadhyay Vichar Darshan, Vol. 5, p-189*
25. *Panchayatiraj: Samkalpaur Sambhavnaayen, Ed. Jagdish Piyush, p-24*
26. *Panchayatiraj: Samkalp aur Sambhavnaayen, Ed. Jagdish Piyush, p-32*

□

Cooperative Constitutional Reform through Institutional Dialogue

—Govind Goel

Sixty-nine years ago, some of the most eminent and dedicated freedom fighters of our nation completed the painstaking task of drafting our Constitution, after an elaborate exercise spanning almost three years.[1] Even to this date, our Constitution remains unparalleled in length and unique in detail.

Despite an elaborate exercise culminating in such a detailed document, the necessity to introduce changes in its provisions was felt within the first few weeks itself. The constitutional courts – the Supreme Court and the High Courts, while still in their post-colonial embryonic stage, sought to give meaning and purpose to constitutional provisions, particularly the fundamental rights. These possible interpretations given by the court prompted the Parliament, which at that point in time was the Constituent Assembly itself, to introduce some watershed amendments in the first year of the Constitution's working itself.

Constitutional interpretation, unlike other exercises of decision-making that a constitutional court undertakes, has been a crucial weapon for constitutional growth in our country. While emphasis in interpretation of ordinary statutes is laid on the words employed, constitutional adjudication is deeply conscious in giving meaning and purpose to the words, sometimes at variance with their literal meaning. One of the duties that courts discharge under our constitutional scheme is that of declaring a law that transgresses constitutional limitations, as unconstitutional. Limitations may be either procedural or substantive.

The most significant substantive limitation with which the constitutional courts has engaged in is the prohibition imposed on governmental action, including laws, to transgress the fundamental rights contained in Part III of our Constitution. It is this power, i.e., judicial review, which gives life and meaning to the Bill of Rights. The court, when confronted with a law alleged to be transgressing one or more fundamental rights, is often tasked with interpreting the true nature, scope and content of such fundamental rights. The eventual outcome notwithstanding, it is this organic process of constitutional adjudication by the court that triggers constitutional dialogue with the Constituent body.

The nature of constitutional interpretation is certainly not a routine judicial exercise, and requires great wisdom, experience and foresight. Constitutional courts in India have played central role in constitutional growth. As the Supreme Court once declared.[2] constitutional court is the sentinel on the qui vive, or guardian, of the Constitution. By interpretation, constitutional courts have amplified rights, protected constitutional virtues, and enunciated the basic principles of democratic governance rooted in rule of law, separation of powers and checks of balances. The courts have also enforced the rule of law and ensured supremacy of the Constitution by exercising judicial review.

In this manner, the constitutional court is not merely a passive interpreter, but an active participant with the Constituent body in this dialogue. This constitutional dialogue has been expressed in two types of situations. First set of situations is when on account of a particular interpretation, the constitutional court has perceivably impeded the political branches from undertaking measures. In such a scenario, the Constituent body steps in to amend the Constitution and undo such an interpretation. A second set of situations occurs when the constitutional court interprets a provision in a manner completely different from either its plain meaning or its intended meaning as discernible from the legislative debates or history. The Constituent body usually has not substituted its interpretation by amending the Constitution. In both these situations, the constitutional text has grown from what it was previously.

Sometimes, this dialogue has been seen as a rivalry between the judicial branch and the Constituent body. In our constitutional scheme, where we have not accorded supremacy to any individual branch, this constitutional dialogue is a larger part of the 'cooperative constitutionalism', where both branches work together towards a common purpose – to give meaning and purpose to the words of the constitutional document to the people.

I. Undoing Constitutional Adjudication for Constitutional Reform

Often, the Constituent body has been impelled to overrule constitutional adjudication which prevents governmental action due to its having been held to abridge fundamental rights.

The very first amendment introduced in the Indian Constitution was a direct result of the Constituent body disagreeing with the interpretation proffered by the constitutional courts, and considering such an interpretation as impeding the social change required to be ushered in for ridding a newly Independent India of the various maladies perceived by the regime.[3] The Constitution (First Amendment) Act, 1951, sought to undo several judgements, including those striking down land reform laws,[4] reservation measures,[5] restrictions on free press[6] and creating state monopoly in certain industries.[7]

There was largely a consensus within the interim Parliament as to the removal of impediment introduction of land reforms immunisation measures by inserting Articles 31A, 31B and Ninth Schedule, as well as enabling the state to undertake reservation measures for Scheduled Castes, Scheduled Tribes and socially and educationally backward classes by incorporating Article 15(4). However, when it came to expanding the restrictions on fundamental freedoms by amending Clauses (2) and (6) of Article 19, the reasoning of the constitutional courts had provided good fodder to debate such amendments, with arguments on both sides having convincing logic.

Validity of the First Amendment was examined by a five-judge Bench of the Supreme Court in Shankari Prasad case,[8] which held that the nature of Constituent power was different from legislative exercise and a constitutional amendment, even if transgressing fundamental rights could not be invalidated and the Constituent power enjoyed immunity from judicial review envisaged by Article 13 of the Constitution. The same position came to be reiterated by the majority in Sajjan Singh case,[9] where, for the first time, the near immunity against judicial review enjoyed thus far by the Parliament's power to amend the Constitution was sought to be reviewed when Justices Hidayatullah and Mudholkar did not emphatically reject the prayer to reconsider the dictum in Shankari Prasad case. In fact, Justice Mudholkar, after quoting Cornelius C.J. of the Supreme Court of Pakistan,[10] pondered on there being some "basic features of the Constitution which are to endure for all times or at least for the foreseeable future", which are more enduring than the incidental and supplemental provisions of the Constitution.

In less than two years, these tiny seeds of departure attained a full-blown curtailment of the Parliament's amending power by an 11-judge Bench in Golak Nath case,[11] which accorded complete supremacy to fundamental rights so as to put them beyond the reach of even the Constituent power. Close on heels, in another watershed decision in bank nationalisation case,[12] another 11-judge Bench decision overturned its earlier decision in Gopalan case[13] to read the fundamental rights together and invalidated the nationalisation of 14 banks. During the same year, another flagship government measure of abolishing the privy purses of erstwhile rulers of princely states, came to be annulled by yet another 11-judge Bench[14] and the court came to be perceived to be standing in the way of the government implementing its policies and programmes.

Faced with severe debilitation of amending power and rendering to naught its important policies, the government of the day sought to overturn the court's position enunciated in these three 11-judge Bench judgements by introducing the 24th, 25th and 26th Constitutional Amendments in the Parliament in July 1971. These amendments were landmark not merely because of the changes they introduced into the Constitution, but also because of the manner in which the court's dictum was sought to be reduced to dust.

The court decision in the famous bank nationalisation case[15] read various fundamental rights together in a composite manner to hold that the validity of law regarding violation of right to property has also to be tested on the principle of reasonableness by reading

Articles 31 and 19(1)(f) together. The said decision was sought to be undone by Constitution (Twenty-fifth) Amendment Act, 1971. It was clearly stated in the Statement of Objects and Reasons[16] that it was in order "to surmount the difficulties placed in the way of giving effect to the Directive Principles of State Policy" by the court in the bank nationalisation case.[17]

By the said amendment, a new Article 31C was added, which provided that laws contemplating effectuation of the Directive Principles contained in Articles 39 (b) and (c) – equitable distribution of resources and diffusing concentration of wealth – shall not be invalidated on ground of them violating the fundamental rights under Articles 14, 19 or 31. The entire purpose of this parliamentary exercise was to accord limited primacy to Directive Principles over and above the fundamental rights as the approach of the court had till this time been to accord primacy to fundamental rights over the Directive Principles.[18]

Similarly, the Twenty-fourth Amendment sought to undo the effect of the decision in Golak Nath case[19] by clarifying that constitutional amendments were not subject to judicial review, as they were distinct from ordinary laws. Therefore, the intention of the Constituent body was to restore the legal position as it existed prior[20] to Golak Nath case.[21]

It was only in the Fundamental Rights case[22] that the largest ever Bench of the Supreme Court till date assembled to authoritatively determine the extent of amending power vis-à-vis fundamental rights, and by a wafer-thin majority of 7 : 6, the basic structure doctrine was laid down, preventing the Constituent body from altering some basic aspects or basic features of the Constitution. While affirming the distinction between legislative and Constituent power, the court held that the Constituent body could amend fundamental rights so long as the basic structure of the Constitution was not altered.

Some such 'basic features' listed in the majority opinions in the Fundamental Rights case[23] include supremacy of the Constitution, rule of law, judicial review, independence of judiciary, federal structure, separation of powers, parliamentary democracy, republican form of government. It was further held that not all fundamental rights formed part of the inviolable basic structure. Right to property was held to be one such fundamental right which did not form part of the basic structure of the Constitution, and consequently its relegation from the status of a fundamental right to a constitutional right, subsequently became conveniently possible.[24] Since the court in the Fundamental Rights case[25] discarded the notion of one set of rights (between the Fundamental Rights and the Directive Principles) being superior to the other, and instead advocated a fine balance between them, the ruling has stood the test of time.

As a consequence of the majority verdict in the fundamental rights case[26], neither has the Constituent body been denuded of its power to amend fundamental rights (which was the result of Golak Nath case[27]), nor is the constitutional court prevented from judicially reviewing constitutional amendments (which was the intention behind enacting the Twenty-fourth Amendment). This fine balance, which was the result of the 23 years of institutional dialogue between the constitutional court and the Constituent body preserves rule of law and has prevented any possible attempt to destabilise the nation from any majoritarian onslaught or numerical tyranny.

II. Constitutional Interpretation towards Constitutional Growth

While the more visible constitutional reform was occurring through constitutional dialogue, all through, the constitutional courts were making far-reaching progress by interpretive techniques in order to give meaning and purpose to the constitutional provisions. An important reason for our Supreme Court being so powerful is its ability and willingness to revisit its decisions in certain situations.[28] The ability to overrule its earlier judgements was not as given in the earlier years. It was only in the Bengal Immunity case[29] that the Supreme Court ruled that it could overrule its earlier decisions. The court, thus, advocated that growth in law must give way to definiteness of legal position, although in exceptional circumstances. Since then, several judgements pronounced by our constitutional courts are critically examined and even long-standing precedents overruled, when they are discovered to be laying down wrong law or found to be outdated.

It is this constant organic exercise of our constitutional courts which gives contemporary relevance to constitutional provisions, in this fast-changing dynamic world, making the Constitution a 'living document'. While the Supreme Court may have held fundamental rights as discreet silos in A.K. Gopalan case,[30] and permitted the right to life to be taken away by a validly enacted law, it revisited this and upset this enunciation in Maneka Gandhi case[31] by holding that not only should the fundamental rights be read together as they inextricably interconnected, but the right to life can be taken away only if the validly enacted law is just, fair and reasonable. Thus, the Supreme Court introduced substantive requirements of 'due process' into Article 21, despite the same having been consciously avoided by our Constitution-makers as evinced in the debates.

Similarly, departing from its earlier position,[32] and also from the plain language, the court held that the President's power to appoint members of the constitutional courts 'in consultation' with the Chief Justice of India, needed to be circumscribed by giving primacy to the views of the Chief Justice and his senior colleagues (known as the Collegium).[33] The court had also to repel the Constituent body's attempt at dislodging this Collegium system of judicial appointments, by holding such an attempt to be destructive of the basic feature of the Constitution, viz., the independence of judiciary.[34]

Right to equality under Article 14 was held permitting reasonable classification with twin test of intelligible differentia having rational nexus with the object sought to be achieved and such classification could be sustained even if it pertained to a single individual.[35] The constitutional court gave life and meaning to the denominational rights of religious minorities by restricting the right to the extent of religious practices[36] and not in respect of secular activities.[37] Rights of minorities in respect of running and administering their educational institutions have been construed in a nuanced manner so as to balance the rights of minorities with standards of education.[38]

The court applied interpretative process to give meaningful content to various fundamental rights even though literally they were not so mentioned in Part III. For instance, freedom of speech and expression was held to contain freedom of press;[39] freedom of movement was also construed to mean the right to go abroad and such right could not in any manner be curtailed except by a valid law.[40] Consequently, Parliament was impelled to enact Passports Act to regulate foreign travel by the citizen. The court acknowledged the singular significance of fundamental rights and their enforceability through high prerogative writs by the Supreme Court as well as the High Court, as the option of the citizen.

An instance of constitutional limitations and limits of powers as well as the principle of separation of powers envisaged by the Indian Constitution was strikingly produced by the seven-judge Bench judgement.[41] Another instance pertains to the court holding the distribution of legislative powers between the Union and the states by means of Seventh Schedule and laying down the principles of interpretation of legislative entries and holding the vesting of residuary power in the Parliament.[42] The legislative power to levy sales tax was also elaborately examined[43] in the light of the freedom of inter-state trade and commerce as also the exclusive power of Parliament to levy sales tax on inter-state trade on account of which Central Sales Tax Act, 1956 was enacted apart from undertaking Constitution (Seventh) Amendment Act, 1956, to insert entry 92-A in the Union List and also amending Article 286 of the Constitution.

Contribution of the Supreme Court in prescribing the significant principles of Constitution and to smoothen the working of the Indian Constitution in respect of administrative law and service jurisprudence is remarkable through its various decisions.[44] Entrenching the principle of 'aid and advice' firmly in our parliamentary system was another important landmark ruling by the Supreme Court in the context of position of executive heads of the Union and the state.[45]

Another contribution of the Supreme Court was to unveil the era of non-arbitrariness[46] and natural justice jurisprudence.[47] Arbitrariness was held to be antithesis to the rule of law and arbitrary action per se violative of the right to equality. Right to fair hearing and right against bias coupled with duty to be informed by reason were ordained to be inalienable parts of rule of law.

III. The Dark Phase and Re-emergence

Twice in a span of three years did the political class of the day launch a direct attack on the Supreme Court by superseding senior judges for the position of Chief Justice of India.[48] What remained was the constitutional court's constant attempt thereafter to re-emerge from this loss of legitimacy, after the dictatorial onslaught on independence of judiciary and muzzling of discordant voice of the court, perceived to be a challenge to unbridled and unrestrained power of the executive.

The first such bold response came in the Election case[49] with the invalidation of the Thirty-ninth Amendment to the Constitution, which had been brought to set at naught the Allahabad High Court decision[50] of nullifying the then Prime Minister's election. By this amendment, a separate tribunal was contemplated to adjudicate election of the President, Vice president and the Prime Minister and to undo the verdict of any court hitherto taken in respect of such election and to oust jurisdiction of all courts including in respect of the pending election appeals. The unanimous court, albeit through separate judgements and by assigning separate reasons, held the said amendment to be violative of basic features of the Constitution such as judicial review, independence of judiciary and rule of law.

But the constitutional court succumbed to the government's pressures soon thereafter, when in Shivakant Shukla case[51] it was confronted with the nature of the fundamental right to life and personal liberty and its enforceability during Emergency.

While the majority upheld such suspension of the fundamental right to life and liberty, Justice H.R. Khanna, who was the senior most puisne judge of Supreme Court, rose to the occasion and gave a sole, yet powerful, dissent by holding that the right to life and liberty are not creations of law or the Constitution but are inherent and natural by virtue of the very existence of a person as a human being. Therefore, such a right could not be suspended or taken away by law or by any means whatsoever including a constitutional amendment. This bold dissent, even though lone, was applauded by the international community[52] in applauding the bravery of Justice Khanna who did not compromise independence even if it cost him the post of Chief Justice of India, the highest judicial office of the country. Justice Khanna met prompt retribution when a judge junior to him was appointed the Chief Justice of India in his place.

This phase, and particularly the majority judgement in Shivakant Shukla case,[53] arguably marks the lowest ebb of the Indian judiciary, since the constitutional court fell far short of its duty as the sentinel on the qui vive.

IV. Consolidation and Expansion

Some of the priorities of the government in independent India had been to alleviate poverty and bridge the gap between the rich and the poor so as to redeem the constitutional pledge of ensuring socio-economic justice. Agrarian reforms were some of the initial steps in this direction. Constitutional measures were undertaken in this regard and as mentioned in the first section of this piece, judicial roadblocks were taken care of by the First Constitutional Amendment in 1951. Over the period, steps such as abolition of 'zamindari' system and estates, denial of market price for compulsory deprival of property,[54] agricultural and urban land ceiling laws, purses and privileges for erstwhile rulers and nationalisation of economic resources were all steps taken by Parliament in this direction. Often, the Supreme Court lent the requisite judicial support to all such steps.

The Twenty-fifth Constitutional Amendment provided for egalitarian society and inserted Article 31C to put laws purportedly giving effect to Directive Principles of State Policy contained in Articles 39 (b) and (c) beyond challenge on the anvil of Articles 14, 19 and 31. By this measure, the directives pertaining to establishment of an egalitarian society were accorded primacy over important fundamental rights. The majority in Fundamental Rights case[55] upheld this measure by holding that both Part III and Part IV of the Constitution constituted the bedrock and the balance of both is of utmost significance.

However, the Forty-second Amendment (colloquially known as mini-Constitution on account of its sweep) amended Article 31C to provide that Parliament could validly legislate to trump the fundamental rights under Articles 14 and 19, if such law envisaged the implementation of any Directive Principle. This amendment, in essence, contemplated to disturb the harmonious balance between Parts III and IV of the Constitution. The Constitution Bench struck down this alteration in Article 31C in the celebrated Minerva Mills case[56] primarily on the ground that the basic features of judicial review and balance between Part III and Part IV stood violated.

Contemporaneous with the political changes in our country, judicial attitudes also underwent a change. With the advent of weak governments confined by coalition compulsions, indecision and laxity in administration began to grow. The ordinary citizen became restless and clamoured for change. The strict procedural rules of locus standi were done away with and constitutional courts frequently began entertaining causes of public relevance and alleging violation of fundamental rights of the unidentifiable citizens at large on account of government action and, frequently, government inaction. Initially, this was in tune with the system of checks and balances envisaged by our constitutional architecture.

Constitutional courts stepped in to fill in legislative gaps.[57] At times, even despite the absence of formal legislative activity, such pronouncements have been treated at par with substantive legislation. This is due to Article 141 envisaging that the law declared by the Supreme Court is binding on all courts within the territory of India. Similarly, Article 144 of the Constitution obligates every civil and judicial authority to act in aid of the Supreme Court. Such exercise not only comprises the acknowledgment of existing right, but also creation of hitherto unacknowledged right.

In the process, constitutional courts frequently resorted to reading Article 21 as a catalogue of unenumerated rights which are concomitant to the right of a person to live as a human being. Some such rights include:

1. The right to go abroad: Satwant Singh Sawhney v. D. Ramarathnam;[58] Maneka Gandhi v. Union of India[59]
2. The right of prisoners against bar fetters: Charles Sobraj v. Delhi Administration[60]
3. The right to legal aid: M.H. Hoskot v. State of Maharashtra[61]
4. The right to bail: Babu Singh v. State of Uttar Pradesh[62]

5. The right to live with dignity: Jolly George Varghese v. Bank of Cochin[63]
6. The right against handcuffing: Prem Shankar Shukla v. Delhi Administration[64]
7. The right against custodial violence: Sheela Barse v. State of Maharashtra[65]
8. The right to compensation for unlawful arrest: Rudul Shah v. State of Bihar[66]
9. The right to earn a livelihood: Olga Tellis v. Bombay Municipal Corporation[67]
10. The right to know: Reliance Petrochemicals Ltd v. Proprietors of Indian Express Newspapers[68]
11. The right against public hanging: A-G of India v. Lachma Devi[69]
12. The right to doctor's assistance at government hospitals and right to medical care: Paramanand Katara v. Union of India[70]
13. The right to shelter: Shantistar Builders v. N.K. Totame[71]
14. The right to pollution free water and air: Subhash Kumar v. State of Bihar[72]
15. The right to speedy trial: A.R. Antulay v. R.S. Nayak[73]
16. The right against illegal detention: Joginder Kumar v. State of Uttar Pradesh[74]
17. The right to a healthy environment: Virender Gaur v. State of Haryana[75]
18. The right to health and medical care for workers: Consumer Education and Research Centre v. Union of India[76]
19. The right to a clean environment: Vellore Citizens Welfare Forum v. Union of India[77]
20. The right against sexual harassment: Vishaka v. State of Rajasthan[78]
21. The right against noise pollution: In Re, Noise Pollution[79]
22. The right to fair trial: Zahira Habibullah Sheikh v. State of Gujarat[80]
23. The right to sleep: In Re, Ramlila Maidan Incident[81]
24. The right to reputation: Umesh Kumar v. State of Andhra Pradesh[82]

25. The right against solitary confinement. Shatrughan Chauhan v. Union of India[83]
26. Right to education: Mohini Jain v. State of Karnataka;[84] Unni Krishnan v. State of Andhra Pradesh[85]
27. Right against exploitation and begar: People's Union for Democratic Rights v. Union of India[86]
28. Right to privacy: K.S. Puttaswamy v. Union of India[87]

With the relaxation of the doctrine of locus standi, the Supreme Court of India became the most accessible constitutional court in the world. The jurisdiction of the Supreme Court of India has been invoked even by sending a letter or a post-card.[88] Nowhere in the world has the judicial process been so informal, accessible and pervasive.

One of the major milestones in the evolution of access to justice jurisprudence is that any public-spirited person or institution either individually or collectively is entitled to approach the highest court for the redressal of grievance of persons who, on account of their inability or lack of means unable to personally seek redress. Besides, the jurisprudence of public interest litigation has gone deep in the entire gamut of administration and governance so as to make rule of law completely all pervasive. Each action of each of the organs of governance is bound by the rule of law and any departure will activate the constitutional courts regardless of the affected persons failing or even consciously deciding not to approach the court. This public interest litigation is a significant and potent check on each public authority against abuse of public power and public funds in any manner whatsoever. This area of jurisprudence is unique in our country and has no parallel in the world. This has made democracy and all democratic institutions workable and ensured them to remain within the bounds of their authority and to be informed by the all-pervasive rationale of public interest.

Even when there is no approach to the court, the court itself takes suo motu cognizance from newspaper report or from any source whatsoever, without waiting for anyone to knock the doors of the court. Instances are numerous where the court took suo moto cognizance against torture, fake encounters, violation of dignity, etc. (Punjab Police vs. Tattoo Taran Taran case)

Evolution of non-arbitrariness as an essential facet of rule of law and equality principle was adapted by the court to be an effective check on exercise of discretion. Even in the matter of conferring largesse, the court insisted that the action of the public authority must be in consonance with non-arbitrariness and informed by rule of law so as to conform to the fundamental guarantee of Article 14 of the Constitution.[89]

Rapid economic development and handling of great amount of material resources including natural and technological resources and by the state in the era of right to information and transparency posed a challenge to ensure integrity in the decision-making process. The approach of the court to act as the ultimate guardian of public interest and to ensure non-arbitrariness in all governmental actions resulted in the directives for disposal of all resources through public auction so as to maximise material return from the economic resources for their utilisation for common good.[90] However, later, the above approach for distribution and allocation of resources only through the means of public auction was modified through a Constitution Bench judgement pursuant to advice sought by the President of India on a Presidential reference and it was authoritatively opined[91] by the court that maximisation of economic value was not necessarily the promotion of public interest and the same may require host of other relevant considerations, such as priority areas and segments and mechanism for dealing with natural resources.

When it becomes difficult to unearth truth and for ensuring fair and impartial investigation, constitutional court also monitors investigations, especially when confronted with allegations of corruption and financial misfeasance at the highest levels of government.[92] This approach can be perceived as the highest watermark in an attempt to uphold rule of law and rule of non-arbitrariness and stringent checks on exercise of discretion.

Conclusion

Through this eventful journey over the past 68 years of its existence, the court has not only reinstated itself to its pre-

Emergency stature of being the sentinel on the qui vive, but has gone much taller and become the strident protector of people's rights and larger public interest or common good. It is no longer a court accessible by men of means and power, but by the very last person on this land. From failing to stand by the citizen during Emergency, the court has become the harbinger of people's rights.

However, there are anomalies galore. While for the sake of people's rights and in public interest, the court frequently decides issues which are conventionally non-justiciable, it is one of the most insulated branches of government. From its composition to its functioning, the judicial Branch has gradually acquired all possible power and is least available to checks and balances by the other two wings of the state.

Another common criticism, which merits introspection by the constitutional court, is its frequent incursion in the field of governance. Judicial review is the power assigned to the constitutional court in our written Constitution to annul a law which abridges a fundamental right. This power is now all-pervasive, and is used by the court to not only check all administrative excess, but also to regulate governance so that the citizens of this country are not deprived of their rights. While it is true that the constitutional court is entitled to check and balance power of a majoritarian government, the arrogation of this power to supervise governance by an unelected and unaccountable wing for purely non-justiciable reasons, may be a cause for concern.

Be that as it may, the Constitutional court and the Constituent body have collaborated to make our fundamental document of governance, workable, and for that purpose, bring changes whenever necessary.

References

1. *From December 9, 1946 to November 26, 1949*
2. *State of Madras v. V.G. Row, AIR 1952 SC 196*
3. *Statement of Objects and Reasons to the Constitution (First Amendment) Bill, 1951*
4. *Sir Kameshwar Singh v. Province of Bihar, AIR 1950 Pat 392*
5. *State of Madras v. Champakam Dorairajan, AIR 1951 SC 226*
6. *Romesh Thappar v. State of Madras, AIR 1950 SC 124; Brij Bhusan v. State of Delhi, AIR 1950 SC 129*
7. *Moti Lal v. Govt. of Uttar Pradesh, AIR 1951 All 257 (FB)*

8. *Shankari Prasad Singh Deo v. Union of India, AIR 1951 SC 458*
9. *Sajjan Singh v. State of Rajasthan, AIR 1965 SC 845*
10. *Fazlul Quader Chowdhry v. Mohd Abdul Haque, 1963 PLD 486 (SC)*
11. *Golak Nath v. State of Punjab, AIR 1967 SC 1643*
12. *Rustom Cavasjee Cooper v. Union of India, AIR 1970 SC 564*
13. *A.K. Gopalan v. State of Madras, AIR 1950 SC 27*
14. *Maharajadhiraja Madhavrao Scindia v. Union of India, AIR 1971 SC 530*
15. *Rustom Cavasjee Cooper v. Union of India, AIR 1970 SC 564*
16. *Statement of Objects and Reasons to the Constitution (Twenty-fifth Amendment) Bill, 1971*
17. *Rustom Cavasjee Cooper v. Union of India, AIR 1970 SC 564*
18. *Mohd. Hanif Qureshi v. State of Bihar, AIR 1958 SC 731*
19. *Golak Nath v. State of Punjab, AIR 1967 SC 1643*
20. *Shankari Prasad Singh Deo v. Union of India, AIR 1951 SC 458; Sajjan Singh v. State of Rajasthan, AIR 1965 SC 845*
21. *Golak Nath v. State of Punjab, AIR 1967 SC 1643*
22. *Keshavananda Bharati v. State of Kerala, AIR 1973 SC 1461*
23. *Keshavananda Bharati v. State of Kerala, AIR 1973 SC 1461*
24. *Constitution (Forty-fourth) Amendment Act, 1978, repealing Articles 19(1)(f) and 31 and inserting Article 300-A*
25. *Keshavananda Bharati v. State of Kerala, AIR 1973 SC 1461*
26. *Keshavananda Bharati v. State of Kerala, AIR 1973 SC 1461*
27. *Golak Nath v. State of Punjab, AIR 1967 SC 1643*
28. *Instances of landmark judgements which have been subsequently overruled include: A.K. Gopalan v. State of Madras, AIR 1950 SC 27, overruled in Sambhu Nath Sarkar v. State of W.B., AIR 1973 SC 1425; State of Bombay v. United Motors (India) Ltd, AIR 1953 SC 252, overruled in Bengal Immunity Co. Ltd. v. State of Bihar, AIR 1955 SC 661; Shankari Prasad Singh Deo v. Union of India, AIR 1951 SC 458, and Sajjan Singh v. State of Rajasthan, AIR 1965 SC 845, overruled in L.C. Golak Nath v. State of Punjab, AIR 1967 SC 1643; L.C. Golak Nath v. State of Punjab, AIR 1967 SC 1643, overruled in His Holiness Keshavananda Bharati Sripadgalvaru v. State of Kerala, AIR 1973 SC 1461; S.P. Gupta v. President of India, AIR 1982 SC 149, overruled in Supreme Court Advocates-on-Record Association v. Union of India, AIR 1994 SC 268; Unni Krishnan, J.P. v. State of Andhra Pradesh, AIR 1993 SC 2178, overruled in T.M.A. Pai Foundation v. State of Karnataka, AIR 2003 SC 355; Islamic Academy of Education v. State of Karnataka, AIR 2003 SC 3724, overruled in P.A. Inamdar v. State of Maharashtra, AIR 2005 SC 3226; Mohd. Hanif Quareshi v. State of Bihar, AIR 1958 SC 731; Abdul Hakim Quraishi v. State of Bihar, AIR 1961 SC 448; Mohd. Faruk v. State of Madhya Pradesh, AIR 1970 SC 93; Haji Usmanbhai Hasanbhai Qureshi v. State of Gujarat, AIR 1986*

SC 1213, overruled in State of Gujarat v. Mirzapur Moti Kureshi Kassab Jamat, AIR 2006 SC 212; Konkan Railway Corporation Ltd v. M/s Rani Construction Pvt Ltd, AIR 2002 SC 778, overruled in SBP & Co. v. Patel Engg. Ltd, AIR 2006 SC 450

29. *Bengal Immunity Co. Ltd v. State of Bihar, AIR 1955 SC 661*
30. *A.K. Gopalan v. State of Madras, AIR 1950 SC 27*
31. *Maneka Gandhi v. Union of India, (1978) 1 SCC 248*
32. *S.P. Gupta v. President of India, AIR 1982 SC 149 (popularly known as Judges' Case-I)*
33. *Supreme Court Advocates-on-Record Association v. Union of India, AIR 1994 SC 268 (popularly known as Judges' Case-II); and Special Reference 1 of 1998, AIR 1999 SC 1 (popularly known as Judges' Case-III)*
34. *Supreme Court Advocates-on-Record Association v. Union of India, (2016) 5 SCC 1 (popularly known as NJAC Case)*
35. *Charanjit Lal Chowdhury v. Union of India, AIR 1951 SC 41; Ram Krishna Dalmia v. S.R. Tendolkar, AIR 1958 SC 538*
36. *Mohd. Hanif Qureshi v. State of Bihar, AIR 1958 SC 731; Tilkayat Shri Govindji Maharaj v. State of Rajasthan, AIR 1963 SC 1638; Shayara Bano v. Union of India, (2017) 9 SCC 1, Indian Young Lawyers' Association v. State of Kerala, 2018 SCCOnline SC 1690 (Sabarimala Temple Entry Case)*
37. *Durgah Committee v. Syed Hussain Ali, AIR 1961 SC 1402*
38. *In re: Kerala Education Bill, AIR 1958 SC 956; Ahmedabad St. Xavier's College Society v. State of Gujarat, AIR 1974 SC 1389; T.M.A. Pai Foundation v. State of Karnataka, (2002) 8 SCC 481; P.A. Inamdar v. State of Maharashtra, (2005) 6 SCC 537; Modern Dental College v. State of Madhya Pradesh, (2016) 7 SCC 353*
39. *Romesh Thappar v. State of Madras, AIR 1950 SC 124; Brij Bhusan v. State of Delhi, AIR 1950 SC 129*
40. *Satwant Singh Sawhney v. D. Ramarathnam, AIR 1967 SC 1836*
41. *Powers, Privileges and Immunities of State Legislatures (Keshav Singh case), AIR 1965 SC 745*
42. *Union of India v. H.S. Dhillon, AIR 1972 SC 1061*
43. *Bengal Immunity Co. Ltd v. State of Bihar*
44. *In re: Delhi Laws Act, AIR 1952 SC 332; Parshotam Lal Dhingra v. Union of India, AIR 1958 SC 36*
45. *Samsher Singh v. State of Punjab, AIR 1974 SC 2192*
46. *E.P. Royappa v. State of T.N., AIR 1974 SC 555; Union of India v. Tulsiram Patel, AIR 1985 SC 1416*
47. *ECIL v. B. Karunakar, (1993) 4 SCC 727*
48. *The first of two such supersessions took place on April 25, 1973, when the three senior-most judges, part of the majority in Keshavananda Bharati case, were superseded, a day after the said judgement was pronounced. Since the majority had affirmed limitations on the Constituent power, it was perceived by the*

political wings of the government to be an obstacle in its assertion for absolute power.

49. *Indira Nehru Gandhi v. Raj Narain, AIR 1975 SC 2299*
50. *Raj Narain v. Indira Nehru Gandhi (Allahabad High Court Judgement dated June 12, 1975 in Election Petition No. 5 of 1971)*
51. *ADM Jabalpur v. Shivakant Shukla, (1976) 2 SCC 521*
52. *Editorial titled 'Fading Hope in India', appearing in New York Times dated April 30, 1976 (digitised version available at https://www.nytimes.com/1976/04/30/archives/fading-hope-in-india.html, last visited: November 16, 2018)*
53. *ADM Jabalpur v. Shivakant Shukla, (1976) 2 SCC 521*
54. *Bhim Singhji v. Union of India, AIR 1981 SC 234. While introducing the Fourth Constitutional Amendment, the then Prime Minister emphasised that not because of inability, but the measure to deny market price is a deliberate design aimed at bringing about egalitarian society and bridging the gap between the rich and the poor.*
55. *Keshavananda Bharati v. State of Kerala, AIR 1973 SC 1461*
56. *S.P. Gupta v. President of India, AIR 1982 SC 149; People's Union for Democratic Rights v. Union of India, AIR 1982 SC 1473*
57. *Laxmi Kant Pandey v. Union of India, (1984) 2 SCC 244; Vishaka v. State of Rajasthan, (1997) 6 SCC 241*
58. *AIR 1967 SC 1836*
59. *(1978) 1 SCC 248*
60. *(1978) 4 SCC 494*
61. *(1978) 3 SCC 544*
62. *(1978) 1 SCC 579*
63. *(1980) 2 SCC 360*
64. *(1980) 3 SCC 526*
65. *(1983) 2 SCC 96*
66. *(1983) 4 SCC 141*
67. *(1985) 3 SCC 545*
68. *(1988) 4 SCC 592*
69. *(1989) Supp (1) SCC 264*
70. *(1989) 4 SCC 286*
71. *(1990) 1 SCC 520*
72. *(1991) 1 SCC 598*
73. *(1992) 1 SCC 225*
74. *(1994) 4 SCC 260*
75. *(1995) 2 SCC 577*
76. *(1995) 3 SCC 42*
77. *(1996) 5 SCC 647*
78. *(1997) 6 SCC 241*
79. *(2005) 5 SCC 733*
80. *(2006) 3 SCC 374*
81. *(2012) 5 SCC 1*

82. *(2013) 10 SCC 591*
83. *(2014) 3 SCC 1*
84. *(1992) 3 SCC 666*
85. *(1993) 4 SCC 111*
86. *AIR 1982 SC 1473*
87. *(2017) 10 SCC 1*
88. *M.C. Mehta v. Union of India, (1987) 1 SCC 395*
89. *Ramana Dayaram Shetty v. International Airport Authority of India, AIR 1979 SC 1628*
90. *Centre for Public Interest Litigation v. Union of India (2G Spectrum Allocation Case) (2012) 3 SCC 1*
91. *In re: Natural Resources Allocation, (2012) 10 SCC 352*
92. *Zahira Habibullah Sheikh v. State of Gujarat, (2006) 3 SCC 374; Common Cause v. Union of India, (2015) 6 SCC 332 (Coal Block Allocation Case)*

□

Indian Constitution and Social Justice

—*Dr. O.P. Shukla*

What the Constitution means to a common citizen? It is primarily the protector and preserver of our most basic freedom, powerful tool for social change and empowerment and, thus, an effective instrument of 'social justice'. The commitment of the founding fathers of our Constitution guaranteeing and ensuring to all the people, justice – social, economic and political, equality of status, opportunity, and equality before law and liberty of thought through constitutional means eloquently finds place in the Preamble to the Constitution.[1] The fundamental rights are designed to foster a social revolution by way of guaranteeing equality (Article 14), prohibiting discrimination (Article 15), equality of opportunity (Article 16), abolishing untouchability (Article 17), banning trafficking in human beings and forced labour (Article 23), and prohibition of employment of children (Article 24).[2] The rights and interest of the minorities have also been protected under Articles 25 to 30, of the Constitution.[3] In Part IV, it provides 'Directive Principles of State Policy' such as (a) state to secure a social order for the promotion of welfare of the people (Article 38), (b) certain principles of policy to be followed by State (Article 39), (c) right to work, education and public assistance (Article 41), (d) provision for the humane conditions of work and maternity leave (Article 42), (e) living wages for workers (Article 43), and (f) promotion of educational and economic interest of the Scheduled Castes (SCs) and Scheduled Tribes (STs) and other weaker sections (Article 46). The principles laid down in Part IV of the Constitution (Directive Principles of State Policy), are fundamental in governance of the country, and it is the duty of the state to apply these principles in making laws (Article 37).[4]

Social Justice

Social justice is the foundation stone of our Constitution. Though the term 'social justice' is nowhere defined in the Constitution, it means equal opportunities for the development of personality to all the people in the society without any distinction of caste, sex or race. The principle of social justice is the basis of providing reservation and other economic opportunities to the disadvantages groups. Social justice is about eliminating the social and economic inequalities between different segments of the society by providing support to those at the bottom of the hierarchical society.[5] The term 'social justice' is very comprehensive and includes various elements, such as right to work, education, justice and humane conditions of work for women, living wages, compulsory education to children, etc., under the Directive Principles of State Policies (Articles 41-46). Special provisions for women and children have been provided [Article 15(3)]. Besides, abolition of 'untouchability' (Article 17) and rights against exploitation (Articles 23-24) finds place in Part-III (Fundamental Rights) of our Constitution. Prof. Upendra Baxi,[6] an internationally renowned legal luminary, emphasises on the special nature of these provisions, as under:

"Article 17 outlaws the practice of 'untouchability'. It is perhaps the only Constitution of the world that declares discrimination-based disability an offence. It certainly inaugurates a post-liberal conception of equality. The entire federal scheme is suspended by Article 35, which endows Parliament alone with the power, coupled with a duty, to make a law for constitutional offence (including rights under Articles 23 and 24 against exploitation)."

These provisions are special in the sense that they ensure protection against social disabilities such as 'untouchability' and 'exploitation' against traffic in human beings and forced labour. The violation of these provisions is a 'constitutional offence'. The primary objective of social justice is to eliminate all kinds of exploitation, inequalities – social, economic and political – and to ensure equal opportunities to all its citizens. The Utilitarians[7] propounded the theory of 'the greatest good to greatest numbers' and consider it as key to the meaning of social justice.

Welfare State and Poverty

Poverty is antithesis of social justice. The makers of our Constitution took all possible steps to ensure removal of poverty and creation of an egalitarian society. Part IV of the Constitution (Articles 36-51) contains certain 'Directives' according to which it shall be the duty of the State to follow both in the matter of administration as well as in the making of laws per se. The Supreme Court in Keshavananda Bharti case while emphasising on the relevance of Article 39(b)(c) inter alia held: These clauses, together with other provisions of the Constitution, contain one main objective, namely building of a 'welfare state' and an egalitarian social order[8] – to fix certain social and economic goals for immediate attainment by bringing about a non-violent social revolution.[9] Through such a social revolution, the Constitution seeks to fulfill the basic need of the common man and to change the structure of the society,[10] without which political democracy has no meaning.[11]

Despite the historical decision in the Keshavananda Bharati case almost 50 years ago, there is no change in the ground realities as such. The fact remains that India has more pro-poor and pro-social justice political leaders than any other country in the world. But the present socio-economic scenario demonstrates that after Independence, no serious attempt has been made to address the real issues of the country. Celebrated columnist Tavleen Singh[12] has brilliantly analysed the poverty alleviation programmes in India and the motive of the government(s) behind it. She has very categorically observed that our leaders have denied the basic tools that are required for the advancement of the poverty-ridden society, such as proper schools, health care, sanitary living conditions and opportunity of employment. Rather, the governments choose to throw scrape of charity like MNREGA. The intention appears to be to keep them in poverty. While questioning the motive, she observed as under:

"...Why is that a Prime Minister who once publically reviled MNREGA now embraced it with open arms? Has he discovered the benefits of glorifying poverty? Absurd though this may sound, there are huge benefits in keeping poverty alive. Very poor people ask no questions. Not even when they see their poverty-

loving leaders strive to become very rich as soon as they enter public life..."

The decision of outsourcing public employment at the lower level (Class-IV) and banning of recruitment in the government sector clearly demonstrates the hostile 'anti-poor' and 'anti-Dalit' attitude of the ruling establishment, per se. This is one example that precisely supports the views of Tavleen Singh.

Nexus between Constitution and Justice

"...Our Constitution is a social document that aims to transform a feudal and social hierarchical society into an egalitarian society...."[13] By the 42nd amendment of the Constitution in 1976, the word 'socialist' was inserted in the Preamble, which inter alia strengthened the constitutional ethos of social and economic justice. Article 14 guarantees every person "equality before law or equal protection of laws within the territory of India." The only exception against the doctrine of equality under Articles 14, 15(1) and 16(1) are provisions for securing social justice to SCs and STs by way of providing reservation in educational institutions, public employment, economic opportunity and legislatures [Articles 15(4), 16(4), 330, 332 and 335] of the Constitution. This discrimination is called 'Positive Discrimination'. The purpose precisely is the welfare and development of the marginalised sections of the society.

However, the guarantee of social justice eventually depends on how effectively we implement the Constitution. Thus, to understand the connection between the Constitution and social justice in its correct perspective, the views of the following distinguished personalities merit attention. Former President Dr. Rajendra Prasad,[14] at the dawn of the freedom, underlines the vision in the Constituent Assembly to create conditions in the country:

"...When every individual will be free and provided with the wherewithal to develop and rise to his fullest stature, when poverty and squalor and ignorance and ill health will have vanished, when distinction between high and low, between rich and poor, will have disappeared... when untouchability will have been forgotten... when exploitation of man by man will have ceased."

Niraja Gopal Jayal, a professor at the Centre for Law and Governance in JNU, New Delhi, has very rightly raised a vital question:[15]

"If state accountability and responsiveness to the needs of citizens are the hallmark of the decent governance, does our Constitution promote such governance practices or does it inhibit them?"

Prof. Jayal further explained that in 2004, two civil servants filed a writ petition in the Supreme Court, seeking, among other things, that good governance be declared a fundamental right under Articles 14, 19 and 21, and a part of the basic structure of the Constitution; and that the independence, integrity and apolitical character of the civil service be constitutionally protected, so that it could become more effective and more accountable. Their contention was that realisation of the fundamental rights depends upon the civil service being protected in this way. Amazingly, the apex court refused to entertain the said petition and held that court will intervene only in specific cases of violation of Constitutional provisions.[16]

Dr. Rajiv Dhavan, an eminent Supreme Court lawyer, begins by asking: "...But age-old questions about our Constitution survive. Who is the Constitution meant for? Who took the Constitution over? In whose hands is the Constitution now?" He sarcastically commented on the electoral slogans that Indira Gandhi's campaign for removing poverty (*garibi hatao*) became an electoral slogan and lost its lustre as a programme. He further said that "the fact that India is shining is meaningless to the poor and jobless voter."[17]

The only surviving member of the Constituent Assembly, 93-year-old Chaudhary Ranbir Singh Hooda,[18] while remembering the day they signed the Constitution, very aptly said:

"It was a special moment. For us, the Constitution was not just a document; it signified hope, progress and good future for the country after years of British rule... That is the best thing about parliamentary system, unlike monarchy where only kings ruled. I am very proud of the Constitution. It was framed to empower the forthcoming generations. Provisions for amendments were included so that it could be changed according to the needs of the changing times."

In our constitutional scheme, the social and economic aspects of 'justice' are left primarily to the lawmakers – members of Parliament and State legislatures. Despite the fact that Parliament and State legislatures have been empowered under the Constitution to make special provisions through ordinary law for the advancement of SCs & STs, nothing substantial has been done to secure justice to these sections. We may recall what Dr. B.R. Ambedkar had said and cautioned the nation almost 70 years ago, while addressing the Constituent Assembly,[19] which read as under:

"On January 26, 1950, we will have equality in politics and inequality in social and economic life. We must remove this contradiction at the earliest moment, or else those who suffer from inequality will blow up the structure of political democracy which Assembly has so laboriously built up."

Unfortunately, Dr. Ambedkar is not alive today to see the present state of affairs, specifically the plight and deplorable conditions of the poor and SCs & STs. Had he been alive, the situation would have been altogether different.[20]

There are around 1,091 castes and 586 tribes in the country. Among them only 4-5 dominant castes and few tribes are disproportionately cornering all the quota benefits meant for the total 1,677 scheduled castes and tribes. The Mahars in Maharashtra, the Malas in Andhra Pradesh, the Pariahs in Tamil Nadu and Chamars in Uttar Pradesh and other Hindi-speaking States are the principal beneficiaries.[21] These dominant castes are being promoted, nurtured and patronised by successive governments while the extremely backward castes are being denied constitutional benefits. J.H. Hutton, who was the Census Commissioner in 1931, had suggested nine tests to identify SCs & STs for the purpose of constitutional safeguards. 'Untouchability' was the predominant test, beside menial occupation, such as scavenging and tanning of animal hides.[22] There are virtually two kinds of untouchables, e.g., 'de facto' and 'de jure'. G.S. Pal, representing United Provinces Hindu Backward Classes League, submitted before the Indian Franchise Commission in the presence of Dr. Ambedkar that:[23]

"Bhangi is the only caste that is universally untouchable, pollution by whose touch is regarded as something very undesirable."

The various other castes or communities, who were not in fact untouchables, were included in the Schedule. Recently, a community, namely Devendrakula Vellaler of Tamil Nadu with 60 lakh population, has represented the Central government praying for their exclusion from the SC list. Their contention is that they were included in the list in 1920 despite their protest. They said that they have been fighting for their exclusion for the last 100 years.[24] Various committees and commissions appointed by the Central and State governments found that the constitutional benefits are not percolating down to the targeted beneficiaries and the sweepers and scavengers are the main losers.

During Round Table Conferences (RTCs) in 1930-31, the main concern of Dr. Ambedkar was how to protect and safeguard the interest of the 'depressed classes' in the Constitution of India. He submitted a memorandum to the Minority Committee of the RTC, wherein he demanded adequate representation in the government services besides other political safeguards.[25] Dr. Ambedkar raised the same demands during the Poona Pact in 1932, which were later incorporated in the Constitution. According to my study and experience, public employment has been a more effective instrument in the development and empowerment of the weaker sections, rather than political reservation. Today, whatever development is visible, it is due to the reservation in government jobs only.[26]

In the backdrop of the Poona Pact, Mahatma Gandhi launched movement against untouchability. After independence, the Congress under the influence of Gadhian philosophy of 'Harijan welfare' was very enthusiastic in perusing various government policies and schemes made for them.[27] But the pre-Independence social reform movement was later abandoned, with the result that lower castes were neglected while the upper castes enjoyed the fruits of the 'socialist' pattern of society which finally culminated into backlash of Mandal I and II.[28] Thereafter, the successive Congress governments encouraged and promoted the dominant and affluent among SCs & STs only with the result that the backward within them were left behind.

Former Deputy Prime Minister Jagjivan Ram was aware of the importance and significance of public employment particularly at the lower level, e.g., Class-IV, jobs. Class-IV embodies around 20 petty and menial jobs or posts, such as peon, *daftery*, *safaiwala* (sweeper and scavenger), *dhobi* (washerman), cobbler and *khalasi*. These jobs were meant for poor, illiterate, semi-educated people and particularly belonging to SC/ST categories. He was conscious about the fact that development of these sections was not possible unless opportunities were provided in public employment. He also knew that these petty jobs/posts were the only source of upward mobility. Therefore, he took a policy decision and issued an office order stating that all Class-IV jobs/posts in Railway Ministry will be filled by SCs & STs only.[29]

The 5th and 6th Central Pay Commissions (CPCs) in 1995 and 2005, respectively recommended merger of Class-IV into Class-III categories and creation of a new Class-III, 'multi-task service' (MTS). Thus, the 2005 CPC recommended abolition of Class-IV jobs. Importantly, Class-IV jobs/posts constitute more than 95% of the public employment in the Central and State governments.

From Social Inclusion to Social Exclusion

The term 'social exclusion' is of relatively recent origin. The notion has, however, already made substantial inroads into the discussions and writings on poverty and deprivation.[30] Former President K.R. Narayanan[31] was apprehensive about the economic reform policy of 1990s and its impact on the marginalised sections. He, thus, observed as under:

"Our three-way fast lane of liberalisation, privatisation and globalisation must provide safe pedestrian crossings for the 'unempowered' India also, so that it too can move towards 'equality of status and opportunity'.

Justice Rajender Sachar has also warned about the impact of globalisation on marginalised sections and opined: "...We need to manage the impact of globalisation better and improve the lot of all the weaker sections. Let us not blame the Constitution." Sachar quoted Joseph Stieglitz and who says, "For most of the world, globalisation as it has been managed seems like a pact with the Devil." Eminent economist Jagdish Bhagwati has also now accepted that "unless steps to ameliorate the growing inequalities, which globalisation implies, are taken, the lot of the worse-off sections would only get worse."[32]

Amazingly, after Independence, as I discussed above, Congress governments claimed that they were pro-poor and pro-Dalit, making inclusive policies for them, but later started ignoring their pre-Independence agenda of social welfare. During 1990s, the ruling establishment went one step further and decided to implement the CPC's recommendations, in the guise of economic reform, knowing fully the socio-economic conditions of marginalised sections. Therefore, the Class-IV jobs including sanitation work was eventually outsourced. This was done without any study of the impact of the policy on these sections and without identifying alternative trade or occupation for them. Besides, while taking policy decision, the government did not consult the National Commission for Scheduled Castes and Scheduled Tribes which is mandatory under Articles 338 and 338A.[33] The government did not comply with the principles of natural justice (Article 14)[34] and did not follow the mandate of Articles 16, 17, 21, 23, 24 (right against Exploitation), 38 and 46.[35] The government also did not comply with Section 10 (Prohibition of Employment of Contract Labour) of the Contract Act, 1970, and other labour laws.[36] Surprisingly, they did not even bother to consult the Ministry of Labour, which is the administrative ministry for various labour laws. Moreover, the government even did not like to consult the National Commission for Safai Karamcharis (NCSK). The mandate of the Commission under Section 8(1)-(a) of the Act is to recommend to the government specific programmes of action towards elimination of inequalities in status, facilities and opportunities under a time-bound action plan.[37]

By way of outsourcing, the ruling establishment eventually abolished substantial part of the reservation. Consequently, SCs & STs at the lower level are the worst loser of several service benefits, financial as well as social security. They are now being forced to work on contract basis. Due to their poverty and illiteracy, the contractors are exploiting them, denying even their bare minimum wages and other facilities. The exploitation of the *Safai Karamcharis*, particularly women, is a major cause of concern.

The survival of these menial workers depends at the mercy of the contractors. Thus, their voice has been suppressed and they are now finding themselves out of the government welfare agenda.[38]

Despite all-round development and progress in the area of economy, infrastructure, science and technology, there is a large section of the population, particularly backward among SCs & STs, has been left behind. The fruits of 'Independence' and 'Constitution' have not reached to them. The gap between rich and poor has widened hugely. No wonder India is placed very low in many indices globally. "In the Global Hunger Index, India's place is 103, denoting severe hunger... In the Human Development Index, the rank is 130 out of 189. India is in the bottom third... In per capita GDP, India's rank is 140, also in the bottom third of 188 countries, etc."[39] The massage '*Sabka saath, sabka vikas*' (collective efforts, inclusive growth) of the present government is a manifestation of its commitment to social justice. But there is no sign even at the end of its tenure towards achieving the said objective. Therefore, it appears to be a hollow promise like the earlier ones – '*Garibi hatao*' or 'Shining India'.[40] Justice J.S. Verma has, therefore, rightly observed that the "State has failed to promote welfare of the people by securing social order with distributive justice and egalitarian ethos."[41]

The 'Constitution' and 'democracy' have been in question from the very beginning. Shrilal Shukla, author of iconic novel *Raag Darbari* published in 1968, had questioned the idea of democracy. He inter alia questioned, "How Indian democracy is far from being, of the people, by the people, for the people, the basic premise of democracy." He further questioned, "Indian democracy is the rule of the people belonging to the powerful castes and not the rule of law."[42] Expressing his displeasure on the issue of governance, eminent jurist Fali S. Nariman supported the view of a foreign journal as under:[43]

"Many years ago (19th November 1990), prestigious British weekly The Economist had expressed an opinion (which was both frank and brutal) and to which (I am convinced) we must all pay heed: 'India will continue to be misgoverned until politics becomes more of a vehicle for policies instead of the other way around' – that is, instead of policies being fashioned to suit the politics of the day!"

Recently, the RSS chief Mohan Bhagwat,[44] while speaking at a function in New Delhi, expressed his views on the Constitution, governance and accountability, and observed as under:

"...that people's organisations have a role to play in holding accountable those in power and should not become subservient to authority... What is the guarantee that the governing system (satta) will follow the Constitution? The guarantee is vigilant citizens led by people's organisations and, hence, they should not be lackeys of power..."

Commenting on the constitutional morality inter alia on the occasion of National Law Day in New Delhi, Chief Justice of India, Ranjan Gogoi[45] observed: "Our Constitution is the voice of the marginalised as well as the prudence of the majority. Its wisdom continues to guide us in moments of crises and stability."

Reservation, Creamy Layer and Distributive Justice

The issue of 'reservation' or 'affirmative action' has been a contentious one since the closing decades of British rule in India. Any student of history would know that government jobs have been the domain of the privileged few, e.g., high-caste Hindus for centuries, whether the country was ruled by native kings, Moghul rulers or the British. Consequently, there were protests against the said monopoly and simultaneously persistent demands for proper representation by different sections of society. The policy of reservation, therefore, was firmly established in India during the British period. It was precisely designed more to address communal inequalities rather than as a social engineering device to address the rooted socio-economic inequalities of the disadvantaged section of the society because of the past societal discrimination. The very first challenge to caste Hindu monopoly in the centre came from Muslims followed by Christians, Sikhs and Anglo-Indians who eventually succeeded in securing a specific reservation more or less in proportion to their population. Between 1874 and 1885 in southern India, the scheme of communal reservation emerged as a result of a revolt by non-Brahmins against Brahmin domination in services.[46]

During 1894 to 1922, in Maharashtra, Chhatrapati Sahuji Maharaj, known as the 'Pillar of Social Democracy', abolished bonded-labour and provided 50% reservation for backward classes in services.[47] Thereafter, Government of Bombay (the parent state of Gujarat) and later Gujarat government appointed OHB Starte Commission in 1928, followed by Justice A.R. Baxi Commission in 1972 and Justice C.V. Rane Commission in 1981. It was Starte Commission who for the first time introduced categorisation of backward classes for the purpose of providing equitable representation to different sections of the society. During 1920 to 1935, the policy of reservation was adopted for the historically deprived sections, commonly known as 'untouchables' or 'depressed classes', which was eventually the result of the endless efforts and struggle of Dr. B.R. Ambedkar. In Gujarat, the Baxi and Rane commissions were entrusted with the job to identify the backward classes and suggest measures for their upliftment. In Karnataka, Justice O. Chinnappa Reddy Commission was appointed in 1990 who suggested, among other things, exclusions of certain advanced and affluent categories of persons from reservation.

While in North India, the Government of Punjab for the first time introduced sub-categorisation of reservation among different sections of SCs & STs. Firstly, the Yash Committee in 1959 recommended 5% separate reservation for sweepers and scavengers.[48] Thereafter, in 1965, B.N. Lokur Committee of Government of India[49] recommended exclusion of some of the affluent and relatively advanced castes and tribes, which came to be known as Creamy Layer, from the Schedule. The Punjab government in 1975 introduced classification among SCs and divided reservation in two blocks with 50% to each. Haryana, Andhra Pradesh, Uttar Pradesh and Bihar later followed Punjab model in 1994, 2000, 2001-02 and 2007-08, respectively.

Challenge to Sub-categorisation

Sharing benefits of reservation with other backward communities within SCs and STs is not acceptable to the affluent and dominant SCs & STs. Therefore, the decision of sub-categorisation was challenged in various courts. Finally, the Supreme Court in E.V. Chinnahaih case[50] in 2006 abolished the sub-categorisation, saying that the SCs are one unit and homogeneous class, therefore, any sub-classification in the list of SCs is violation of Articles 14, 15 and 16 of the Constitution.

On the other hand, the Supreme Court in 1976, while discussing the dangers of reservation, for the first time laid down the principle of 'Creamy Layer'. Justice Krishna Iyer observed in N.M. Thomas case[51] inter alia in Para 124 of the judgement as under:

"...Its benefits, by and large, are snatched away by the top creamy layer of 'backward' caste or class, thus keeping the weakest among the weak always weak and leaving the fortunate layers to consume the whole cake..."

Justice Iyer[52] further underlines the purpose of reservation policy and opined as under:

"...Obviously, Article 16(4) was not designed to get more Harijans into government as scavenger and sweeper but as 'officers and bosses', so that administrative power may become the common property of the high and low, homogenised and integrated into one community..."

The Supreme Court applied 'Creamy Layer' principle for the first time in Indira Sawhney case[53] in 1992. The case was pertaining to reservation for Other Backward Classes (OBCs). This principle was extended to SCs & STs in M. Nagraj in 2006[54] and in Jarnail Singh case in 2018.[55] Both these cases inter alia deal with reservation in promotion for SCs & STs. The purpose of the N.M. Thomas case was altogether different, i.e., to ensure equitable representation of the 'weak and the weakest' in government jobs. But the irony is that despite the decision in N.M. Thomas case in 1976, the dominant and powerful SCs & STs, whom Justice Iyer was referring to as 'Creamy Layer', eventually grabbed all the positions, from the lower level to the top, in the bureaucracy and, thus, monopolised it. In as much as, the economically backward sections (EBSs) among SCs & STs were denied their legitimate share in government services.

For instance, Justice Gurunam Singh Committee (1990) of Haryana found serious anomalies in the distribution of public jobs. It found that there was 'over-representation' in employment and other spheres. The total population of SCs (as per 1991 census) was 24,64,012 – Chamars 12,97,339, Balmikis 4,88,649 and Dhanuks 2,69,436. Population of the rest of 34 castes was 4,08,588. While the caste-wise representation in the public employment was as under: total posts of IAS 34 – Chamars/Jatavs got 32 (94%) while Balmikis and Dhanuks got one each (2.94%). The total posts of IPS were 5 – Chamars/Jatavs got 3 (60%), Balmikis 2 (40%) while Dhanuks and rest 34 castes got none (0%). The total posts of IFS were 7 – Chamars got 5 (71%), Balmikis 2 (28%) and Dhanuk and rest 34 castes none (0%). The total posts of Class-I were 147 – Chamars/Jatavs got 121 (83%), Balmikis 20 (17%) and Dhanuks 6 (8%). The total posts of Class-II were 399 – Chamars/Jatavs got 368 (93%), Balmikis 18 (4%) and Dhanuk 13 (3%). And, lastly, the total posts of Class-III was 18,434 – Chamars/Jatavs got 16,608 (90%), Balmikis 1,107 (6%), Dhanuks 554 (3%) and the rest 34 castes got 183 (1%). The rest of the 34 castes were having (0%) share in first 3 categories.[56]

The Committee report showed 'severe under-representation' of different sections within SCs in public employments and other spheres. It, therefore, recommended sub-categorisation of SCs into two blocks – A and B. A-block was consisting of 42 castes and B-block had only one caste (and its 6 sub-castes). Accordingly, 50% reservation was given to Chamars, Jatavs, etc., falling in B-block and the second half to the rest of the 42 castes in A-block like Balmikis and Dhanuks. The distribution of quantum of reservation was precisely based on population rather than the backwardness per se.

This is precisely the true picture of inequitable distribution of benefits of reservation in the whole country. The aforesaid findings demonstrate that the presence of 'weakest among weak' is negligible in the bureaucracy and elsewhere. Therefore, the decisions of Indira Sawhney, M. Nagraj and Jarnail Singh cases are of no use to those who have no representation in public employment and other spheres. This was exactly the sections to which Justice Iyer was referring to in N.M. Thomas case in 1976.

Surprisingly, the results of sub-categorisation in Punjab and Haryana were incredible and the EBSs among SCs & STs were getting opportunities in public employment and in other spheres. Unfortunately, sub-categorisation was withdrawn due to the Supreme Court decision in E.V. Chinnaiah case in 2006. During the 10 years' period between 1994 and 2006, the EBSs had made substantial progress in all walks of life.[57] But ironically, the dominant and powerful Chamars and Jatavs opposed the sub-categorisation and sharing of reservation benefits with EBSs, and finally had their way.

Similarly, following the Punjab and Haryana model of sub-categorisation, Andhra Pradesh government decided in 2000 to subcategorise SCs & STs into four groups, e.g., A, B, C and D. The Mala community of Andhra Pradesh was against the sub-categorisation like Chamars of northern India and Mahars of Maharashtra. E.V. Chinnaiah belonging to Mala community challenged the government decision in Andhra Pradesh High Court. The court decided in favour of sub-categorisation. Thereafter, he approached the Supreme Court, which finally decided against sub-categorisation, as discussed above. To neutralise the adverse effect of E.V. Chinnaiah case on the OBCs of Andhra Pradesh, Justice Usha Mehra Commission was appointed by Government of India in 2006-07. Justice Mehra, in her report in 2008, inter alia opined[58] that the SCs and STs are not one unit or a homogeneous caste, rather it is heterogeneous and plural one. Supported by sub-categorisation, she observed that it was a legally sustainable method of distribution of benefits of reservation.

Social Justice and Supreme Court

Justice Kurian Joseph's incredible comments in his farewell address at the time of his retirement from Supreme Court[59] needs attention. He said that "the silence of 'law man' does more harm than the violence of 'layman'. Justice Kurian said that "every case he handled engaged him fully, and enabled him to stand for the disadvantaged, poor and powerless." His central idea was to move beyond the law and ensure 'justice beyond law.'[60] He further said that judges should practice "constitutional compassion." "Compassion from the court is not the charity of a judge; it is the bounden duty of a constitutional court."[61] The Supreme Court Bar Association termed Justice Joseph a 'compassionate humanitarian judge'. It reminds me of Justice P.N. Bhagwati, Justice Krishna Iyer, Justice D.A. Desai and Justice K.K. Mathew, when compassion and commitment for justice to poor, untouchable and Harijan was very much visible in their decisions. Justice Iyer in N.M. Thomas case laid down the golden principle of social justice, e.g., creamy layer, while Justice Bhagwati in 1980s opened the doors of the courts for poor, destitute and untouchables.

After the Indira Sawhney case, the Supreme Court had an opportunity in E.V. Chinnahaih case to deliver justice to the neglected sections as laid down by Justice Iyer in N.M. Thomas case, recommended by various committees and commissions appointed by the Union and state governments from time to time and enshrined in the Constitution of India. But, unfortunately, the court did exactly the opposite and lost the opportunity of addressing the irregularities in the affirmative action policy. Thus, the poor and the untouchables were back in square one.

Faizan Mustafa, VC, NALSAR, University of Law, Hyderabad,[62] while commenting on the behaviour of the apex court on the issue of reservation, inter alia observed as under:

"...The judiciary has not been keen supporter of reservation and, therefore, in a number of cases, in the name of 'merit', it has tried to put restraints on the state's power to make reservations, i.e., excluding promotion from reservation, catch up rule, creamy layer..."

The concept of reservation is primarily based on the principle of 'distributive and re-distributive justice' as propounded by John Rawls and other social scientists.[63] 'Distributive Justice', in other words, is 'Social Justice' as such. Therefore, I am personally of the view that the whole issue of reservation today has become a 'mess' due to the apathetic and hostile attitude of the judiciary as well as the ruling dispensation. Thus, the objective of distributive or social justice has been eventually defeated.

What the Constitution and Independence Has Given to the Untouchable?

A small booklet in Hindi titled 'What the Constitution and Independence has given to the Untouchables?' was published in 2017.[64] The book contained the discussion as to how extremely backward groups have been unfairly treated and unjustly denied the constitutional benefits. It was, thus, concluded that the untouchables were cheated and betrayed by the successive ruling establishment. Ironically, whenever 'Ati-Dalits or 'Vanchit-Dalits'

(EBSs) demanded their share in the affirmative action policy, the dominant groups opposed the move vigorously and branded them as Anti-Ambedkar or Anti-Dalit unity.[65] As discussed above, the sub-categorisation was abolished in 2006 by the court in E.V. Chinnahaih case. Therefore, there was no other option available with us except seeking exclusion of dominant and affluent castes/ tribes from the Schedule (Articles 341 & 342). Thus, in 2011, a writ petition (PIL) was filed by me in the Supreme Court seeking the said relief.[66] The main objective was to get justice for the neglected sections among SCs & STs. The people who believe in social justice appreciated and supported my PIL. Ironically, I was abused by Dalit scholars, activists and political leaders. Prominent Dalit scholar and writer Anand Teltumbde wrote an article with the heading "Dismantling 'Dalit' with a Poisonous PIL."[67] The headline was enough to appreciate his anger and frustration against the PIL and also against those who question their monopoly in reservation.

In a statement in September 2015, RRS chief Mohan Bhagwat said that there should be a review of the reservation policy to know who benefited from it and how much? We supported the stand of the RRS chief and observed: "What is wrong in saying that reservation be reviewed? Everyone has a right to know what each caste got in these 68 years. We welcome this effort by RRS chief Mohan Bhagwat."[68] There was hue and cry among SCs & STs. One can understand why they are afraid of review of reservation policy. Firstly, they believe in status quo. Secondly, they may get exposed with regard to their socio-economic and political conditions via-à-vis the extremely backward among SCs & STs. Thus, their fear is that the review may go against them.

In our country, the delivery of social justice has become a political issue. All political parties use to view it through political glasses. For them, political and electoral considerations are paramount. Those who are at the bottom of the pyramid are the worst victims of the hostile social and political environment. Maharashtra government recently announced 16% separate reservation for Marathas. Tamil Nadu government had provided 70% reservation despite the cap of 50% ceiling. The Patels of Gujarat, Jats of Haryana and Kapus of Andhra Pradesh are also demanding the same treatment.[69] These dominant castes are politically relevant for political parties in power. But for the sections that are politically insignificant and not relevant for the parties, social justice is merely a mirage. The de facto untouchable, for whom the constitutional safeguards were provided, has been neglected, whereas the dominant has been favoured. Therefore, this is a unique country in the world which primarily helps those who are affluent and powerful and ignore those who are poor and deprived.

The death rate of the sewer and sanitation workers is very high in the country. Manual scavenging and untouchability is still continuing despite its abolition long ago. People are losing faith both in the ruling establishment and the Constitution. For every petty grievance, people have being forced to approach the courts. But judiciary is inaccessible and expensive, whereas bureaucracy is not responsive and accountable. Therefore they are not concerned whether people get justice or not. There is alarming increase in crime against Dalits. Data released by National Crime Record Bureau shows that the BJP-ruled states have recorded highest rates in terms of crime against Scheduled Castes.[70] Anti-poor, anti-Dalit policies like outsourcing, reduction in the allocation of funds, educational grants, scholarships, huge unemployment and health care, etc., are few instances of misgovernance and failure of implementation of the Directive Principles of State Policy. It appears that this country is no more a 'welfare state' now. Hence, in the present scenario, the word 'social justice' has become a mockery and, thus, redundant.

Conclusion

Many renowned luminaries have raised some very relevant questions: (a) Who is the Constitution meant for? (b) What did happen to the dreams of the framers of the Constitution? (c) Why can't good governance be a fundamental right? (d) Why did legislature fail to implement Directive Principles of State Policy? and (e) Why did the apex court, despite celebrated decision in Keshavananda Barati case, fail to ensure social justice? Rajiv Dhavan[71] has rightly cautioned about the collapse of Constitutions in our neighbouring countries. This reminds us what Dr. Ambedkar had said in the Constituent Assembly 70 years ago. It appears that the decisions of the Constituent Assembly to entrust the powers to legislatures to implement the 'Directives' was not correct. These directives could have been made part of the 'Fundamental Rights' as such.

The apex court's decisions on 'Creamy Layer' and 'Exclusion' (B.N. Lokur, A.R. Baxi, C.V. Rane, Chinnappa Reddy case verdicts of Karnataka and Gujarat High Courts, 2004)[72] from the Schedule is primarily an act of 'de-reservation'. This will in ultimate analysis reduce the existing quantum of reservation which SCs, STs and OBCs will not be ready to afford right now. The best mechanism according to me could be, to first include, then review and then exclude from the Schedule, e.g., include those who need affirmative action, and then review the policy periodically and then exclude those who do not need it. This cycle will have kept repeating till the time an egalitarian society, the mandate of the Constitution, is achieved.[73] This will help the SCs & STs or OBCs assimilate themselves in the mainstream of the society. This will put an end to the monopoly of dominant social groups and provide equal opportunities to others. The existing quantum of reservation will also remain intact as such. Alternatively, Creamy Layer coupled with sub-categorisation could be a good method to address this issue. Therefore, the country needs a national policy on exclusion of Creamy Layers for all types of reservation. Since this has not happened, it is high time the adjudicatory leadership indicate this as a legal prescription.

References

1. *See Part-IV of the Constitution of India, 1950, [As amended through the Constitution (102nd Amendment) Act, 2018, p xxxiv]. See K.I. Vibhute, 'Social Justice: Constitutional Scheme And Spirit', in Mohammad Shabbir (Ed.), 'B.R. Ambedkar, Study in Law and Society, (1997) pp. 42-58.*
2. *Part III of the Constitution of India.*
3. *Part III of the Constitution of India.*
4. *See, Fali S. Nariman, The State of the Nation, in the context of India's Constitution, (2013) p. 112.*
5. *See, K.C. Suri, Dialectic of Social Justice, in 'Dividing Dalits, writings on Sub-Categorisation of Scheduled Castes' (2009), pp. 172-187.*
6. *Upendra Baxi, 'Jurisprudence of inverted comas, Biology does not trump human rights', The Hindu, September 3, 2018, p 9.*

7. *See, Julius Stone, 'Human Law and Human Justice', (1966), pp. 122-146.*
8. *Keshavananda Bharti v. State of Kerala, AIR 1973 SC 1461.*
9. *Keshavananda Bharti v. State of Kerala, AIR 1973 SC 1461.*
10. *Keshavananda Bharti v. State of Kerala, AIR 1973 SC 1461.*
11. *Keshavananda Bharti v. State of Kerala, AIR 1973 SC 1461. See also, See Durga Dass Basu, Shorter Constitution of India, pp. 443-453.*
12. *Tavleen Singh, Poverty, glorious poverty, The Sunday Express, January, 15, 2017, p 15.*
13. *Dr. O.P. Shukla, 'Reservation Issue', The Hindustan Times, Saturday, December 25, 1989, p 8.See, also Granville Austin, 'The Indian Constitution Cornerstone of Nation', (ed.) (1972), p. 50.*
14. *J.S. Verma, the former Chief Justice of India, quoted in 'The Power of the Letter', The People's Republic, The Indian Express, January 26, 2007, p 4.*
15. *See, for detail discussion, 'Holy grail, not a holy book', The People's Republic, The Indian Express, January 26, 2007, p 5.*
16. *Id*
17. *Rajiv Dhavan, In whose hands is the Constitution?, The People's Republic, The Indian Express, January 26, 2007, p 6.*
18. *Shilpa Venkatramn, 'Not just a document...it meant hope, good future', The People's Republic, The Indian Express, January 26, 2007, p 6.*
19. *Dr. B.R. Ambedkar's address to the Constituent Assembly, November 25, 1949.*
20. *Ibid. foot note 13. See also, O.P. Shukla, Indian Express, November 19, 1986, p 8.*
21. *Vikas Pathak, 'Making a case for sub-quotas' Hindustan Times, June 9, 2008, p 8. See also Yagati Chinna Rao (Ed.), Dividing Dalits, writings on Sub-Categorisation of Scheduled Castes (2009), p 9.*
22. *Marc Galanter, Competing Equalities, Law and the Backward Classes in India (1984), pp. 120–153. See also Yagati Chinna Rao (Ed.), Dividing Dalits, writings on Sub-Categorisation of Scheduled Castes (2009), p 7.*
23. *Ibid. Marc Galanter, pp. 127 onwards.*
24. *Nav Bharat Times (Hindi), 'Why 60 Lakh People Want to Leave Reservation?', April 23, 2018, p 16.*
25. *Dr. B.R. Ambedkar, What Congress & Gandhi have done to the Untouchables, (Writings and Speeches), Vol. 9, (1991) pp 41-52.*
26. *Dr. O.P. Shukla, Legislative Reservation and Social Development under the Indian Constitution, (unpublished thesis), Delhi University, (1999).*
27. *See Gandhi's philosophy on Harijan Welfare, Mukut Behari Verma, 'History of the Harijan Sevak Sangh', 1932-1968, (1971) pp. 173 onwards.*

28. *See, Meghnad Desai, 'The Rock and The Ark', The People's Republic, The Indian Express, January 26, 2007, p 2.*
29. *See Rail Bandhu, The magazine published by Ministry of Railways, Government of India, (2006).*
30. *Amartya Sen Social Exclusion, Concept Application Scrutiny, (2004) pp. 14-16.*
31. *The Hindu, November 26, 2018, p 9.*
32. *Justice Sachar, 'We are all minorities', 'The People's Republic', The Indian Express, January 26, 2007, p 7.*
33. *Since outsourcing of Class-IV jobs is a matter which affects SCs & STs, our organisation sought information under the Right to Information Act from Department of Personnel and Training (DoPT), Ministry of Home Affairs, Ministry of Social Justice and Empowerment, NCSC and NCSK, regarding consultations before implementing Pay Commission Recommendations. They all informed us that they did not consult any of the ministries or departments on this issue.*
34. *Upendra Baxi (Ed) 'K.K. Mathew on Democracy, Equality and Freedom', (1978), pp. 26-51.*
35. *See, Constitution of India, 1950 (As amended by the Constitution – One Hundred and Second Amendment), Act, 2018.*
36. *Contract Labour (Regulation and Abolition) Act, 1970, Equal Remuneration Act, 1976, Minimum Wages Act, 1948 and Works Man Compensation Act, 1923.*
37. *See, in detail, Section 8, the National Commission for Safai Karamcharis Act, 1993.*
38. *The grievances and problems of the Safai Karamcharis and Sanitation Workers have been raised in various reports of the National Commission for Scheduled Castes and National Commission for Safai Karamcharis, but none of the report has been placed on the tabled of the both Houses of parliament, ana if placed, no action so far has been taken on the reports.*
39. *See for detail, P. Chidambaram, 'Those who are left behind', the Indian Express, November 11, 2018, p 13.*
40. *See Rajiv Dhavan, Ibid foot note 17.*
41. *Ibid. foot note 14.*
42. *Prakash Rajan, 'Vikas Has Missed the Bus', The Sunday Express Magazine – 'Eye' November 18, 2018, p 2.*
43. *Fali S. Nariman, Ibid. foot note 4, pp. 257-261.*
44. *The Times of India, November 11, 2018, p 10.*
45. *The Indian Express, November 27, 2018, p 8.*
46. *Dr. Parmanand Singh, 'Equality, Reservation and Discrimination in India', (1985), pp. 80-96.*
47. *P.B. Salunkhe, (ed.) 'Chhatrapati Sahuji Maharaj, the Pillar of Social Democracy' (1994-95), pp. 230-248.*
48. *Yash Committee Punjab 1959-60.*

49. *B.N. Lokur committee 1965.*
50. *E.V. Chinnaiah v. State of AP, (2005) 1 SCC 394.*
51. *State of Kerala & Anr. v. N.M. Thomas and Ors. (1976) 2SCC 310.*
52. *Id.*
53. *Indira Sawhney v. Union India, 1992 Supp. (3) SCC 217.*
54. *M. Nagraj v. Union of India, (2006) 8 SCC 212.*
55. *Jarnail Singh & Others v. Laxmi Narayan Gupta & Other, SC (DOJ: 26. 9 2018).*
56. *See Gurunam Singh Commission Report, 1090.*
57. *Id. See also Dr. O.P. Shukla, 'What the Constitution and Independence has given to the Untouchables'? 2017. See also Justice Grunam Singh Committee Report Haryana, 1990.*
58. *Justice Usha Mahra Committee Report, 2008.*
59. *The Hindu, November 30, 2018, p 10.*
60. *The Indian Express, November 30, 2018, p 10.*
61. *The Hindu, November 30, 2018, p 10.*
62. *The Tribune, October 16, 2018.*
63. *See Dr. O.P. Shukla, 'Political Reservation and Distributive Justice', (Unpublished dissertation submitted to Delhi University for the award of the degree of Master of Laws) 1982, pp. 60-77.*
64. *'Mission Justice' is a mini publication venture to make available relevant material on social, economic and political issues that affect directly or indirectly SCs & STs. Therefore, the objective is not only to inform and enlighten the readers but also to expel them towards emancipatory engagement with the society at large.*
65. *See in detail emerging intra-caste conflict on the issue of sub-categorisation, Chandraiah Gopani, 'New Dalit Movement, An Ambedkarite Perspective', in The Radical in Ambedkar, Critical Reflections, 2018, pp. 181-200.*
66. *The Times of India, August 24, 2011, p 9.*
67. *Economic & Political Weekly', October 8, 2011, Vol. XLIV No 41, pp. 10-11.*
68. *The Hindu, September 25, 2015, p 12.*
69. *See editorial page, The Indian Express, November 20, 2018, p 12.*
70. *The Indian Express, November 20, 2018, p 6. See also, India Today, October 17, 2018.*
71. *Rajiv Dhavan, ibid foot note 17.*
72. *See Samasta Gujarat Rajya Mochi Samaj v. Union of India Through Secretary Ors. Gujarat Law Herald, (2004) p. 67.*
73. *See Dr. O.P. Shukla 'Reservation issue' The Hindustan Times, December 25, 1989, p 8.*

□

Constitution of India and Princely States

—Devesh Khandelval

A meeting of the Chamber of Princes or Narendra Mandal was convened on 17-18 January 1946.[1] Nawabs, Rajas or Maharajas of more than 50 princely states gathered in Delhi. It was decided that all possible help would be extended to address their grievances regarding the Indian Constitution.[2] Affirming his faith in the Constitution in his address, the Maharaja of Bikaner said, "We are not less patriotic than any other King of India. I can say that this matter is of reconciliation. Further, I do not think there will be any obstruction in this reconciliation. Powered by the goodwill on both the sides, while taking into consideration the pragmatic situation, we would be able to ring in a just and unbiased Constitution which would safeguard the interests of princely states."[3]

A new chapter was about to unfold in the history of India. The next 18 months were to witness euphoria of freedom interspersed with the tragedy of division. Confusion was almost certain arising from the pre-planned ideologies of the British government and the communal policies of the Muslim League. Irrespective of all of this, India that was divided into 565 princely states was unified. And a Constitution written by Indians was enforced throughout the country, which is considered to be an important part of the world's largest democracy.

The Secretary of State for India, Pethick Lawrence, on 19 February 1946, took a step in the direction of self-government under which the British parliament decided to take three steps: (1) Preparatory discussions with the elected representatives of British India, and with the Indian States, in order to secure the widest measure of agreement as to the method of framing a Constitution; (2) The setting up of a Constitution-making body; and (3) The bringing into being of an Executive Council having the support of the main Indian parties.[4] The British parliament decided that Indians must prepare the new Constitution of India. Only Indians would join the Constituent Assembly, the necessary conditions for which would be decided by the British parliament.

On 24 March 1946, a Cabinet Mission constituting of three senior British officers came to India. They started meeting the Indian leaders, princes of the states and their representatives. Most princely states pledged support to the mission in supporting widespread changes that were taking place in India.[5] After numerous meetings and raising memorabilia, the British parliament on 16 May 1946 informed the Constituent Assembly in India on the basis of the report of the Cabinet Mission that the British India be divided into three sections, which included Chief Commissioner's provinces which was to be given 296 seats.[6] Apart from this, the princely states got 93 seats, and it was decided that a committee should be made to decide the distribution of these seats among the states. The mission had also prepared a basic format for the Constitution. Its main point was that a Union of India would be created, which would include both British India and the princely states, and whose sole concern would be to deal with foreign affairs, security and communication, as well as the mandatory power of collecting the necessary capital for these subjects.

The Mission was welcomed at the meeting of the Standing Committee of the Chamber of Princes. Some conditions were considered necessary for clarification and for the following, a discussion forum was made on 21 November 1946. Members of the Chamber included Chancellor, Nawab of Bhopal, Maharaja of Patiala, Jamsaheb of Nawanagar, C.P. Ramaswamy Iyer, Sultan Ahmed, Mirza Ismail, D.K. Sen, A. Ramaswamy Mudalir, K.M. Panikar, Raja of Bilaspur (in place of Manubhai Mehta), Meharwal of Dungarpur (in place of Maharaja of Dungarpur, Vidarbha Singh), V.T. Krishnamachari and Ramchandra Kak. The chamber, however, did not fully represent all the princely states. Some kings did not want to be included in it. Cochin and Baroda were such states that felt the need to negotiate personally.[7]

The Muslim League's demand for a separate and an autonomous sovereign country took an unprecedented turn. Mohammad Ali Jinnah called the elected members of the League to Delhi. They undertook to unite Bengal, Punjab, Sind, the North-West Frontier Province, Assam and Balochistan along with the demand for Pakistan and pledged not to take part in the Constituent Assembly ever.[8] This was a bewildering moment as it was debated widely that what would be the format of the Constituent Assembly if India was to be divided? How could the representation of princely states be decided? The matter was discussed at length in the British parliament.[9]

After three months, the Mission returned and the Congress accepted all its conditions. Jawaharlal Nehru, who presided over the working committee held in Bombay on July 6, 1946 opined that the question is not of accepting the conditions of the Mission by the Congress but, in a simplified manner, it's a matter of coming to an agreement to enter the Constituent Assembly.[10] The League was adamant to go ahead with the segregation, whereas the British government also made it clear that without the League, the Constituent Assembly would not be convened.[11] The Congress was not ready for this delay and it wanted to call the first session in September 1946. After many ups and downs, the first session was finally called on 9 December 1946, but neither the League nor any representative came from any state.

Notably, states' inclinations were different from each other as seen before in Cochin and Baroda's approach of direct talks, while in the meantime, other states preferred to wait for the next stand of the committee. Nevertheless, efforts were made to ensure participation of the states in the process of making of the Constitution between December 1946 and early 1947. One of the members M.R. Jayakar suggested that the discussion should be postponed not only for the League, but also till the representation of states is affirmed in the Constituent Assembly;[12] a suggestion that found support from the Diwans of Hyderabad, Mysore, Travancore and Bikaner, along with the Chamber secretary Sultan Ahmed, from outside the Constituent Assembly.[13] Another member K.M. Munshi on 21 December 1946 proposed that a committee of Constituent Assembly should be formed to negotiate with the princely states. Its members included Abul Kalam Azad, Jawaharlal Nehru, Vallabhbhai Patel, B. Pattabhi Sitaramayya, Shankar Rao Dev and N. Gopalaswamy Ayyangar. Eventually, the Constituent Assembly was adjourned till 20 January 1947.

The process of mutual negotiation between both the committees continued for long and the results were amiable and satisfactory. However, some reactionary states of the Chamber passed a resolution on 29 January 1947, which took everyone by surprise. They began demanding for a Constitutional assembly which would only make Constitution of the Union and would have nothing to do with the internal administration or Constitution of its princely states or their groups. At the same time, when British paramountcy would end with the British Crown, it would go directly to the states and princely states would become sovereign. The Maharaja of Bikaner opposed this proposal saying that some kings were creating obstacles in the political development of India.[14]

There were two types of factions in the Chamber. One group was led by the Maharaja of Bikaner and Patiala, and they were in favour of joining the Constituent Assembly at the earliest. Pitted against this was the Nawab of Bhopal who devoted his energy in seeing that the princely states should not be able to become a part of the Constituent Assembly. On the other side, Sardar Patel also became active and Nawab had to disintegrate from the Chamber. Now the Constituent Assembly gradually started to take finite contours. Till 28 April 1947, representatives from Baroda, Bikaner, Cochin, Jaipur, Jodhpur, Patiala and Rewa had joined it.

During this time, the British Prime Minister Clement Attlee said on 20 February 1947 that Britain would leave India before June 1948. Louis Mountbatten arrived in India on 22 March 1947, and two days later, became the next Viceroy and Governor-General. The British government was now ready to make laws in its parliament for the partition of India. On 13 June 1947, the Governor-General convened a meeting of Indian leaders in which discussions were made about establishing relations between the two new countries of the princely states. On 25 June 1947, a decision was taken for the creation of a new State(s) Department whose minister and secretary were Sardar Patel and V.P. Menon, respectively.[15]

It should be kept in mind that India was not yet partitioned, and the British Crown had not finished its alliance with the princely states. States started joining the Constituent Assembly of India. A law was proposed to be made for the division. Keeping in mind the future partitioning, Sardar Patel started contacting the Maharajas to ensure the timely compilation of the Constitution. Jai Narayan Vyas from Rajputana Regional Council, Jodhpur, on 29 June 1947, suggested Sardar to go for a free and integrated India.[16] This is an example that demonstrates that there were many princely states that made every possible contribution in uniting India.

A meeting was held in London on 26 June 1947, under the chairmanship of Atlee. In the aftermath of power shifting, the practice of establishing relations between the UK and the states was quickly initiated to come to some conclusion. The British government assured that the princely states would be assembled in either one or the other from the two new countries. He was not ready to give any state the status of an independent country.[17] Atlee proposed Indian Independence Bill in the second week of July 1947 in the House of Commons. This Bill was passed on 18 July 1947, which carried the official announcement of the partition of India.

During the discussion of Bill, Stanley Reed, a member of the British parliament, recalling the days of Viceroy Curzon, said that Lord Curzon used to say that the base of the Crown is the King and his princely states.[18] This foundation was conscientiously shaken by Britain itself. According to the Seventh Section of the Act, British dominion was over from the princely states. This led to serious problems in not only the political relations of the Central government and the princely states, but also in the coordination between economic and other areas. However, it was not mentioned in the Act that the princely states were independent or there would be separate arrangements for them. Whatever the provisions were made, it was in relation to two new countries, i.e., India and Pakistan. Some Maharajas were individually ambitious. It was just their imagination; they had no legal or solid basis.

The British Crown was amiable with 40 princely states. With the other kings, it had signed other types of agreements.[19] Thus, there were a total of 565 princely states in terms of the properties and fiefdoms. On 25 July 1947, the Governor-General called a special meeting of the Chamber at the end of British occupation. Mountbatten advised the Maharajas that they can merge with one country with respect to three subjects, namely foreign affairs, security and communication.[20] On the basis of the Government of India Act 1935, the accession letter or merger agreement was prepared. There was no deadline for merger, hence, the Maharajas signed only after 15 August 1947. The British government provided a tentative facility to the princely states. If a Maharaja wanted, he could make a stand-alone agreement with either one or both of India or Pakistan to look after the local administrative system and general matters. The Government of India had made such an agreement till conjunction or merger with several princely states.

According to the above Act, a separate Constituent Assembly was formed in Pakistan the first session of which was called on 10 August 1947. As a result, the number of members in the Constituent Assembly of India decreased to 299, in which the princely states represented were 89. In order to maintain their representation in the Constituent Assembly with the convergence, there was an increase in mutual negotiations. Sardar Patel had said that in India, they could neither live in isolation, nor could they live outside the Constituent Assembly.[21] The situation was clear in his mind as he wrote, "If the work of the princely states is settled and peace prevails in India, then there is a need to start the second work of creation of the future. All would be well by God's grace."[22]

A meeting was held on 17 July 1948, under the chairmanship of Sardar Patel in the presence of some princely states' chiefs, co-heads and representatives. It included officers of the Constituent Assembly along with the State Department. Here one or more seats were given to those 15 princely states whose population was over 10 lakhs. Thus, 49 seats went into their account. For the remaining 550 princely states, only 40 seats were left. In such a situation, they had to form groups and their representatives were to be sent to the Constituent Assembly by combining two or three or twenty to fifty states.[23] By this time, all the representatives of Jammu and Kashmir and Bhopal had been decided.

The making of the Constitution reached its last phase. Finally, in the presence of Dr. Rajendra Prasad, representatives of Jammu and Kashmir, Mirza Mohammad Afzal Beg, Maulana Mohammad Sayeed Masoodi and Moti Ram Bagda, along with Sheikh Mohammed Abdullah, became members of the Constituent Assembly on 16 June 1949. One rule was that the states had to make their own internal Constitution through their Constituent Assembly.[24] It was later realised that differences could arise if all the princely states formed their Constitution without the help of the Centre.[25] Hence, a committee headed by B.N. Rao was appointed to get a solution for this problem. It was decided that on the basis of the provincial Constitution, a uniform Constitution of these states would be made. The committee submitted its report on 22 March 1949. It said that there was a problem in forming of the Constitution because Constitutional assemblies were not made in Rajasthan, PEPSU, Vindhya Pradesh and Central India. The reason for this was that many princely states were struggling with initial problems since the convergence.

Time was deficient since the Constitution of entire India was to be implemented latest by January 1950. It was considered that a separate Constitution for everyone could not be possible in a democracy. The meeting of the heads of states and princely states was convened on 19 May 1949 to resolve the matter. It was decided that the Constitution created by the Constituent Assembly of India shall be the Constitution of all the states. This Constitution would be restored by princely states through a suitable process.[26] Under the leadership of M.K. Velodi, a committee was formed with N. Dandekar and S.N Mookerjee. They were to investigate the draft of the Indian Constitution and suggest its amendment in accordance with the states. The amendments that came from the draft committee and the Velodi Committee's mutual consultation were sent to the first sitting assemblies in Saurashtra, Travancore-Cochin and Mysore. Saurashtra adopted the constitutional draft on 13 November 1949 completely. The other two constitutional bodies proposed some reforms. Eventually, some of these were included in the amendment accepted by the Constituent Assembly of India while other suggestions were discarded based on the discussions with the representatives of these meetings.[27] In the places without the Constituent Assembly, the Constitution of India was adopted by the head of the state.[28]

Now the question comes of Jammu and Kashmir, for which a tentative provision – Article 370 – was incorporated in the Constitution of India on 17 October 1949. Gopalaswamy Ayyangar, who presented it, said that the situation there was not reasonable, so this Article had been presented before the Constituent Assembly. On being asked by a member as to why such discrimination was being made, his reply was that Jammu and Kashmir was not yet ready for the accession, but soon it would be a part of India like other princely states.[29] Ayyangar drafted this Article. Abdullah did not like it and he sent a draft from his side. It was again sent to Sheikh on 15 October 1949, after some rectification. Even this time, he rejected it. Sardar Patel also gave some suggestions which were equally sidelined. Later, he wrote a letter to Ayyangar on 16 October, after backing from the matter himself, "There is no question of my consent in these circumstances. If you think it is okay to go ahead with it, then you do that."[30]

Sheikh's real demand was to restrict the power of Indian Parliament to make laws for the state and prohibit the three subjects mentioned in the Accession form for the provision of a Constitution directly related to defence, foreign affairs and communication. Sheikh made this disclosure in a letter to Ayyangar on 17 October 1949, in which he also said that Prime Minister Nehru had promised him for this.[31] This was not possible with the presence of Sardar Patel around. The article was finally submitted on 17 October 1949.

Another change was made at the last moment. Sheikh was present in the Constituent Assembly that day and he did not approve of the change being made. In order to make the situation favourable, he wrote a letter to Ayyangar in which he threatened to resign from the Constituent Assembly. In fact, Sheikh could not imagine that there would be such a change in the final draft of the amendment list. However, he was told before the final decision. He left the meeting and went on to believe that it would be presented in the same format as acknowledged by him. However, this did not happen and a change was made in the clarification of sub-section B of Section 1 of the paragraph.[32]

Article 370 was the last provision of the Constituent Assembly. The Constitution of India was adopted on 26th of the following month. All the members, including the princely states, signed their Constitution on 24 January 1950, and the very next day, it came into effect throughout the country. Thus, the Constitution was completed in two years and eleven months. It is true that princely states did not have much special contribution in the Constitution. The reason behind this was that a lot of time was spent in incorporating them, which was solely the doings of the British government. They created an ambience of disorganisation and confusion that it became increasingly challenging to fathom as to which direction should be sought to make a humble beginning. Nevertheless, the princely states were included in the Constituent Assembly which shows that their contribution in the integration of India was very important.

References

1. *Chamber of Princes was founded on February 8, 1921. In 1946, approximately 140 States became its members.*
2. *Meeting of Chamber of Princes, January 17-18, 1946, Delhi, p. 3*
3. *Ibid., pp. 22-23*
4. *Parliament of United Kingdom, Cabinet Mission in India, February 19, 1946*
5. *V.P. Menon, The Transfer of Power in India, Longman : Bombay, 1957, p. 264*
6. *Section A: Madras, Bombay, United Province, Bihar, Central Province and Orissa with 187 seats, Section B: Punjab, NWFP and Sind with 35 seats, and Section C: Bengal and Assam with 70 seats. In addition, each member from Chief Commissioner Provinces in Section A's Delhi, Ajmer-Marwar and Kurg and Section B's British Balochistan was to attend the Constituent Assembly.*
7. *S.M. Gokhale, Indian States and Cabinet Mission Plan, p. 61*
8. *Choudhry Khaliquzzaman Pathway to Pakistan, Longman: Lahore, 1961, pp 340-41*
9. *Parliament of United Kingdom, India: Statement of Cabinet Mission, May 16, 1946*
10. *V.P. Menon, The Transfer of Power in India, Longman: Bombay, 1957, p. 280*
11. *Elections were held in British India in July 1946 for the Constituent Assembly. The Congress got a majority in the general seats, while*

the Muslim League won 72 of the 78 seats in Muslim dominated areas. These results of the League gave rise to the fire of partition of India which the British Government accepted as per Mountbatten Plan (June 3, 1947).

12. *Constituent Assembly of India, Aims and Objectives, December 16, 1946*
13. *V.P. Menon, The Transfer of Power in India, Longman: Bombay, 1957, p. 331*
14. *S.M. Gokhale, Indian States and Cabinet Mission Plan, p. 67*
15. *Nicholas Mansergh, The Transfer of Power 1942-7, part XI, His Majesty Stationery Office: London p. 620*
16. *Durga Das, Sardar Patel Correspondences, 1945-50, Part 5, Navajivan: Ahmadabad, p. 393*
17. *Nicholas Mansergh, The Transfer of Power 1942-7, part XI, His Majesty Stationery Office: London p. 662-663 (36th meeting of India and Burma Committee)*
18. *Parliament of United Kingdom, Indian Independence Bill, July 10, 1947*
19. *White Paper on Indian States, Ministry of States, 1950, p. 21*
20. *Ibid., p. 35*
21. *V. Shankar, Sardar Patel: Chuna Hua Patra Vyavhaar, part 1, Navajivan: Ahmadabad, p. 588*
22. *Maniben & G.M. Nandurkar, Sardar Shri ke Vishisht aur Anokhe Patra-1, p. 86-87*
23. *Princely states with 10 lakhs population: Hyderabad (16), Mysore (7), Travancore (6), Jammu and Kashmir (4), Baroda and Jaipur (each 3), Jodhpur (2), Cochin, Bikaner, Bhopal, Kohalapur, Mayurbhanj, Sikkim + Kunchbehar, Tripura + Manipur + Khansi Sates and Rampur + Banaras (each 1); and groups of princely states included Orissa (4), Central India and Berar (3), Madras (1), Bombay (4), Himachal Pradesh (1), Kathiawar (4), Matasya (2), Rajasthan (4), Vindhya Pradesh (4), Malwa (7), PEPSU (3), Kutch and Junagrah (each 1) and other (1) were became members of Constituent Assembly.*
24. *Mysore, Travancore, Baroda, Cochin, Jammu and Kashmir, Hyderabad, Undh, Banswara, Gwalior, Jaipur, Indore, Rampur, Banaras, Puddukottai, Jind, Sangli, Sawantwari, Nayagarh, Saraikela, Sirmaur, Bhor, Probandar, Jamkhandi, Miraz Senior, Miraz Junior, Devas Senior, Devas Junior, Mudhol, Phaltan, Sitamau, Kolahapur, Mayurbhanj, Bhopal, Kunchbehar, Bhavnagar, Bharatpur, Tihari-Garwahl, Palanpur, Raigarh, Akalkot, Kurundvaad Senior, Tripura and Idar has own Assembly.*
25. *B.N. Rao, The Framing of India's Constitution, part 4, Delhi: IIPA, 1968, p. 547*
26. *Ibid., p. 548*
27. *White Paper on Indian States, 1950, p. 109*

28. *B.N. Rao, The Framing of India's Constitution, part 4, Delhi: IIPA, 1968, p. 554 (Rajasthan and Hyderabad on November 23, 1949; PEPSU and Central India on November 24, 1949; and Jammu and Kashmir on November 25, 1947 made such proclamation)*
29. *Constituent Assembly of India, Article 306A, October 17, 1949 (Jammu and Kashmir became part of India on October 26, 1947. However, war from Pakistan side was started in September 1947.)*
30. *V. Shankar, Sardar Patel: Chuna Hua Patra Vyavhaar, part 1, Navjivan: Ahmadabad, p. 305*
31. *Sardar Patel Correspondences, 1945-50, Part 5, Navajivan: Ahmadabad, p. 306*
32. *V. Shankar, Sardar Patel: Chuna Hua Patra Vyavhaar, part 1, Navjivan: Ahmadabad, p. (Letter from Sheikh Abdullah to Gopalswami Ayyangar – October 17, 1949)*

□

'Minority' in Indian Constitution

—Ashutosh Kumar Jha

Bharat is a shining example of a geo-cultural entity existing since thousands of years. In its *dharmic* principle, it has always stood for welfare and humanism. As an age-old civilisation and seat of almost all major religions of the world, a basic innate unity has always existed in our country amidst diversity. The innate cultural unity is manifested in the strength of our culture that integrates all the pluralistic thinking of human beings.

Understanding Minority in the Indian Context

The expression 'minority' is an alien concept for India. Historically speaking, reference in the binary of majority-minority has been non-existent in this piece of land. Instead of identifying things by division, Indians have found a way to live in mutual harmony. In the West, the notion of diversity is always understood in terms of 'difference'. In the present times, 'multiculturalism' has acquired a great significance because of its connotation of pluralism and diversity. It is being hailed as a solution to cultural and identity-related differences emanating as a problem in many countries of the West.

India took upon the task of organising itself as a modern state post Independence. So, modern Indian state began to grapple with concepts like 'minority' and its safeguard in the scheme of its Constitution. But the issue of minority in India was an attempt to shape India and look at its society through a Western and imperialistic lens. There is a practical problem with such an approach. In the post-Westphalian world, the Westerners began constructing their territory with a sense of 'othering' creating their respective nation-states in Europe – a resolve to construct its nation-state on the ideals of minority rights, minority safeguards and multiculturalism. But, India, instead of creating sense of 'other', has believed in the innate unity of everyone. One fundamental problem that religiously differentiates the West and India is the concept of 'religion' itself. Christianity is a dogmatic religion based on the concept of a God/Messenger and a holy sacred text. But the same could never be reciprocated for Hindus in India as it consists of several Gods (Western connotation) with diverse texts sacred to diverse seekers of truths (West calls it 'believers'). So, making sense of 'minority' in India through the Western way would see India as the land of minority and a majority.

The issue of minority gained special significance in the context of India's freedom which led to the emergence of a politico-religious state of Pakistan. So, the 'appeasement of minorities' became a tool for negotiation to the makers of our Constitution in their resolve to create a so-called modern, liberal, democratic and secular India. So, the issue of the rights of minorities was considered to be central to a sensitive interpretation of democracy in a state that is devoid of an understanding of 'majority'. In West, minority rights became essential because they had a religious majority ruling the state.

Minority Rights in Historical Perspective

There is no internationally accepted definition or a definite yardstick to define the term 'minority'. The 'minority' as a legal and constitutional group emerged during demarcating new boundaries between the European countries after the First World War. The term appears in international legal documents as 'Minorities Treaties' that accompany the post-WWI Peace Settlement. The Minorities Treaties mentioned only 'racial, linguistic or religious minorities', avoiding the category of 'national minorities'.[1]

Gradually, protection of minorities came to be covered within the concept of human rights and fundamental freedoms as enshrined in the Charter of United Nations. So, after WWII, the rights of minorities did not remain the guiding principle, but the principle of human rights was accepted instead. In the new world, the United Nations charter and Universal Declaration of Human

Rights and Freedoms and the principle of non-discrimination and equality replaced the previous arrangement.

The UN concept and protection of minorities came to be incorporated in its Covenant on Civil and Political Rights[2], and India is a party to it. Article 27 of the Covenant explicitly recognises the rights of 'ethnic, religious or linguistic minorities'. Although we lack an accepted definition of the term, the United Nations, through its Sub-Committee on the Prevention of Discrimination and Protection of Minorities, has undertaken on several occasions to define 'minority' in a satisfactory international legal sense. The most thorough such effort has given rise to the Capotorti Report in 1979.[3]

Concept of Minority in Indian Constitution

The word 'minority' in India has a colonial legacy. The architects of the Indian Constitution guaranteed to minorities all necessary rights and freedoms but have nowhere defined the expression 'minority'. There is no parliamentary legislation either defining a 'minority'. The Motilal Nehru Report (1928) showed a prominent desire to afford protection to minorities, but did not define the expression. The Sapru Report (1945) also proposed, inter alia, a Minorities Commission but did not define the word.

The British colonialists systematically followed policies leading to evolution of the concept of minority after the 1857 Sepoy Mutiny. They evolved schemes to classify minority groups by dividing Indians on the basis of religion. The first such effort was made to divide Bengal in 1905. The Government of India Act 1909 gave separate electorate to Muslims. The Act of 1919 created further division as the Sikh and the Anglo-Indian communities were also extended separate electorate.

The constitutional proposals of 1909 instituting separate electorate for Muslims and further reforms creating such benefits for other groups had allowed these religious groups to be the prime beneficiary of the colonial state's policy of group preference. As soon as the Constituent Assembly began its proceedings as scheduled on 9th December 1946, with the Muslim League boycotting its sessions, political safeguards encompassed provisions for reserved seats in legislatures, quotas in government employment, reserved posts in the Cabinet and the creation of administrative machinery to ensure supervision and protection of minority rights, in all the constitutional drafts and deliberations. It is important to note that all the minority groups were part of the initial proposal and in the first draft of the Constitution published in 1948. But in a remarkable turnaround, by the final draft, religious minorities were rightly excluded from the purview of all political safeguards, which were restricted mainly to the 'scheduled castes' and the 'scheduled tribes'. These radical changes in minority safeguards are explained mainly in terms of the Partition of the country in the literature on the Constituent Assembly debates.[4]

The House, instead of giving preference for preservation of a distinct cultural identity, preferred to follow the nationalist vision. In the vision, backwardness of a group was considered as legitimate ground for group preference provisions. The House rejected the idea of political safeguards for minorities as a rule. For them, legitimacy of any such safeguard entails a specific purpose ameliorating the social and economic disabilities of backward sections. This marked a shift from the manner in which communal safeguards had been envisioned and defended in colonial policy.

It is believed that the vent of Partition created a strong feeling against communal forces and, hence, the Assembly never attempted on any occasion to define 'minority' in precise words. The strength of the feeling could be understood from the fact that the words 'certain classes' were substituted for the word 'minorities' wherever it occurred in the text of the Constitution. In our Constitution, the use of the term 'minority' is rarely used and no group is explicitly mentioned as a minority therein. The term 'minority' is mentioned in only two Articles – 29 and 30.

Political Representation

The chief mechanism proposed in the Constituent Assembly to facilitate representation of minorities on the legislature were separate electorates, reserved quotas for communities in the legislatures in proportion to population and various forms of proportional representation. Muslim representatives were at the forefront of such demands, although similar claims were put forward by Sikh and backward advocacy of caste representatives.

The Muslim League was at the forefront of a demand for a separate electorate as a safeguard for religious minority. But the House deliberated on the issue and rightly rejected demands for a separate electorate. The prominent argument for rejection of such a demand was based on the consideration of nationhood and national unity. Separate electorates were also opposed on secular grounds, as they involved the introduction of religious considerations into the political sphere.

Reservation in Employment

The debate regarding quota in service revealed a similar pattern to the debates regarding special representation provisions. The general consensus in the House was in favour of quotas in the services for the backward classes. The criteria of 'fairness' was also implied in such a decision as it was seen as reparation of history of injustices against the Scheduled Castes and Scheduled Tribes. It emerged that the state was willing to compensate against the historical injustices inflicted upon the lower castes and tribes. There was also scope of indigenous belief system of atonement of one's past action playing a dominant role in evolving a consensus on the said issue.

Nehru applauded the Assembly's decision to give up reserved seats for the minorities. He accepted that such a safeguard was required under an autocratic or foreign rule. But since India was going to be a self-governing democracy, it needed to entail equal voice for all its constituting citizens. Nehru's definition of democracy was: "If it is a democracy, in the long run or in the short run, it is the will of the majority that will prevail." Given this, minority safeguards, such as reservations, would perhaps protect the minorities "to a slight extent but at the cost of forfeiting that inner sympathy and fellow feeling with the majority, which is dangerous", since as Nehru repeated, "in the very nature of things, in a democracy, the will of the majority will ultimately prevail.[5]

Right to Worship or Practice

When the issue of right to religious freedom was first discussed in the Fundamental Rights Sub-committee of the Constituent Assembly in April 1947, there was sharp disagreement between members of this sub-committee over the way in which religious freedom was to be defined. The concern was with regard to whether religious freedom was to be defined as a freedom to 'worship' or as a freedom to the 'practise' of religion. Rajkumari Amrit Kaur argued that since "infringement of the rights of women and of Dalits was part of the practice of several religions of India, and so to have a right to 'practice' religion in a chapter guaranteeing the fundamental rights of all Indian citizens would be an anomaly." She recommended granting a much narrower right to religious 'worship'. Kaur was representing the 'statist' nationalist position in the Assembly. The task at hand before the House was to constitute Indians into a nation by making them members of the same state. The new Indian citizen was to be identified as just that – a citizen of India, with all markers of extra-political identity, like sex, religion, language and culture, being attenuated by conscious state policy. If this was the goal, the worst mistake the Constituent Assembly could make would be to highlight the extra-political aspects of one's person, by giving cultural and educational rights to minorities or by consciously placing religion in the public domain by defining religious freedom widely as a right to the 'practice' of religion.

K.M. Munshi, while advocating a broad right to the 'practice' of religion as well as educational and cultural rights for religious and linguistic minorities, rejected outright any reservations for these minorities in any legislative bodies of the new state on the grounds that such a step would dangerously strengthen extra-political identities.

An interesting explanation is contained in the following words of H.C. Mookerjee, chairman of the Minorities' Sub-committee, in the advisory panel's 11th May 1949 report on reservations in the legislatures for religious minorities. Expressing his disapproval of those members protesting the rejection, he said, "There are certain people who really feel alarmed over the future of their communities. Such people want to come to the legislatures because they think they can safeguard the interests of the groups to which they belong... But when we have passed the different fundamental rights which guarantee religious, cultural and educational safeguards which are justiciable, safeguards which can be decided in a court of law, I feel that the presence of people belonging to certain groups is not necessary."

Cultural Rights for Linguistic Groups

Today, minorityism is recognised with religion but the Constituent Assembly had discussed that cultural rights should be provided for linguistic groups alone, and not for religious groups. Jai Prakash Narayan, held that the "secularisation of general education... necessary for the growth of a national outlook and unity" required that the cultural and educational rights guaranteed in the Constitution should be confined only to linguistic minorities. On the same lines, Damodar Swarup Seth suggested that "minorities should be recognised based on language. Recognition of minorities based on religion or community was not in keeping with the secular character of the state. If such minorities were granted the right to establish and administer educational institutions of their own, it would not only block the way to national unity, but also promote communalism and an anti-national outlook." His words reverberate in modern India which has become a land of competitive minorityism.

G.B. Pant had earlier, in an April 1947 meeting of the sub-committee, suggested that the cultural and educational rights of minorities be included among the non-justiciable directive principles. Kaur had similarly proposed that religious minorities not be allowed to set up separate educational institutions, nor state aid be provided to these institutions. So, we also find in the Constitutional Assembly debates a rejection of recognition of cultural rights based on religion. But the Indian Constitution, acting under the impression of creating an India safer for the Muslims who did not move to Pakistan, recognised these rights for both linguistic and religious minorities in the final Constitution.

Articles 29 and 30

The Constitution had not adequately defined the term 'minority'. Though it mentions the cultural attributes of religion and language, there is no detail on the geographical or numerical specification of the concept. The Constitution does not specifically mention any language and religion under the minority category. In the Constituent Assembly Debate on Article 23, Dr. B.R. Ambedkar said that the word was used not merely to indicate the minority in the technical sense of the word, it is also used to cover minorities which are not minorities in the technical sense, but which are nonetheless minorities in the cultural and linguistic sense.[6] It seems from the above exploration that the scope of Article 23 of the draft, now Article 29, was broadend by dropping the word 'minority' to include all such minorities that were not minority in technical sense but were minority nonetheless.

The National Commission for Minorities Act, 1992 enabled the Centre to notify minorities for the limited purposes of that Act only and in exercise of that power, the government had notified five religious communities – Muslims, Christians, Sikhs, Buddhists and Parsis – to be regarded as minorities. These five communities constitute roughly 17% of the country's population.

It seems that the Constitution makers were not willing to incorporate the colonial legacy of separate representation based on the idea of minority, but agreed to recognise minority right for cultural preservation based on religious and linguistic identity. Even this proposition was not without its fair share of problem as it has made minority a fluid identity which keeps changing with space and time. But the biggest danger that has led to the politics of pseudo-secularism in the country has emanated from the fact of recognising religious minority opposed by many Constitution makers.

Minority in Judicial Pronouncement

Article 30 for the first time came up for interpretation before a seven-judge Constitution Bench constituted to consider the reference made by the President under Article 143 with regard to the Kerala Education Bill, 1957-59. It held, "The existence of minority community should in all circumstances and for purposes of all law of that state be determined on the state basis only when the validity of law extending to whole state is in question or it should be determined on the basis of the population of the particular locality, for the Bill in practice before us extends to the whole of state of Kerala and consequently the minority must be determined by reference to the entire state. By this test, Christians,

Muslims and Anglo-Indians will certainly be minorities in the state of Kerala."[7]

The Supreme Court suggested the technique of arithmetical tabulation of less than 50 per cent of population for identifying a minority. It was to be applied on the applicability of the law in question. If the law has to be applied nationally, then the applicability has to be decided on national figures and, if it has to be applied in a state, it has to be decided on state figures.

In DAV College, Jullunder's case (1971), a Constitutional Bench of the Supreme Court reaffirmed its earlier decision maintaining that minorities has to be determined only in relation to the particular legislation which is sought to be impugned, namely if it is the state legislature, the basis of determination of minority would be the population of the state.[8] As far as language is concerned, the case of DAV College, Jullunder v. State of Punjab is considered important because in defining a linguistic minority, the court observed, "A linguistic minority, for the purpose of Article 30(1), is one which must at least have a separate spoken language. It is not necessary that language should also have a distinct script for those who speak it." The importance of the verdict can be understood from the fact of linguistic minority being a very fluid identity.

The Supreme Court held in Bramchari Sidheswari Shai v. State of West Bengal (1995) that the Ramakrishna Mission a Hindu sect under Article 26 of the Constitution cannot be considered a religious minority under Article 30. This makes it clear that court decision of granting protection of Article 30(1) is available only to religious groups.[9] This judgement clarified that the recognition of minority status is available to religious group only and not available to denominations or sect of a religion.

In TMA Pai Foundation v. State of Karnataka (2002), the 11-judge Bench of the Supreme Court delivering the judgement in above case held by majority that "minority in Article 30(1) covers linguistic and religious minorities." For the purpose of determining 'minority', the unit will be the state and not the whole of India, i.e. minorities have to be considered state wise.[10]

The concept of minority is still evolving, as the issue resurfaced in Bal Patil v. Union of India's case (2005) and Anjuman Madarsa

Noorul Islam Dehra Kalan Ghazipur v. State of Uttar Pradesh (2007) case. But subsequent judgements have further complicated the question of definition of minorities, as both these judgements relate, for the most part, to definitional issues. Bal Patil judgement questioned the identity of Jains as a religious minority while in the above said UP case, judge S.N. Srivastava ruled that Muslims, by virtue of their numbers, cannot be considered a minority in Uttar Pradesh. The Patna High Court announced Arya Samaj in Arya Pratinidhi Sabha v. State of Bihar (1958) case, a minority distinct from the Hindus. However, in 1976, Delhi High Court in Arya Samaj Education Trust v. Director of Education decided against providing benefits of Article 30 to denominations and sects.

There is a potential for increasing demands of different denominational sects within Hinduism to declare themselves as a distinct religious group. The judicial verdict above shows inconsistency in the approach of judges on similar question. There is no doubt that 'competitive minorityism' has the potential to further divide the already fragile Hindu unity in this country.

Conclusion

The recognition of a Western notion of 'minority' and its use as a means to attain power has manifested the fears of our Constitution makers. Hinduism is a multi-religious identity, so in a majority Hindu state, the idea of religious minority has created fertile grounds for communal politics to grow and prosper. The imperialistic scheme had devised the word 'minority' to rule over India. The minorityism that grew out of it led to the division of India. But India failed to learn its lessons well. So under the garb of 'minority', the politics of minorityism is creating havoc for national unity and integrity. India's unity and integrity would have been strengthened if we would have avoided concepts of religious minority in the India Constitution. The communal basis of it in a secular country has not left the lasting imprints of separation visible in the polity today. India needs a constitutional amendment in this regard so that idea of religious minority is erased. As a first step towards the attainment of socio-political unity, uniform civil code should be implemented ushering a new zeal of national unity in the country.

References

1. *Andre Liebich, Minority as Inferiority: Minority Rights in Historical Perspective Review of International Studies, Cambridge University Press, Vol. 34, No. 2 (April 2008), pp. 243-263.*
2. *International Covenant on Civil and Political Rights, adopted on December 16, 1966, entered into force on March 23, 1976, G.A. Res., 2200 (XXI), 21 U.N. GAOR Supp. No. 16 at 52, U.N. Doc. A/6316 (1966).*
3. *Frank Capotorti, Study on the Rights of Persons Belonging to Ethnic, Religious and Linguistic Minorities (New York: United Nations, 1979), para. 568.*
4. *Rochana Bajpai, Constituent Assembly Debates and Minority Rights, Economic and Political Weekly, Vol. 35, No. 21/22 (May 27-June 2, 2000), pp. 1837-1845.*
5. *Shefali Jha, Rights versus Representation: Defending Minority Interests in the Constituent Assembly, Economic and Political Weekly, Vol. 38, No. 16 (April 19-25, 2003), pp. 1579-1583.*
6. *Constituent Assembly Debates, Vol. II, pp: 922-923.*
7. *AIR 1958 SC 956*
8. *AIR 1971 SC 1737*
9. *(1995) 4 SCC 646*
10. *(2002) 8 SCC 481*

□

History of Struggle for Women's Rights in India

—Alisha Dhingra

The gender equality enshrined in the Indian Constitution is the outcome of long struggle by women activists and progressive male leaders in general and the efforts of women leaders and women's organisations within the Indian National Congress in particular. The image of unified national movement overlooks the movement for women's rights since the formation of Congress till Independence. Right from the end of the nineteenth century, women like Tarabai Shinde[1] and, during twentieth century, radical men like Periyar have challenged the patriarchal ideology, questioning the subordination of women in the family. Moreover, it is assumed that only after complete legal and political equality is achieved, the demand for equality in family arises. This was not the case in India. By 1930s, women's organisations began to claim equality in family and started campaigning for reform of personal laws.

It is remarkable to note the presence of women in 1889 Congress session just four years after the formation of Congress. The report of the session specifies that "no less than ten lady delegates graced the assembly – one elected by men at a public meeting and the others by various ladies associations like the Women's Christian Temperance Union, Bengal Ladies' Association and the Mahila Arya Samaj."[2] It was on the enterprise by Ramabai[3] that women delegates participated in this meeting. Charles Bradlaugh recommended to her that women delegates should join the Congress from this time on so that their concerns are considered when Congress forms independent India's Parliament. The report, however, does not disclose the fact that though women delegates were allowed to sit in the meeting, they were neither allowed to speak nor to vote for resolutions. During 1890 session, one woman was given the chance to present a vote of thanks to the president. She expressed her gratitude for being allowed to speak, asserting that this "raised the status of our Indian women."[4]

Annie Besant[5] became the first woman president of Congress in 1917. It was during her term that Congress articulated the belief that the "same tests be applied to women and men with regard to education",[6] Her valorisation of strength of women is strikingly similar to Gandhiji and, in her judgement, the Home Rule Movement was "rendered ten-fold greater by the adhesion to it of large numbers of women who bring to its help the calculating heroism, endurance and self-sacrifice of the feminine nature."[7]

All-India delegation of prominent women met with Montagu and Chelmsford on December 15, 1917. They demanded for the franchise on same terms as men. The next year, at the special session of Congress held in Bombay, Naidu[8] spoke on behalf of suffrage for women. She said:

Never, never, for we realise that men and women have their separate goals, separate destinies and that just as man can never fulfil the responsibility or the destiny of a woman, a woman cannot fulfil the responsibility of man... We ask for the vote, not that we might interfere with you in your official functions, your civic duties, your public place and power, but rather that we might lay the foundation of national character in the souls of children that we hold on our laps, and instil into them the ideals of national life.[9]

This special session was attended by 5,000 delegates and the resolution was approved by 75 per cent majority.

Sarladevi Chaudhrani[10] presented the resolution advocating the vote for women at the thirty-third session of Congress in December 1918. She asserted that women had as much right to map their own destinies as men in this era of human rights, justice, freedom and self-determination. She held that the world has outgrown certain ideas, predominantly the "fanciful division of intellect and emotion being the respective spheres of men and women."[11] She asserted that the "sphere of women included comradeship with men in the rough and tumble of life and to being the fellow-workers of men in politics and other spheres."[12]

Kumar[13] argues that nationalism and feminism shared an ambiguous relationship. On the one hand, nationalism had a beneficial effect on feminism as it drew it out of its upper-class enclave but, on the other hand, it created a rift among feminists. Begum Shah Nawaz[14] and Radhabhai Subbaryon[15] raised the demand for women's reservation in legislatures at the First Round Table Conference (from November 1930 to January 1931) arguing that women can reach equality with men only through initial reservation. Nationalist women fervently opposed this argument and demonstrations against the participation of Nawaz and Subbaryon in the conference held by Rashtriya Stree Sabha and Desh Devika Sangh.[16]

During the Second Round Table Conference, a memorandum was presented by nationalist feminists which discarded all recommendations of concessions to women, whether reservation, nomination or co-option, and declared that "to seek any form of preferential treatment would be to violate the integrity of the universal decision of Indian women for absolute equality of political status."[17]

The period between 1917 and 1927 saw the emergence of three womens organisations at the national level: Women's Indian Association (WIA), All India Women's Conference (AIWC) and National Council for Women in India (NCWI). The most prominent issues which appeared in the campaigns of these organisations were related to marriage, divorce and inheritance as well as towards extending educational and economic opportunities to women. WIA was formed by Annie Besant, Dorothy Jinarajadasa,[18] Malati Patwardhan,[19] Ammu Swaminathan,[20] Mrs. Dadabhoy and Mrs. Ambujammal.[21] In 1932, Rajkumari Amrit Kaur[22] hailed this organisation as the "first purely feminist organisation to arise in India."[23] The association was the first women's organisation to take up the demands of women workers. The demand for maternity leave was first put to the fore in the 1921 Jamshedpur strike. It was also brought up in the charter of All India Trade Union Congress (AITUC) in the year the organisation was formed. The Bombay Maternity Benefit Act was passed in 1929, which was followed by analogous legislation in other provinces.[24]

Once it became apparent that the Bengal Congress was not

concerned about women's issues, women leaders called for a meeting to form a separate women's Congress. In May 1931, Bengal Women's Conference was held where Sarladevi Chaudhrani made a provoking speech with a clearly discernible feminist agenda. While she recognized men's role in getting women in the freedom movement, but raised doubts whether they were actually concerned about improving women's status. She emphasised that though women were remunerated with ornamental speeches, but were not appointed to sub-committees and councils. She alleged that Congress allotted to women only "the position of law-breakers and not law-makers."[25] She proclaimed that the moment has come to voice overtly the status of women and join the worldwide women's movement. She questioned why the Congress on no occasion considered of an anti-brothel campaign. She called for legal, economic, social and educational equality. The audience, which Sarladevi spoke to, was not as radical as her and, in their concluding session, they restated the usual demands, precluded resolutions favouring birth control and equal treatment for women and decided not to form separate women's Congress.[26]

The AIWC was dissatisfied with both the Sarda Act and the proposed India Act. In 1934, it asked the government to appoint an all-women commission to reflect the legal disabilities of women. The concerns they brought to the fore were inheritance, marriage and guardianship of children. Their eventual objective was to pass a new law. AIWC legal secretary, Renuka Ray[27] wrote a pamphlet titled "Legal Disabilities of Indian Women: A Plea for a Commission of Enquiry" and spoke in support of a new law for all women, irrespective of community. She penned that the legal position of Indian women was one of the most unequal in the world today. Ray demanded for new personal and family law that would make women autonomous and fully prepared to partake in public life.[28]

In 1937, a National Planning Committee was instituted with Jawaharlal Nehru as its chairman. Lakshmibai Rajwade,[29] Sarojini Naidu, Vijaya Lakshmi Pandit,[30] Hansa Mehta,[31] Mrs. Maneklal Premchand,[32] Begum Shah Nawaz,[33] Begum Hamid Ali,[34] and Radhabhai Subbaroyan were members of the sub-committee to analyse women's role in planned economy.[35] The final report

(Women's Role in Planned Economy or WRPE) of the sub-committee was presented before the plenary session of the National Planning Committee in 1940. Some of the rights that were recommended by the sub-committee were "equal voting right as individual, right to hold public office or employment, right to work as implied in the demand for equal access to public services and equal wages for equal work without endangering employment opportunities for women, right to choose one's nationality and equal rights to health, leisure and recreation."[36] The thought enshrined in the report was that "housewives were also working women."[37] "The concept of fixed hours of work, adequate relief from duties in the kitchen, cooperative efforts to relieve/sharing household duties, etc. sought to expand the scope and meaning of women's work."[38]

In the report, economic independence was understood not only in terms of equal access to employment, but more significantly in "making women co-sharers in the collective income and resources of the family."[39] Moreover, the report emphasised the economic value of women's work at home and demanded for recognition for their contribution in family production. There were several recommendations in the report for enhancement of the state of working women by asking for equal wages, equal work opportunities, child care services, etc. The WRPE report noted that "economic rights of women were contingent on each woman being recognised as a separate and an independent unit within the economic structure."[40] The report emphasised on the provision of crèche facilities and this is noteworthy since this crucial provision was not recognised till as late as 2006, when Mahatma Gandhi National Rural Employment Guarantee Scheme (MNREGS) was implemented. The report suggested that "there should be cessation of all work during the day so that the mid-day meal can be conveniently taken and the housewife is released from the duties in kitchen."[41] The report also condemned "prioritisation of male workers over women" and sought "equal guarantee for women at work regardless of their marital status."[42]

Roy points out that though the report made several recommendations which widened the opportunities available to women, the sub-committee based their claims to gender equality on the special contribution women made to the nation and community as "reproducers, sustainers and the guardians and trustees of the future generations."[43]

During this time, various measures pertaining to women's rights were introduced between 1937 and 1938, such as the Hindu Woman's Right to Property Bill, an amendment to the Child Marriage Restraint Act, a Bill to allow inter-caste marriage, the Hindu Woman's Right to Divorce Act, the Muslim Personal Law Bill, the Prevention of Polygamy Bill and the Muslim Women's Right to Divorce Bill. These were accompanied by anti-dowry Bills, marriage laws and Bills allowing women to inheritance were introduced in the provincial legislatures.[44]

The Bills which were introduced were defeated one by one. The opposition's intractability reflected in the debates shocked women members. Begum Hamid Ali lamented the "utterly unsympathetic attitude of the men in the Assembly and concluded they were afraid they might lose half of their land, power and money."[45] She argued that though legal reform is incompetent in itself to resolve all women's problems, nonetheless it will endow financial security to some women who might live their own lives and take care of their children. It is significant to note that women increasingly contained their pleas in vocabulary of human rights and spoke less often about the special contribution of politics. Begum Hamid Ali asserted, "Women are asking nothing more than just and humane treatment and to be liberated from their disabilities."[46]

The government's decision to appoint a committee of distinguished lawyers to study Hindu law and make recommendations was delayed till 1941 owing to the war and political disturbances. Sir B.N. Rau was chosen to be the chair of the committee in January 1941. The appeal to include a woman to the committee was uncared for. Despite this, women's organisations worked hard to support the measure. It was for the first time that all women's organisations worked together to collect information for the Rau Committee.[47] In order to draft a statement to the Rau Committee, the AIWC held a meeting of the Standing Committee in Bombay in May 1941. In the draft, AIWC demanded equal rights for women in inheritance, marriage, guardianship, prohibition of polygamy and legalisation of divorce. The AIWC petitioned provincial legislatures to extend the Hindu Women's Right to Property Act to agricultural land.[48]

In 1941, when Congress boycotted the legislatures, the women activists – who were both nationalist and feminist – faced the dilemma whether they should cooperate with Rau Committee to protect rights for women or join the Congress boycott? Gandhi was dismissive about the committee as a government ruse to distract attention from genuine issues, but he did not ask women activists to boycott it. His compromise solution was that women who desired to work with Rau Committee might do so in their individual capacity, but women should refrain from acting as spokepersons for any group. Though Mridula Sarabhai admitted that this proposed reform was the "equivalent to what a Temple Entry Bill would mean to Harijan workers", she asked women to stand firmly behind the Non-cooperation Movement.[49] On the other hand, some women Congress leaders like Sarojini Naidu, Vijaylakshmi Pandit and Amrit Kaur unrelentingly called for legal reform. Moreover, Mrs. Renuka Ray and Mrs. Radhabhai Subbarayan, the Congress women who were in the Central Legislative Assembly, spoke in praise of Rau Committee's work.[50]

In their struggle for rights, women leaders employed the nationalist vocabulary. Despite the fact that there was marked difference in the living conditions of women across different regions, castes and classes, the construction of unified image of 'Indian womanhood' was crucial for the construction of the idea of 'Indian nation'. The speeches by women members of the Constituent Assembly clearly reflect the nationalist discourses on womanhood. In the Constituent Assembly, a marked consensus was observed on those issues which were agreed upon during the nationalist movement such as granting women the right to vote. The women members opposed special representation on identity basis and spoke against women's reservation. Their views were influenced by nationalist vocabulary which viewed any special representation as hindrance to national integration. The nationalist vocabulary, thus, both advanced and constrained the agenda of transformation. Women members based the premise of equality on their responsibilities towards the nation. Within the nationalist discourse, special representation was antithetical to national unity. What is interesting to note is that many of the progressive proposals which had the potential of transforming gender relations were either ignored or defeated. Some of these proposals had explicit mention of abolishing of Devdasi system, removal of discrimination between legitimate and illegitimate children, removing impediments to equality in the sphere of marriage, reforming personal laws, extending equality to private sphere. These provisions would have struck at the root of patriarchal structure and would have gone a long way in transforming gender relations in society. Thus, only those rights were incorporated in the Indian Constitution on which consensus was achieved during the nationalist movement, such as the right to vote. Even the right to vote could not become part of the fundamental rights and was shifted to Part XV of the Constitution. The amendment moved by one of the members of the Constituent Assembly to explicitly mention the right to get elected was rejected. Despite the fact that many progressive proposals were not accepted, but the anxiety expressed by certain members of the Constituent Assembly that women may compete with them testifies to the transformative potential of the Constitution. Gender discourses prevalent at the constitutive moment of Indian democracy are resonant in the post-Independence era in interpretation of the Constitution by different organs of the state, i.e., judgements by the courts, reports of committees set up by the governments and legislative debates on reservation and uniform civil code.

Bibliography

1. *Arya, Sadhna. 2000. Women, Gender Equality and the State. New Delhi: Deep and Deep.*
2. *Forbes, Geraldine. 1996. Women in Modern India. New York: Cambridge University Press.*
3. *Kumar, Radha. 1993. The History of Doing: An Illustrated Account of Movements for Women's Rights and Feminism in India 1800-1990. New Delhi: Zubaan.*
4. *Roy, Anupama. 2005. Gendered citizenship. New Delhi: Orient Longman.*
5. *Report of the Committee on Amendments to Criminal Law 2013, accessed on February 5, 2015, available at: http://www.thehindu.com/multimedia/archive/01340/Justice Verma_Comm_1340438a.pdf*

References

1. *Tarabai Shinde is the author of 'Stree-Purush Tulana' (A Comparison Between Women and Men), originally published in Marathi in 1882. The pamphlet is a critique of upper-caste patriarchy, and is often considered the first modern Indian feminist text.*
2. *Radha Kumar. 1993. The History of Doing: An Illustrated Account of Movements for Women's Rights and Feminism in India 1800-1990. New Delhi: Zubaan.*
3. *Ramabai was the first woman to be accorded the titles of 'Pandita' as a Sanskrit scholar and 'Sarasvati' after being examined by the faculty of the University of Calcutta. She is the author of 'The High-Caste Hindu Woman', published in 1888. Originally written in Marathi, it was translated into English and sold in America.*
4. *Radha Kumar. 1993. The History of Doing: An Illustrated Account of Movements for Women's Rights and Feminism in India 1800-1990. New Delhi: Zubaan.*
5. *Annie Besant was a British socialist, theosophist, women's rights activist, writer, orator and a supporter of both Irish and Indian self-rule. She led the Home Rule Movement in India.*
6. *Radha Kumar. 1993. The History of Doing: An Illustrated Account of Movements for Women's Rights and Feminism in India 1800-1990. New Delhi: Zubaan.*
7. *Radha Kumar. 1993. The History of Doing: An Illustrated Account of Movements for Women's Rights and Feminism in India 1800-1990. New Delhi: Zubaan, p.48.*
8. *Naidu became the first President of Indian National Congress and later she was appointed as the Governor of the United Provinces, now Uttar Pradesh. Known as the 'Nightingale of India', she was also a noted poet.*
9. *Geraldine Forbes. 1996. Women in Modern India. New York: Cambridge University Press, p.94.*
10. *Sarla Devi Chaudhrani was the founder of the first women's organisation in India, the Bharat Stree Mahamandal, in Allahabad in 1910. One of the primary goals of the organisation was to promote female education, which at that time was not well developed.*
11. *Geraldine Forbes. 1996. Women in Modern India. New York: Cambridge University Press, p.94.*
12. *Geraldine Forbes. 1996. Women in Modern India. New York: Cambridge University Press, p.94.*
13. *Radha Kumar. 1993. The History of Doing: An Illustrated Account of Movements for Women's Rights and Feminism in India 1800-1990. New Delhi: Zubaan.*
14. *Begum Jahanara Shah Nawaz was a Muslim League activist and*

a politician. She succeeded in bringing All India Muslim Women's Conference's resolution against polygamy.

15. *Radhabai Subbarayon served as a member of the All India Women's Conference. In the Round Table Conference of 1930, she and Begum Jahanara Shahnawaz were the only two active members of women's organisations nominated to the conference. They argued unsuccessfully for a 5 per cent reservation for women in the legislatures. Radhabai also participated in the Second Round Table Conference and was a member of The Lothian Committee which was appointed to gauge public opinion over reservations. She was elected unopposed to the Council of States from a general constituency in 1938 and became the first woman member of the Council of States.*
16. *Radha Kumar. 1993. The History of Doing: An Illustrated Account of Movements for Women's Rights and Feminism in India 1800-1990. New Delhi: Zubaan, p.81.*
17. *Radha Kumar. 1993. The History of Doing: An Illustrated Account of Movements for Women's Rights and Feminism in India 1800-1990. New Delhi: Zubaan, p.81.*
18. *Dorothy Jinarajadasa was an English feminist and Theosophist, who married C. Jinarajadasa, the fourth president of the Theosophical Society (Adyar). She co-founded the Women's Indian Association.*
19. *Malati Patwardhan served as the secretary of Women's India Association (WIA) and editor of Stri Dharma, the journal of Women's Indian Association which was first published in January 1918 by two theosophist feminists – Margaret Cousins and Dorothy Jinarajadasa – and continued until August 1936.*
20. *Ammu Swaminatahan was a social worker, freedom fighter and political activist. She was a member of the Constituent Assembly. She was also a member of Lok Sabha during 1951-57.*
21. *Mrs. Ambujammal was a freedom fighter and women's rights activist. A Gandhian, she participated in the Civil Disobedience Movement and served as Vice president of the Tamil Nadu Congress Committee. Ambujammal was awarded the Padma Shri in 1964.*
22. *Rajkumari Amrit Kaur was the first Health Minister of India and served for 10 years in the capacity. She was an eminent Gandhian, freedom fighter and social activist. Kaur was also a member of the Constituent Assembly. She co-founded the All India Women's Conference in 1927, became its secretary in 1930 and president in 1933.*
23. *Radha Kumar. 1993. The History of Doing: An Illustrated Account of Movements for Women's Rights and Feminism in India 1800-1990. New Delhi: Zubaan, p.81.*
24. *Radha Kumar. 1993. The History of Doing: An Illustrated Account*

of Movements for Women's Rights and Feminism in India 1800-1990. New Delhi: Zubaan.

25. *Radha Kumar. 1993. The History of Doing: An Illustrated Account of Movements for Women's Rights and Feminism in India 1800-1990. New Delhi: Zubaan.*
26. *Geraldine Forbes. 1996. Women in Modern India. New York: Cambridge University Press, p.143.*
27. *Renuka Ray was a noted freedom-fighter, social activist and politician. She was member of All India Women's Conference and served as its President in 1952-53. She was also a member of the Constituent Assembly.*
28. *Geraldine Forbes. 1996. Women in Modern India. New York: Cambridge University Press, p.143.*
29. *Rani Lakshmibai Rajwade served as the secretary of AIWC for two years and thereafter its President. Jawaharlal Nehru appointed her as the head of the section of Women's Welfare, Education and Advancement under the National Planning Committee. Rajwade went to the US as a member of a delegation led by Prime Minister Jawaharlal Nehru.*
30. *Vijaya Lakshmi Pandit was the first Indian woman to hold a Cabinet post in pre-Independent India. In 1937, she was elected to the provincial legislature of the United Provinces and was designated minister of Local Self-government and Public Health. In 1946, she was elected to the Constituent Assembly from the United Provinces. In 1953, she became the first woman President of the United Nations General Assembly.*
31. *Hansa Mehta was a reformist, social activist, educator, freedom fighter, feminist and writer. She was a member of the Constituent Assembly. She became the president of All India Women's Conference in 1945-46. In her presidential address at the AIWC convention held in Hyderabad, she proposed a Charter of Women's Rights. She was a member of the Advisory Committee and Sub-Committee on Fundamental Rights.*
32. *Mrs. Maneklal Premchand led a delegation of 10 women to attend the International Council of Women (ICW) conference in Paris in 1934. In 1936, she became one of the Vice presidents of ICW.*

33 *Begum Shah Nawaz was a politician and Muslim League activist. In 1918, she successfully moved the All India Muslim Women's Conference to pass a resolution against polygamy. In 1935, she founded the Punjab Provincial Women's Muslim League.*

34. *Begum Hamid Ali was the only Muslim woman who worked with women's sub-committee of National Planning Committee.*
35. *Geraldine Forbes. 1996. Women in Modern India. New York: Cambridge University Press, p.143.*
36. *Anupama Roy. 2005. Gendered citizenship. New Delhi: Orient Longman, p.214.*

37. *Anupama Roy. 2005. Gendered citizenship. New Delhi: Orient Longman, p.214.*
38. *Anupama Roy. 2005. Gendered citizenship. New Delhi: Orient Longman, p.214.*
39. *Sadhna, Arya 2000. Women, Gender Equality and the State. New Delhi: Deep and Deep, p.48.*
40. *Report of the Committee on Amendments to Criminal Law 2013, p.34.*
41. *Report of the National Planning Committee, 1948, p.224 cited in Report of the Committee on Amendments to Criminal Law 2013, p.34.*
42. *Report of the National Planning Committee, 1948, p.224 cited in Report of the Committee on Amendments to Criminal Law 2013, p.34.*
43. *Anupama Roy. 2005. Gendered citizenship. New Delhi: Orient Longman, p.215.*
44. *Geraldine Forbes. 1996. Women in Modern India. New York: Cambridge University Press.*
45. *Geraldine Forbes. 1996. Women in Modern India. New York: Cambridge University Press, p.146.*
46. *Geraldine Forbes. 1996. Women in Modern India. New York: Cambridge University Press, p.146.*
47. *Geraldine Forbes. 1996. Women in Modern India. New York: Cambridge University Press, p.116*
48. *Chitra Sinha. 2012, Debating Patriarchy: The Hindu Code Bill Controversy in India (1941-1956). New Delhi: Oxford University Press, p.56.*
49. *Geraldine Forbes. 1996. Women in Modern India. New York: Cambridge University Press, p.116.*
50. *Geraldine Forbes. 1996. Women in Modern India. New York: Cambridge University Press, p.116.*

□

Indian Constitution and Institution of Family

—*Prof. Bhagwati Prakash Sharma*

Family is the greatest and the most precious gift of our rich cultural heritage. The reciprocity of self-sacrifices made in the family by each member for the wellbeing of the other is the most pious penance. For this reason alone, in our classical scriptures like Padma Puran,[1] Narad Puran[2] and Skanda Puran,[3] the idea of family is accorded very high esteem, and the performing of one's duties towards his/her parents and elders, as well as between the spouses is considered to be more pious than what one gets from the most sacred pilgrimage. In the Vedas, especially in Rig Veda and Atharva Veda, utmost emphasis has been given on sustaining harmony, reciprocity and dutifulness *inter se* in a family. The cultural values we inherit in the family, cooperation we receive and helps that we derive in our family, help us in developing and harnessing our abilities and potentials. The support that we get from our family, starting from childhood up to the old age throughout the entire span of our life is nothing short of a heavenly elixir of life. In India, the tradition of living together of the three generations happily in a joint family with utmost reciprocal cooperation voluntarily and with mutual respect, as well as the selfless performance of duties without expecting anything in return is a mysterious puzzle for the people in other societies.

The Constitution and the Institution of Family

In spite of the family being the core unit of the society, the State and the nation since time immemorial, our Constitution has no mention of the family institution, internal as well as external dynamics of families, including the mutual duties, responsibilities and vividness of relations *inter se* the members. Family, which is a basic unit for intimate and live relations for mutual and reciprocal cooperation, constituting the ecosystem for an individual in the society as well as of the family with the society and nation and which always provides the fundamental and doctrinal support for all the crucial decisions into our lives. Yet, there is no mention of the role, importance and contribution of family, familial relations, duties or even a meaningful mention of this vital institution in the Constitution. It is strange that this basic cultural unit constituting the society and a determinate of societal dynamics, influencing the national integrity, unity and economy is missing from our Constitution. All the more, Hindu Undivided Family (HUF) is considered as a form of business entity in the Income Tax Act for taxing it as an 'enterprise'. The HUF, which has always been the fundamental unit of our social, cultural and economic structure and conduct, has also been treated as a commercial unit for the purpose of taxation under the Act.[4] Nowadays, even that HUF is losing its sheen. To the contrary, undermining the family, the Indian Constitution best upholds individual sovereignty by acknowledging and protecting personal freedom and individual rights of its citizens. The Constitution focusses on a person's individual rights may be because of two reasons: first, at the time, when our Constitution was being framed, the discussions and deliberations on human rights were at their peak in the world as during that time alone, the United Nations Declaration on Human Rights was in the process of adoption.[5] Therefore, the framers of our Constitution were so overwhelmed and influenced by those discussions that they focussed upon individual sovereignty and overlooked the family institution, which otherwise could curb part of individual sovereignty by family duties and reciprocities, and there underlying cultural heritage. It also seems that their vision was swayed by the idea of socialism, imported from the erstwhile Soviet Union and China. This Soviet influence got more pronounced in 1976, during the Emergency when by virtue of the 42nd amendment of the Constitution, the word 'socialism' was added to the Preamble of the Constitution. In the Directive

Principles of State Policy as well as familial doctrines of economic conduct, Gandhiji's 'trusteeship' theory as well as family values could not get any space, which could be done. As a result, even in 1976, during enlisting of ten fundamental duties of citizens, no mention of any family related duty(ies) was/were incorporated in it.[6] It was only in 1986s, when through the 86th amendment of the Constitution, the guardian's duty towards the education of dependents was assertively added as the 11th duty.[7]

In fact, in mid-1950s, the Hindu Civil Code was enacted through four separate laws. Even in that, the family as an institution and doctrine of familial reciprocity was grossly overlooked. Article 44 in the Constitution rather gives a clear directive for uniform civil code for all citizens and not for Hindus alone.[8] But the provision of this Article was grossly neglected and 4 Acts were made for the Hindu society alone, leaving the Muslims to be governed by Sharia laws, i.e., their communal law. The attachment to Sharia laws has been solely responsible for the blood-letting division of Bharat. Even in those 4 Acts of Hindu laws, instead of making any provision or mention of and empowerment of the family institution, indirect attempts were made to weaken it. The four Acts enacted in mid-1950s are:

- Hindu Succession Act, 1956
- Hindu Marriage Act
- Hindu Minority and Guardianship Act
- Hindu Adoption and Maintenance Act

Recently, the Supreme Court, in the name of ensuring full and proper execution of constitutional provisions and its smooth functioning, has even abolished the punitive clauses meant for punishing against the acts of homosexuality[9] and adultery[10] by repealing of the relevant provisions from Indian Penal Code and decriminalised both of them. Until now, under the provisions of Sections 377 and 497 of IPC, homosexual relations and adultery (a man having illegal relation with a married woman without the permission of her husband) were punishable offences. In two separate decisions on 6th and 27th September this year respectively, the apex court declared the provisions of punishment for these two offences as unconstitutional. These two decisions will have long-run implications for the family institution in

India. Moreover, on 23rd July 2015, the same court, which is the custodian of our Constitution, also had legalised the live-in relationship between unmarried couples.[11] Such verdicts may lead to unimaginable amount of perversion in the family life and family structure. Because of this, family relation, morality and public order might get affected. Today, in many Western countries, high rate of divorces, unwed cohabiting couples, the increasing number of children of such of cohabiting adult couples, fragmentation of such families of cohabiting couples, multiple marriages, increasing number of families with step parents, have contributed to rapid accumulation of mental diseases in pre-teen and adolescent children, as young as 7 to 14 years. It is necessary to be cautious of such distortions here in India as well. That's why, the society is becoming vocal and coming forward to insist on inclusion of positive provisions on morality, family, family responsibility, ethics, and our culture in our Constitution.

Problem of Pre-teen and Teenage Psychiatric Disorders as a Result of Family Splits in Western Countries

In America, Australia and European countries, one can see increasing percentage of divorces, multiple marriages, resultant cases of single parenthood, single-member families and step parent families with either a step-mother or father and step children. As a result of that, there is an ever-increasing number of child psychiatric problems, where a large number of children as well as adolescent-age patients are with mental diseases. Mental diseases among the children are spreading like epidemic in disturbed, fragmented or separated families. In such fragmented or step families, ailments like 'attention-deficiency hyper-activity' (ADH) syndrome and criminal mentality caused by them; lack of culture; live-in relationships; unmarried motherhood or fatherhood; and many other such unimaginable sociological problems are increasing fast. In the last two decades, India too has seen 15-fold increase in the rate of divorces. And it is increasing at an accelerating pace. In 2001, the rate of divorce was one in 1,000 couples. It has now gone up to 15.1 per 1,000 couples (1.51%) in 2017.[12]

In England, the Marriage Foundation and University of Lincoln has conducted a survey on the mental ailments of children below 14 years of age (who had to be admitted in psychiatric word), wherein 10,929 mothers were surveyed and published its results in November 2017. The survey shows that the kids, whose parents get separated or live without marriages, get the symptoms of mental diseases even before their adolescence. In another survey, the researchers found that in situations where there is a single parent or there is a step-mother or step-father in the family, the serious problem of child mental disease is rampant.[13] The foundation found in its survey that 27% children of unmarried live-in couples, who have not separated yet, and 38% kids of the ones who have separated, suffer from mental ailments. In case of the divorced couples, 32% of the kids are found to suffer from mental illness.

In America, the Lincoln Prairie Behavioural Health Centre studied 154 pre-adolescent individuals suffering from psychiatric ailments, between July and December 2012. The study found that out of those children who are suffering from mental illness, only 11% were such who were living with their natural parents while rest of the 89% kids were such whose family structure was fragmented in some way or the other. Out of them, 71% kids were such whose parents or siblings had also been suffering from mental illnesses due to any disturbance or fragmentation in family.[14] Because of the ADH disorder problem of the majority of kids from disintegrated families, their academic performances were also found to have been adversely affected. Jeremy Orca studied this effect on children from 7 to 14 years of age. He found that the academic performance record of these children started to show sharp decline even 2 to 4 years before the divorce of their parents.

In a similar study, it is seen that even when the parents are not divorced, and only because of the family disputes, the academics and the overall behavioural condition of children are adversely affected. In the Euro-American countries, it is seen that among the adult mental patients, the percentage of such people is higher than others who, in their childhood or teenage had gone through mental problems due to family disputes, divorce of parents, or step-parents or step-siblings in the family. The tension and conflicts between the husband and wife seriously affect the life and health-wise development of their children. That is why, couples should not push their children into a hellish life because of their own ego clash.

Increasing Rate of Family Disputes in India

In 2011 census, 13,60,000 respondents mentioned 'divorced' as their marital status. This comes to 0.2 percent of total married population and 0.11 percent of total population of the nation. Ten years ago, in 2001, this percentage was 0.07 percent. In 2011, the percentage of divorced and separated people increased from 0.07 to 0.08 percent. That means, out of total married population, 0.08 percent had already divorced or separated by then. However, 0.56 percent of them re-married. As a result, the percentage of people living lonely life due to divorce is found to be 0.02 percent. By the end of 2016, divorce or separation rate became 1.3 percent, i.e., 13 people in every 1,000. The increase in divorce rate from 0.01 in 2001 to 0.8 in 2011 and then to 1.3 in 2016 indicates a serious situation. So, considering the epidemic of psychiatric mental diseases in India like in the Euro-American nations, married couples and their family members should try to fully stop any possibilities of divorce or disputes in the family. Harmony in family is absolutely essential for the development of the next generation. In Indian tradition, the ancient scriptures have assigned extreme importance to the family unit. At this point, it is necessary to furnish a brief description of the role of family in ancient Indian scriptures.

The Place of Family in Our Ancient Heritage and Scriptures

Vedas are the oldest texts in the world and the Rig Veda has been declared to be world's heritage even by UNESCO. According to Vedic thought, family is formed by individuals and, in turn the society and nation are formed by families. According to the Vedas, sages, well-versed in religious austerity initiated the nation formation process for the purpose of social welfare and successful householders have always been instrumental in enhancing its radiance, vigour and empowerment. In this way, since the Vedic era, family life along with its values has been considered for a strong nation and a healthy society. Rig Veda considers family as a beautiful sanctuary and respect for women as the highest form of devotion in that sanctuary. [Rig Veda 3(53/6)]. In Padma Puran, one's gratification and respect to wife is also said to be of the penance of same importance as the pilgrimage. Parents, teachers and spouses have been described as important as a pilgrimage or '*teerth*'. In family, if mutual respect and harmony are missing, then their visit to holy place is held to be ineffective like the uselessness of the presence of fish and other water creatures living in holy water.

Family Life and Dutiful Family Reciprocities in Vedas

The way all the members should live in a family and maintain the limits is clearly mentioned in the Vedas and other texts. Each member of family is related to different relations. A man is either someone's son, father, brother, uncle, husband or son-in-law. Similarly, a woman can be someone's mother, sister, aunt, wife or daughter-in-law. In Vedas, this mutuality is beautifully described.

Family Relations, Mutual Duties and Responsibilities Need to be Empowered by Law and Constitution

Institution of family needs to be strengthened and its glory be restored by all-round efforts. Even Japan, bearing in mind the importance of family, is considering provisions related to the respect of family and mutual harmony inside the family to be added to their Constitution. The Liberal Democratic Party there has proposed inclusion of family duties in their Constitution.[15] In India, it is high time to develop a code of conduct regarding family harmony and mutual cooperation as well as to begin a discourse for the empowerment of the family institution, by all kinds of social, legal and constitutional initiatives and endeavours.

References

1. *Padmapurana, bhoomikhand 53. 11-14, 24 Padmapurana, Bhoomikhand 63. 14, 19, 21 Padmapurana 1, Bhoomikhand 95. 12-14/ Padmapurana 41. 12-14*
2. *Naradpurana.*
3. *Skandapurana, Kashikhand, chapter-6*
4. *Income Tax Act 1961, Section 80C*

5. *Human Rights Under Indian Constitution http://www.lex-warrier.in/2010/08/human-rights-under-indian-constitution/*
6. *Constitution of India, Article 51A*
7. *Clause (K) added in 2002 in Article 51A of the Constitution of India*
8. *Constitution of India, Article 44A https://www.jagran.com/haryana/bahadurgarh-14908806.html*
9. *https://khabar.ndtv.com/news/file-facts/ipc-section-377-supreme-court-verdict-on-decriminalising-gay-sex-today-10-points-1912079*
10. *https://www.livehindustan.com/national/story-adultery-verdict-live-updates-supreme-court-strikes-down-adultery-as-offence-under-section-497-of-ipc-2193873.html*
11. *"Adult couple can live together without marriage: Supreme Court" https://www.hindustantimes.com/india-news/adult-couple-can-live-together-without-marriage-supreme-court/story78VUJpqqqLVlLm7EqSfeBK.html*
12. *"Divorce Rate in India Increasing" https://marriagelane.com/divorce-rate-in-india-increasing/*
13. *"Attention deficit hyperactivity disorder (ADHD) in phenotypically similar neurogenetic conditions: Turner syndrome and the RASopathies" https://www.ncbi.nlm.nih.gov/pmc/articles/PMC5502326/*
14. *"Short-Term Residential Treatment: Effectiveness of Intensive Intervention for Children with Complex Mental Health Needs" "Evaluation of the Short Term Residential Treatment Unit Serving Children and Youth Ages 6-13" Shannon, L. Stewart, Ph.D., C. Psych. Christine Cullion, M.A. Chloe Hamza, B.A. http://www.excellenceforchildandyouth.ca/sites/default/files/gai_attach/PEG-657_Final_Outcomes_Report.pdf*
15. *"LDP announces a new draft Constitution for Japan" https://www.jimin.jp/english/news/117099.html Purposed new draft Constitution for Japan announces by LDP, Chapter III, Rights and duties of the people "This chapter prescribes the conditions for universal suffrage at the national and local levels: universal suffrage shall be given to Japanese adults. It newly prescribes that a family shall be respected as a basic unit of a society and that family members should help one other. New articles regarding responsibilities of the state include conservation of environment, protection of Japanese overseas in the case of emergency, and providing consideration to victims of crime."*

□

Saga of a Struggle: The Authorised Hindi Text of Our Constitution

—Brij Kishore Sharma

The Authorised Text and the Translation

At the very outset, it would be apt to make it clear that there is a world of difference between an authorised text and a translation. When a Bill is passed in both the Houses of Parliament, it is signed by the President to transform it into an Act. Whatever is written in the Act is the authorised text of it. If an amendment is called for, the same process is to be employed as was done in the original Bill. English is the language of the Bills in Parliament, so what we read is the authorised English text.

The process of preparing an authorised text in Hindi is given in the Official Languages Act. The English text is translated into Hindi and, after the consent of the President, it is published in the Gazette of India. After publication, it becomes the authorised Hindi text of the Constitution. The courts can give their verdicts on the basis of it. So, there can be more than one authorised texts. The Constitution of Canada has two authorised texts—one in French and the other in English. The authorised texts of the United Nations Charter are in five languages.

The Question of Hindi in the Constituent Assembly

On the very first day of the Constituent Assembly (9 December 1946), Raghunath Vishnu Dhulekar tendered a request to run the proceedings in Hindi and insisted on framing the Constitution in Hindi. Dr. Sachidanand Sinha was the interim President on that day. After two days, Dr. Rajendra Prasad was elected as the permanent President. His heart's desire was to frame the Constitution in Hindi.

The Constitution Drafted in English

The first draft of the Constitution was circulated in October 1947. It was prepared by B.N. Rao. The second draft was circulated by the Draft Committee on 21 February 1948 after a thorough debate and amendments. A bit-by-bit debate of the third draft began on 4 November 1948. All three drafts were in English. Seth Govind Das asked: "Whether the Articles we are going to pass will be passed again in Hindi or not?" The President replied that after the Articles are passed, a Hindi translation will be made available to the members for their approval. Balkrishna Sharma 'Naveen' suggested that the debate should continue over the Hindi parts as well so that after some time, the Constitution stands approved in Hindi and the same is taken as the authorised text.

Dr. Rajendra Prasad said, "Keeping in view the capability of the people who were entrusted with the job to prepare the draft of the Constitution, we could not but make the draft in English. When the matter of the language will be settled, it will be translated and put before the House."

Dhulekar, on the same day again, said that it is insulting to adopt a Constitution translated from English. No country has done it till date. Algurai Shastri seconded him. Ultimately, the President said that our Constitution would be framed in our own language and there was no room for more discussion on the subject.

But the events took such shape that the wish of Dr. Rajendra Prasad could not but remain just a wish.

Dr. Rajendra Prasad and the Translation of the Constitution

In the very year of 1947, Dr. Rajendra Prasad had constituted an expert committee to translate the Constitution. Following were the members of the committee:

1. **Ghanshyam Singh Gupt, Chairman:** He was the Speaker of the Legislative Assembly of the Central Provinces and Vidarbha and a member of the Constituent Assembly. (Madhya Pradesh was not as state till then).
2. **Pandit Kamlapati Tripathi:** Member, Constituent Assembly Afterwards, the Chief Minister of Uttar Pradesh.

3. **Raghuvir:** Eminent linguist, historian and lexicographer.
4. **HariBhau Upadhyaya:** Freedom fighter. Afterwards, the Chief Minister of Rajasthan.
5. **Dr. Nagendra:** Advisor in Akashvani. Professor and Head of the Department of Hindi, Delhi University.
6. **Balkrishna:** Lecturer in Political Science in Pilani. Afterwards Member-Secretary, Official Languages (Legislative) Commission.

This committee prepared the Hindi draft of the Constitution which was then sent to the members of the Constituent Assembly. Meanwhile, Sundarlal and Mahapandit Rahul Sankrityayan had got published the translations of the draft Constitution. Rahulji was very critical of the translations of the Gupt Committee. What was sad was that Babu Purushottam Das Tandon, too, over a small flaw, became vocal in his opposition.

The Hindustani Translation

We need to understand that the translators of the translations, done outside the sphere of Gupt Committee, had no knowledge of legal principles and their interpretation. They did not keep in view that the legal principles involve a specific style. The aim of drafting is to ensure the unequivocality of the meaning. Courts decide the meaning of the draft. The draft must be interpreted as per the rules of interpretation. Even the common people in England with English as their mother tongue cannot understand the real meaning of the legal Acts.

Sundarlal and Kaka Kalelkar were of the view that some words and grammatical forms can be taken from other languages to give rise to an altogether different language. The equivalents used by Sunderlal are noteworthy. These words tell their tale (or agony) theirselves. Such language can never be in practice.

International	Antarqaumi
Discipline	Qaydadari
Legislature	Kanoonkari
Chairman	Masnadi
Broadcasting	Dhunpasar
Socialise	Samaajiyana
Controller-General	Sarpartaliya

Reaction	Palatkari
Central	Bichbindi Kholi
Individualise	Ekjaniyana
Citizen	Nagra
Compensation	Yatjana
Residuary powers	Rahi Sahi Shakti

Gandhiji's idea of Hindustani language seems to be active behind this. On 23 May 1917, he had written to the editor of the journal *Saraswati* that Hindi only can be the language of Hindustan. In 1945, Gandhiji changed his view and, instead of Hindi, presented Hindustani that could be written in both Devnagri and Persian scripts, and the words of Arabic, Persian, Sanskrit and other languages were included in it. The Muslim League wanted Urdu to be made the official language. So, Gandhiji tried to create a new language in the form of Hindustani. Ananthashayanam Ayangar (ex-Speaker of Lok Sabha) was Gandhiji's disciple. While delivering the chairman's address in the Meerut session of Hindi Sahitya Sammelan, he said that to forge unity among Hindus and Pakistan-minded Muslims, Gandhiji agreed to sacrifice his own language, but the opposers did not care a fig about it and they chose their own path of separation.

The exercise to replace Hindi with an artificial language failed just like the attempts to grant facilities and special powers to Muslims so that they remain with us. Languages can never be manufactured in laboratories but take shape in everyday usage. A language can never be separated from culture. We cannot accept the usages like '*Badshah* Ram' and '*Begum* Sita'.

Afterwards, Rahulji accepted that his translation was flawed as he had no knowledge of constitutional rules. This speaks for his grace and humility which are so characteristic of a thorough and great scholar like him.

Another Translation Committee

When not only Tandon but Jawaharlal Nehru and Maulana Azad as well expressed dissatisfaction over the quality of the Hindi translation, Dr. Rajendra Prasad constituted another translation committee that was as follows:

1. Ghanshyam Singh Gupt, Chairman.

2. Dr. Suniti Kumar Chatterjee, eminent linguist.
3. Mahapandit Rahul Sankrityayana.
4. Pandit Jayachandra Vidyalankar, eminent historian.
5. Moturi Satyanarayana, member of Constituent Assembly, worked tirelessly to spread Hindi, master of many languages.
6. Yashwant Ramakrishna Date, Marathi lexicographer.
7. Justice W.R. Puranik, High Court of the Central Provinces.
8. Professor Mujeeb, Department of Urdu, Jamia Millia.
9. Balkrishna, Secretary.

The Resolution for the Translation of the Constitution

The framing of the Constitution was getting delayed. It had exceeded much beyond the limit estimated in the beginning. So, it was decided that the Constitution will not be approved in Hindi. On 17 September 1949, the Constituent Assembly passed a resolution authorising the President to get the Constitution translated into Hindi and other Indian languages.

On the same day, Dr. Rajendra Prasad instructed the members to suggest the names of the scholars from their language and province to enable him to decide the glossary for the Constitution. Rajendra Babu was somewhat disconcerted as his dream to see the Constitution being approved in Hindi was shattered. Seth Govind Das and Ramnaryan Singh too, were not in favour.

A Conference of Language Experts

Dr. Rajendra Prasad called a conference of language experts to decide about a glossary to translate the Constitution which could be used in Hindi and other languages whenever possible. He was of the view that this move could ensure administrative, legal and judicial unification of the country. This conference was attended by the representatives of all languages included in the Eighth Schedule of the Constitution. It was presided over by Ghanshyam Singh Gupt. The glossary for the Constitution was decided and used to translate the Constitution into Hindi. Rajendra Babu did this to enable the Constitution to be passed in Hindi also. But all these things took time and, till then, the decision had been taken to complete the process of creation of the Constitution at the earliest. So, no time was left to discuss the Hindi text bit by bit. Had this been done, the delay of a year or two may have occurred.

When the translation was completed, Dr. Rajendra Prasad was in Wardha. Ghanshyam Singh Gupt and Balkrishna were called there. Rajendra Babu went through the whole draft of the translation and suggested amendments.

Signatures on the Hindi Translation

The Constitution had been passed on 26 November 1949. The session of the Constituent Assembly on 24 January 1950 was the concluding session. Till then, the translation was complete and available in printed form. The President told Ghanshyam Singh Gupt to present the Hindi translation. After that, the President invited the members to put their signatures on English and Hindi copies. There are 282 signatures including that of Nehru on the Hindi version. The English version was signed by 278 members. Then the Hindi version was published in the Gazette of India.

The Legal Status of the Hindi Translation

The Official Languages (Legislative) Commission was established in 1961. It was around 1968 that the legal status of the Constitution, written in Hindi and signed by the members of the Constituent Assembly, was questioned. A sub-committee of the commission was of the view that the translation was without any legal status. The question was sent to Attorney-General Niren Dey who opined that the translation was not an authorised text and, as the Constituent Assembly stands dissolved, no Hindi text of the Constitution was possible. The Ministry of Law and Justice constituted a Hindi Advisory Committee with Satish Chandra (ex-Chief Justice, Patna High Court), Ved Vyas, Dr. Laxmimal Singhvi and Gopi Nath Dixit (all senior advocates) as the members. The committee was of the view that the Hindi translation is the authorised text of the Constitution. Separate opinions were sought from M.C. Sitalwad (former Attorney-General) and Pandit Kanhayalal Mishra (former Advocate-General Uttar Pradesh). Their opinion was primarily based on the fact that the Hindi text had not been debated upon Article by Article. So, it has not been passed by the Constituent Assembly.

The members of the Constituent Assembly who were alive had established an organisation with Manulal Dwivedi as its head. He felt pained by the opinions. The matter was raised in the Central Hindi Committee. Prime Minister Indira Gandhi, the Chairman of the Committee, requested the Law Minister to pay attention to the matter. The same subject came for discussion in the Committee of Parliament for Official Languages. On 19 June 1981, a meeting of the committee was held in the Parliament House Annexe. It was chaired by Om Mehta. The Secretary of the Official Languages Department, Jainarayan Tiwari was also present. I, being the In-charge Joint Secretary of the Official Languages section of the Legislation Department, was called as a 'special invitee'. The members of the committee were sad and shocked over the fact that an authorised text of the Constitution was not available in Hindi. Dr. Lokesh Chandra, Jagannath Rao Joshi and Rambhagat Paswan participated actively and offered suggestions. The second meeting of the committee was attended by Legislative Secretary, R.V. Perishastri and me, along with others. Perishastri made it clear to the committee that he cannot assure how an authorised Hindi text of the Constitution could be made available, but he would try his best with genuine sincerity and commitment to ensure it.

The Role of Law Minister, Jagannath Kaushal

Whatever was the opinion of the legal experts about the Hindi text, I personally felt very guilty that the Constitution of our country was not in our own language. As far as I know, no country has ever been in this situation. This is our unique situation and we only have to find the solution to it. We can get no precedents from any other country. Normally, our Law Ministers never felt the need to consider this problem. When Jagannath Kaushal became the Law Minister, I requested him to take up the matter. Manulal Dwivedi and Balkrishen had already talked to him. Sudhakar Pandey (M.P. and secretary of Nagri Pracharini Sabha) and Gangasharan Singh had raised the matter more than once. Fortunately, Perishastri too was an ardent supporter of Indian languages. He forwarded the matter to the then Attorney-General, S.K. Parasharan, to whom he had already conveyed his opinion. Parasharan suggested that the

Constitution should be amended to include proper provisions and when there are provisions, the validity will be assured.

The Constitution was Amended

After this suggestion from the Attorney-General, I had a detailed discussion with the Legislative Secretary. It was decided that a copy of the Constitution duly signed by the members of the Constituent Assembly must be honoured. This is a historical document. Besides, the changes in language, style and diction used in the authorised Hindi texts of the Central Acts in the last 40 years must be taken into consideration and the Hindi text of the Constitution be made according to these texts. The amendments made in the Constitution till date may also be included. Provisions should also be made for the authorised texts of the future amendments. To keep the dignity of everything intact, all this should be done through the authority of the President. The declaration will be there in the Constitution itself that the text published in this way shall be the authorised Hindi text of the Constitution. The Cabinet appointed a Group of Ministers (GoM) to discuss the resolution of inclusion of provisions for the authorised Hindi text of the Constitution. This GoM approved the resolution on 19 March 1986.

After the inclusion of all these points, the then Home Minister Buta Singh introduced the Bill on 27 February 1987. It was passed by Lok Sabha on 24 November 1987 and Rajya Sabha on 26 November 1987. The President gave his assent on 9 December 1987.

Preparing the Authorised Text

After the Constitution amendment was passed, the massive responsibility to prepare the authorised text fell on my shoulders. The whole Constitution was to be studied minutely and linguistic and stylistic changes were to be done along with the changes in diction. The legal parlance had undergone a significant change in the last 40 years and those changes were to be incorporated. The syntactic structure was to be made comprehensible. The Constitution is a document of utmost importance. So, it was just expected that a sizeable number of people will read the text.

The minutes of the resolution to amend the Constitution was sent for publication. For this, a new section was required in the gazette. In the government press, publication of books takes a lot of time. After taking due permission to get the document printed in a private press, tenders were solicited and a press chosen. The Hindi translation of the Constitution was examined minutely. The glossary was assorted and compared with the words used in the legal Acts. The terms, sentences, expressions and provisions used more than once were marked to ensure uniformity. Everything was looked at from the point of view of usage as well. Then the changes were made with utmost care. All amendments till 58th one were incorporated.

It will be apt to give some examples here. In the Hindi translation made available by the Constituent Assembly, the 'Council of States' was translated as '*Rajya Parishad*'. It was quite appropriate as the synonym for 'council' is nothing but '*parishad*'. But at the insistence of the first Lok Sabha Speaker Mavalankar, 'Rajya Sabha' was used in all proceedings of Parliament. This was being used in English as well. So, in Article 80 and everywhere, the phrase 'Rajya Sabha' was incorporated.

For 'Reserve Bank of India', they had written '*Bharat Ka Aarakshit Bank*'. But "*Bharatiya Reserve Bank*" was printed on every currency note. So, in the associated Act also, the name was changed to 'Bharatiya Reserve Bank'.

Some More Examples

Word	Translation by the Constituent Assembly	The New Text
Bail	Zamin	Zamanat
Banking	Mahajani	Banking
Civil	Vyavhar	Civil
Decree	Agyapti	Decree
Jurisdiction	Kshetradhikar	Adhikarita
Justice	Nyayadhipati	Nyayamurti
Police	Aarakshi	Police
Scheduled Tribe	Janjati	Aadim Jati
Survey	Bhooparimap	Sarvekshan

Panthanirpeksha for 'Secular'

With the Constitution Act 1976, 42nd amendment to the Constitution of India was enacted, in which two words, 'secular' and 'socialist' were added to the Preamble. For the word 'socialist', the Hindi equivalent '*samajwadi*' was acceptable to all, but the equivalent for the word 'secular' needed contemplation. '*Dharmanirpeksha*' is the common Hindi usage for 'secular' which is used in newspapers also. But, this usage has its flaws. The sphere of meaning of Dharma is really vast. Eminent poetess Mahadevi Verma had said that Dharma is the duty that remains obligatory from birth till death. How can we be '*nirapeksha*', i.e., live a life independent or irrespective of it. Reverend Madhav Sadashiv Golwalkar 'Guruji' always used the word '*panthnirapeksha*' for being 'secular'. I was well aware of his diction and the background in which the use of such words had evolved. Perhaps, since 1953, he had been using the word '*panthnirapeksha*' (See the collection of Guruji's writings on his philosophy, Shri Guruji Samagra Darshan, Vol. 3, pp. 119, 126, 127). He has explained Dharma as the eternal law of life. I chose three words as Hindi synonyms for 'secular' — '*panthnirapeksha*', '*sampradayanirapeksha*' and '*matanirapeksha*'.

I discussed these synonyms with Kanshiram Sharma who had translated the Constitution in Sanskrit. He had been the Director in Central Translation Bureau. I took the opinion of Balkrishna, who had shouldered the responsibility of creating the Hindi version of the Constitution as well. At last, '*panthnirapeksha*' was chosen and put to use as I was in charge of the final decision and the responsibility was mine. No other opinion but of these two gentlemen was taken and no suggestion came from any other quarters.

The word 'secular' is also used in Article 25(2) of the Constitution. There they have put the word '*laukik*' as its equivalent. 'Secular' has a third meaning, in the banking sector. In my Banking glossary, I have used '*dirghakaleen*' as the equivalent.

The Acceptability of the Authorised Hindi Text

In this way, every word, phrase and sentence was translated carefully. On 9 December 1987, the Amendment Act was passed and the Hindi translation was published in the Gazette of India under the authority of the President on 23 August 1988. It was published in book form on 25 August 1988 and after that, the bilingual edition (Hindi and English side by side) was published on 1 November 1988.

The result of our commitment and hard work was that this authorised text was well appreciated and put to use. Some gentlemen claimed that '*panthnirapekshata*' was accepted on their suggestion. There was not even an iota of truth in this, but this really filled me with a sense of pride that people were trying to own a minute part of my work. This also is a kind of appreciation. In fact, whatever are the virtues and vices in the text, all is my responsibility. Long experience, genuine hard work and scientific method lessens the possibility of any error, but only God can make things perfect, not a human being. Despite that, thousands of copies of the translated Constitution are in use and there has been no criticism from any quarter so far.

During my tenure in the ministry, the Constitution was published in more than 14 Indian languages other than this authorised text. Multilingual glossary of the Constitution was also published in which technical words used in the Constitution have been given in 13 Indian languages. Five editions of the Legal Dictionary have already been published. Since 1 October 1976, Rajasthan and Madhya Pradesh made use of Hindi essential in legal services up to the district court.

But, Indian languages are yet to get their due place in the field of law and justice.

□

Colonial Background of Indian Constitution and Some Immediate Correctives[1]

—J.K. Bajaj

The Colonial Hangover

The Indian Constitution was created under extremely difficult circumstances. In the initial phases of the work of the Constituent Assembly, it was not clear whether the Muslim-majority areas of the country would remain within the Indian Union or not. After formalisation of partition of the country, the Assembly worked under the shadow of chaos and violence associated with this climactic event in the history of India. This, along with the prevailing uncertainty about the position of the princely states, created fears about the unity and stability of the country.

Under the circumstances, keeping the administrative machinery intact became the main concern of the makers of the Constitution. This perhaps was the major reason why the Government of India Act of 1935, under which the colonial administration was functioning, became the basis of the Constitution of free India.[2] The concern with keeping the machinery of colonial administration intact is strongly reflected in the debates that took place on those parts of the Constitution which went beyond the 1935 Act, especially the parts relating to Fundamental Rights and federal structures. In these debates, the members seem to be constantly worried that granting various freedoms and rights to citizens and the states of the Union may weaken the administrative apparatus inherited from the colonial administration. They seem to be constantly hedging the rights of the individuals and the states with a variety of provisos and limitations.

Besides the fear of loss of administrative control, the other major concern that informed the makers of the Constitution was their firm belief that the Indian people needed to be guided towards economic and political maturity through the intervention of the state. This belief was partly a hangover of the arguments advanced by the British, who had always pretended that they were in India to provide a paternalistic administration since the people of India themselves were incapable of governing and improving themselves. The belief was reinforced by the socialist milieu of the times. Those were the times when almost everyone in the world believed that the economic and political development of nations was the responsibility of the national bureaucracies.

This fear of the 'political and economic immaturity' of the Indians led the makers of the Constitution to not only provide constitutional protection to the colonial administrative machinery, but also to give extraordinary powers to the judiciary to oversee the functioning of the legislatures. The founding fathers, it seems, were not sure that the legislatures chosen by the people of India, who they believed were largely illiterate and politically immature, would always act wisely. So they created a judiciary that is known to be more powerful than any other judiciary in the world.

The concern with keeping the colonial administrative machinery intact combined with the fear of the immaturity of the Indian people led to emasculation of the political executive. The Constitution first placed all the initiatives in the hands of the Central government. And then the initiatives of the Centre were so hedged in by the sanctity accorded to the bureaucratic structures and the all-pervasive judicial overseeing that the political executive at the Centre itself became powerless to initiate anything substantive. The government that came into being under the Constitution was, thus, a caricature of the colonial government; the colonial administrative machinery remained intact, but the power and initiative that vested in the Viceroy and even the provincial Governors to direct and purposely utilise this machinery, the so-called steel-frame, evaporated.

The emasculation of the central political executive did not become too tangible till men like Patel and Nehru, who were looked upon as respected peers by the bureaucracy and judiciary, led the government. Though even for Nehru and Patel, the struggle to defend political legislature and executive from judicial intervention began from almost the beginning. Later, Prime Ministers and their governments felt the lack of constitutional space for any political initiative at every step. The situation has deteriorated further and, further, and today the political executive seems to have ceded much of its authority to the various bureaucratic and judicial structures created by the Constitution. This is how India has come to be the proverbially 'soft state' of the world.

The makers of the Constitution also seem to have believed, along with the colonial British administrators, that India is not one nation: it is a conglomerate of numerous minorities placed alongside an uncaring and orthodoxy-ridden caste-Hindu majority. Therefore, there was a deep concern to provide extraordinary constitutional protections for the minorities on the one hand, and on the other hand, to give powers to the state to act in order to 'reform' the Hindu majority. The provisions regarding the minorities were fortuitously kept under some control because the Partition had made it imperative for the leaders of diverse minorities to be somewhat accommodative. But, the enthusiasm to reform Hindu society through the instrumentalities of the state remained unbounded.

Many of the concerns and beliefs that we have outlined above perhaps were inherent to the process that was adopted for making the Constitution. The Constituent Assembly was chosen by an electorate that constituted less than one-third of the adult population of India. The members of the Assembly largely came from the section that was familiar and conversant with the functioning of the colonial administrative and legal machinery. At that time, there were probably a few thousand Indians who had acquired such familiarity with the colonial apparatus, and the Constituent Assembly was drawn mainly from these. The Constituent Assembly further left the detailed work-out and drafting of the constitutional provisions to a select group of legal and administrative luminaries of the time. There were perhaps about 21 experts who directed all facets of the making of the Constitution; ranking members of all significant committees of the Constituent Assembly were drawn from these. Of these 21 experts,

12 were lawyers, another four were career administrators, and one had been a medical doctor. At least six of this select group had never had any relation with the Congress, and several of them were known to be opposed to the spirit of the freedom movement. It seems that from the beginning the making of the Constitution was taken not as a political task, but as an exercise in legal and administrative expertise.[3]

Possibility of Correction

The concerns that informed the making of the Indian Constitution have become irrelevant today. Though there continue to be some fissiparous tendencies on the borders of India, the unity and integrity of India is hardly in doubt. The people of India have shown extraordinary political maturity and sagacity in most circumstances. And, the belief that national bureaucracies would guide the nations to economic and political strength has become outdated all over the world.

India today is strong enough to let the different constituents take the initiative in matters of political, social and economic development. The times, in fact, demand that such initiative is encouraged at all levels. Through the process of economic liberalisation, we are trying to squeeze some economic initiative out of the clutches of the bureaucratic machinery. But, in the absence of thorough-going changes in the colonial administrative and judicial arrangements enshrined in the Indian Constitution, the political executive at the national and lower levels is likely to remain emasculated. And the initiative of the Indian people at all levels is likely to remain tied down in the maze of bureaucratic and legalistic rules and regulations. There is, therefore, an urgent need to review the Constitution from this perspective.

In the following, we outline some of the fundamental changes that, we believe, are minimally required to restore some dynamism in the constitutional arrangements and at least begin chiselling away at the colonial legacy that our Constitution carries not only on its core but also in its entirety.

Preamble of the Constitution

A Constitution is not meant to merely create the legislative, administrative and judicial structures and establish the necessary balance between these institutions. The larger objective of a Constitution is to remind the nation of its civilisational genius, urges and seekings. By thus reminding the nation, a Constitution motivates the people to make the necessary effort so that the genius of the nation may find a forceful expression and the urges and seekings may be abundantly fulfilled in the present-day world. The legislative, administrative and judicial structures that a Constitution creates are mere mechanisms to facilitate such expression and fulfillment of the national genius and urges. This mechanism, of course, has to be made powerful and appropriate to the seekings of the nation. But the main objective of the Constitution is to define the seekings and give expression to the national resolve to fulfill these.

The Preamble to a Constitution is the appropriate place for defining the civilisational genius, urges and seekings of a nation. Thus, the Preamble of the modern Chinese Constitution makes lofty references to the history, culture and geography of China. 'China', the Preamble begins, "is one of the countries with the longest histories in the world. The people of all nationalities in China have jointly created a splendid culture and have a glorious revolutionary tradition." And it states that, "Taiwan is part of the sacred territory of the People's Republic of China. It is the lofty duty of the entire Chinese people, including our compatriots in Taiwan, to accomplish the great task of reunifying the motherland."[4]

The Japanese, while promulgating a modern Constitution for themselves in 1898, went to great lengths to relate their new Constitution with the deepest past of Japan. The promulgation of the new Constitution was made to coincide with the 2549th anniversary of the supposedly mythical founding of Japan. On the morning of that day, the Emperor presented himself in front of his imperial ancestors to assure them on oath that the new Constitution was being promulgated to "the end of preserving the ancient form of government bequeathed by them to the country." Later, a Shinto priest delivered this message to the 'myriad gods' at the palace shrine. And, special imperial messenger, who had been previously dispatched, reported the message to the Ise shrine and to the spirits of Emperor Jimmu, the founder of Japan, and Emperor Komei, father of the then Emperor Meiji. Only after thus informing the gods and the ancestors was the Constitution of Japan published for the world in a glittering secular ceremony held in the afternoon. And, even this secular ceremony was designed to convey and preserve the mythical significance of the promulgation of the Constitution.[5]

The Preamble of the Indian Constitution, unfortunately, makes no such effort to relate itself to the civilisational history or the sacred geography of India. It makes no reference to the genius, urges or seekings of the Indian people. On the contrary, it refers loftily to the concepts of Justice, Liberty, Equality and Fraternity derived from the French revolution. These sentiments can raise no resonance in the hearts of the people of India, who are hardly expected to be acquainted with the history of Europe or to be moved by the European ideals.

If the Constitution of India is to strike a chord in the hearts of the people of India, the Preamble must be amended to include appropriate references to the deepest urges of our civilisation. Much thought shall have to be given to the appropriate phrasing of this part of the Constitution. But it shall have to include words to the effect that: "The Republic of India is dedicated to the service of the sanatana civilisation of India. The Republic is founded to preserve and project the great glory of the sanatana Indian civilisation in the modern times. Keeping this objective in view, the Republic shall persistently endeavour to further develop the unmatched spiritual and material capabilities of the Indian people. The Republic shall endeavour to ensure that all people of India get the opportunity to exercise these capabilities of theirs and, thus, to powerfully manifest their civilisational genius, urges and seekings."

Citizenship

Citizens constitute the basic units of a nation. Constitutions of different nations expect those who would be citizens to have a certain commitment to and faith in the civilisational genius, urges and seekings of the nation, and to acquire virtues appropriate to the spirit of the nation. Most nations impart training in citizenship and patriotism to their young in diverse ways.

Soon after the promulgation of its Constitution in 1889, the Emperor of Japan issued a Rescript on Education, which sought to lay down the personal and moral virtues expected of a citizen of Japan. Issued in 1890 after much deliberation and extremely careful drafting, the Imperial Rescript was soon enshrined as the core of moral education. Bowing before the Rescript and ceremonially reading it out became part of the morning ritual in the schools. The Rescript aroused such interest and devotion amongst the people of Japan that by 1940, there were as many as 595 book-length commentaries interpreting and explaining its intentionally terse and heavily meaning-laden phrases.[6]

Meiji Japan, of course, pursued the task of patriotism training, nation building and inculcation of virtue extremely vigorously. Other nations, however, do not neglect the task. The Constitution of India is probably unique in not expecting any particularly Indian commitment or virtue from its citizens. The main clause regarding citizenship in the Constitution – Article 5(c) – laid down that every person who had been ordinarily resident in India for not less than five years immediately preceding the commencement of the Constitution was entitled to be a citizen of India. According to this clause, almost all the Britishers staying in India at the time of Independence could have chosen—if they so wished—to stay on as citizens of Independent India and continue to occupy the administrative and other positions they were holding.

Excepting for providing such guarantees of citizenship to various classes of persons, the Constitution makes little provision regarding citizenship. Most of the matters concerning citizenship are left to the discretion of the Parliament and future judicial interpretations. The chapter on Fundamental Duties (Article 51A) introduced through the much maligned 42nd amendment of 1976 does lay down some expectations from the citizens, but these are in the nature of common platitudes and hardly anyone seems to pay any attention to these duties.

The citizenship provisions of the Constitution need to be tightened up so that being a citizen of India becomes both a high honour and a sacred responsibility. We can probably add words to the effect that "It is expected of the citizens of India that they shall have faith and loyalty towards the sanatana civilisation of

India and shall be ever ready to sacrifice their all for defending the glory and greatness of India and the Indian civilisation." The exact virtues to be defined and the words to be used shall, of course, have to be selected after much thought and discussion.

But, it is not merely a matter of adding a few high-sounding words to the Constitution. Having made the enabling provisions in the Constitution, we must introduce proper citizenship and patriotism training in our schools, so that the future citizens begin to realise the glory and the responsibility of being an Indian.

States of the Union

Just as the Constitution makes little attempt to define the specific virtue of being an Indian citizen, similarly it gives little recognition to the specific identity of the Indian states that together constitute the Union. As far as the Constitution is concerned, the states of India are such amorphous entities that the Parliament has been given the right to increase or diminish the area of a state, alter its boundaries or change its name. And for doing all this, the Parliament needs to only ascertain the views of the legislatures of the concerned state(s); their consent to the changes is not necessary. The Parliament can effect such far-reaching changes in the boundaries and names of the states under its normal legislative powers; such changes do not even have the sanctity of a constitutional amendment. (Articles 3 and 4)

At the time the Constitution was promulgated, it was perhaps necessary for the Parliament to be given such overriding powers concerning the states. After the princely states were merged into the Union, reorganisation of state boundaries drawn by the colonial administration and renaming of many states had become essential to accommodate the legitimate regional and linguistic identities and aspirations. But, there is no justification for the Parliament to retain this untrammelled right to reorganise and rename states after 70 years of Independence. There is a need to seriously review these provisions.

The states of India are not mere administrative units. Indian civilisation has manifested in diverse linguistic, historic, literary and cultural forms in the diverse regions of India. One of the greatest achievements of the Indian civilisation is in having kept these diverse forms together within the umbrella of an overarching and essentially unified Indianness. Therefore, the greater glory of Indian civilisation is best sought in the further development and blossoming of the diverse forms in which it manifests in different regions of India.

We should, therefore, now endeavour to provide constitutional stability to the boundaries of the states of India so that their specific identity receives formal recognition. The responsibility of accommodating sub-regional cultural or linguistic aspirations of groups within the states can then be legitimately left to the states themselves. In this context, it should be recalled that Mahatma Gandhi had always insisted that the boundaries of the Indian states are not a matter of mere administrative convenience; there existed natural cultural boundaries, which he felt were best determined on a linguistic basis. And, in the first Constitution of Indian National Congress that he drafted in 1920, he provided a list of provinces on the basis of language.[7] How can we keep such natural boundaries administratively fluid after so many years of independent functioning?[8]

There are several provisions in the Indian Constitution that regulate the relations between the Union and the states, and most of these tend to vest the Union with overriding powers. Articles 249 to 254 vest the Union with the power to legislate on subjects in the State List under various circumstances. Articles 256 and 257 give the Union executive the power to issue directions to the states on various subjects. Articles 268 to 280 make provisions for the distribution of resources between the Union and the states, and these provisions establish an explicit ascendancy of the Union over the major sources of revenue. All these and related provisions need to be reviewed, so that the states may acquire the greatest possible responsibility in legislative, judicial, administrative and fiscal matters.

The list of subjects in the Union List, State List and Concurrent List also need to be reviewed. These lists originated in the 1935 Act. The British delegated certain subjects to the states, and then circumscribed the responsibility of the states by creating several provisions that vested in the Union the authority to intervene in these matters. In addition, they created a Concurrent List of subjects in which the responsibility of the states was made explicitly subject to the higher control and supervision of the Union.

We should arrive at a clear assessment of what issues and subjects may be handled by the states, and the entire responsibility for these should be placed on them. Central intervention in such matters should then be restricted only in case of clear and imminent emergency. Duality of responsibility in most matters, as is the case today, seems only to breed irresponsibility all around, with the states blaming the Union for their failures and the Union doing likewise.

Making the states thus clearly and solely responsible for matters that fall within their domain shall help the states contribute effectively to the development of the Indian civilisation in its diverse forms. This shall also greatly reduce the burden on the Union executive, and, thus, give it the freedom to energetically pursue the larger national and international objectives that necessarily fall within the domain of the Union. Vesting the states with such clear and well-defined responsibility is particularly apt in the current international situation, when there is intense pressure on the Union to cede larger and larger areas of national sovereignty to multilateral control, supervision and direction. With the states becoming solely responsible for matters falling within their domain, the Union shall be forced to effectively consult the states before opening any new area of national economy and polity to global access. This shall help the Union withstand pressure in multilateral negotiations. For this strategy to succeed, it is important that the states should have no power to deal directly with foreign or international agencies. The states ought to be autonomous within India, but their economic or other dealings with the rest of the world must take place only through the Union. The current tendency of allowing the states to seek and negotiate foreign collaborations directly needs to be curbed.

Provisions Concerning the Minorities

Every self-confident nation makes provisions for the protection of minority groups. Such protection is accorded so that the diverse cultural, linguistic and other capabilities of minority groups may contribute to and, thus, enrich the national mainstream, which naturally is constituted of the majority. Section 29 of the Constitution that guarantees protection of the minorities, however, almost invites diverse groups to claim special rights in the name of their distinct language, script or culture. The other provision regarding minorities – Article 30 – gives the minorities the right to establish and administer educational institutions of their choice and, thus, creates an invidious distinction against the majority. The right to establish and administer educational institutions of their choice is a natural right of all communities, whether constituting a minority or a majority. The Article does not, in fact, give any special right to the minorities, but takes away a valuable natural right from the majority.

These two Articles together have created a premium upon various groups to break away from the national mainstream. Groups that would have been happy and proud of being distinct yet inseparable, parts of the mainstream have, therefore, begun to discover and claim separate identities. These constitutional provisions, instead of providing protection to the minorities, have had the effect of creating new minorities and vitiating the integrity and depth of the national mainstream.

There is an urgent need to seriously review both these provisions. The minorities, of course, must be provided guarantees of protection. But such guarantees must be such as not to create pressures on diverse groups to separate from the mainstream. Article 29 certainly needs redrafting. And, the protection of Article 30 needs to be equitably extended to all people of India.

Provisions Concerning Freedom of Religion

Article 25 grants "freedom of conscience and the right freely to profess, practise and propagate religion." Freedom to profess and practise the religion of their choice is, of course, a natural right of all citizens in a secular state. But the freedom to 'propagate' that has been included in this clause is highly unusual. No secular state guarantees the freedom to propagate and convert people from other faiths. This freedom has been fortuitously circumscribed by the judicial interpretations of the term 'propagate', which have held that 'propagation' does not mean 'conversion'. But the phrasing of the original clause leaves much scope for intense proselytising activity on behalf of various religions and sects.

The second clause of the Article makes two provisos to the freedom of religion. The first proviso gives the state the authority to regulate or restrict 'secular activities' associated with religious practice, and the second proviso vests in the state the power to make laws for 'social welfare and reform' of Hindu religious institutions.

The first of these provisos is applicable to all religions, but in practice, it has been used to control and regulate the functioning of only the Hindu institutions. The second proviso is specifically aimed at Hindus and their institutions alone. Judicial interpretations of these provisos have so extended the definition of "secular activities associated with religious practice" as to allow the state to take over control of all aspects of the Hindu religious institutions, and directly interfere with the established rituals and customs. In several states, especially in the South, under the protection of these provisos, temple properties have been frittered away, temple incomes are being applied towards the salaries of highly paid government officers, and temples are being run more or less as departments of the state government. The states do even claim and exercise the right of not only prescribing the qualifications and conditions of service of the priests, but also the language and form of the ritual.

This certainly amounts to invidious interference in the religious affairs of the majority of the Indian people. Religion is at the core of Indian civilisation. Provisions concerning religious freedom in the Indian Constitution should, therefore, be the ideal for the world. India ought not to restrict or control the religious practice of any group, whether that of the majority or minority. The first clause of Article 25 already makes the freedom of religious practice subject to public order, morality and health. The only other proviso we need to add is that such practice may not interfere with the security and integrity of the nation; and that the religious affairs and religious institutions of no religion in India may be subject to foreign control or domination.[9] The right to freedom of religious practice ought not to be circumscribed by any other provisos. People of India ought to be left free to organise, institutionalise and practise their religious affairs themselves, neither the state in India nor any foreign agencies or bodies need have any say in it.

The current provisions of Article 25 instead of granting religious freedom have the effect of taking away the right of the Hindus to run their own religious institutions and affairs. These also give the state the right to aggressively interfere with the custom, rituals and beliefs of the Hindus in the name of social reform. This Article, therefore, needs to be reviewed seriously.

Judiciary and Administration

The Constitution of India is perhaps the longest Constitution in the world. This extraordinary length of the Indian Constitution arises in large part from the detailed provisions it makes regarding the public services and the judiciary. The Constitution records in great detail the structure of administrative and judicial institutions, and the rights, privileges and also the salaries and allowances of public and judicial officers at various levels. Most democratic Constitutions of the world record only the fundamental principles of governance, and leave such detailed working out of the administrative and judicial arrangements to the wisdom of the parliaments. Such institutions are almost always created by legislative Acts of parliaments, not by constitutional fiats.

The leaders of the Constituent Assembly deliberately chose to include detailed administrative and judicial arrangements in the Constitution. One reason for this decision was that in the prevailing circumstances, the leading founding fathers were keen to retain intact the administrative and judicial arrangements of the colonial administration. And, therefore, they found it necessary and expedient to provide constitutional guarantees to the high administrative and judicial officers that their domain of authority as well as their salaries, perquisites and privileges would remain unaltered in independent India. But perhaps even a more pressing reason was that many of the leading founding fathers had little faith in the wisdom and maturity of the people of India and the Parliament chosen by them. They were afraid that the Parliament and the state legislatures might choose to make drastic alterations in the administrative and judicial structures of the colonial administration, which many of them believed were ideal for the governance of India.

Dr. Bhimrao Ram Ambedkar, known as the father of the Indian Constitution, expressed his fears openly, declaring that the details of administrative and judicial arrangements must be enshrined in the Constitution because "it is perfectly possible to pervert the Constitution without changing its form by merely changing the form of administration."[10] Dr. Ambedkar, in fact, was of the view that independent India does not need a new constitution; the Government of India Act of 1935 could itself form the Constitution of India.[11] Eventually, as we have mentioned earlier, the 1935 Act did become the basis of our Constitution.

The extraordinary sanctity provided to the administrative and judicial structures in the constitutional arrangement has served to severely restrict the initiative and authority of the Indian people and their elected representatives. That these arrangements were going to so restrict the initiative of the political authorities in carrying out any fundamental changes in the social milieu left behind by the British became clear at the very beginning. Several judgements of various High Courts and the Supreme Court in the very first year of the coming into force of the Constitution challenged the authority of the Parliament and state legislatures at a level that leaders of the stature of Patel and Nehru began to feel frustrated. And they felt the need to effect the first amendment of the Constitution to get around judicial pronouncements rather soon. The process to carry out the amendment was initiated in October 1950 and the amendment was passed by the provisional Parliament in May 1951, even before the first election under the new Constitution was held.[12]

It is possible to read the constitutional history of India as a tug of war for supremacy between the judiciary and the political authority, as a meticulous scholar of Indian Constitution seems to do in a recent study of the working of the Constitution during the first four decades.[13] This tug of war has given rise to traumatic events in the recent history of the nation. But more than anything else, it has diverted the attention and energies of the nation from the primary task of nation building to legalistic debates that have occupied the centrestage in the life of the nation.

The same level of controversy has not arisen about the constitutionally sanctified public services. But, clothed with constitutional protection, the administrative services have continuously expanded their areas of influence and curbed the initiative of the people at all levels. Only in the recent decades, under the influence of the global tilt towards free-market principles, has some effort been begun to lessen the rigours of the all-encompassing bureaucratic apparatus.

Whatever the reasons of the Constituent Assembly for enshrining the colonial administration and judiciary in the Constitution of free India may be, these arrangements cannot be allowed to be permanent. It is now high time to begin altering these arrangements and making them appropriate to the genius and seekings of the Indian people. As a first step towards this restructuring of the administrative and judicial apparatus of India, we need to bring these arrangements out of the Constitution and recreate these through legislative Acts of the Parliament and the state legislatures, as is done everywhere in the world.

We need to remove the constitutional protection provided to the administrative and judicial arrangements, even if we chose to keep the arrangements entirely intact and unaltered at this stage. Such changes in the Constitution shall probably change nothing immediately, but shall restore dynamism in the development of administrative and judicial structures, and open the way for far-reaching changes in the future.

Sources for Rethinking the Constitution

The constitutional changes that we have suggested above are the minimal changes that we need to undertake to alter the colonial ways and structures that we inherited. Even after all these and similar other changes, the resulting Constitution shall remain European in content and spirit; its basic structures shall remain unaltered. But it shall at least be an indigenously adapted European arrangement, which shall give due respect to the identity, dignity and initiative of the Indian people and their civilisation.

In order to bring the Constitution in consonance with the Indian sensibilities and the classical Indian ways of governance, we shall have to draft a new Constitution. That exercise probably lies far in the future. Meanwhile, we can certainly carry out an intensive study of various sources that may be of help in moving in that direction.

One of the major sources of such rethinking about the Indian Constitution is the life and works of Mahatma Gandhi. Indian freedom movement under the leadership of Gandhiji was aimed at restoring initiative in all matters to the people of India and to the basic political and economic unit of *grama* (village) around which they were organised. Gandhiji was not much enamoured of the European and socialist ideal of the state taking responsibility for social and economic revolution. He preferred to leave the initiative in such matters with the people and their *gramas*. Mahatma Gandhi gave much consideration to how the *grama* was to be revived and restored to its central position in the Indian polity. It is indeed tragic that the leading founding fathers, entrusted with the task of drafting a Constitution that was to formalise the freedom won under the leadership of the Mahatma, gave so little importance to *gramas* and their *panchayats* (local self-government). The first draft of the Constitution did not even include the terms '*grama*' or '*panchayat*'. When several members vociferously objected to the omission, a single clause expressing the wish that the states would "take steps to organise *grama panchayats* and endow them with such authority as may be necessary to enable them to function as units of self-government" (Article 40) was included amongst the Directive Principles of State Policy.[14]

The Gandhian thought on polity was to a large extent derived from the basic principles of Indian civilisation concerning polity and governance. There is a vast corpus of classical Indian literature on these issues. And this literature is unanimous on the basic principles of political and social organisation.

In addition to the Gandhian and classical Indian thought, the experience of other nations of the world can also be of help in rethinking about the Indian Constitution. Many other countries of the world, during the last couple of centuries, have tried to build modern nations through the constitutional process. Some of these, like Japan in 1890, created a modern Constitution with the deliberate intention of protecting themselves from the colonial influences that had subdued most nations around them. Other countries, like China in the 1980's, have created Constitutions to celebrate the revival of their civilisational greatness at the end of a couple of centuries of submission to alien civilisations. It shall be of help to look into these various Constitutions. Within Europe, countries like Germany have created modern constitutional arrangements that continue to protect the traditionally high status and crucial role of the local communities in the functioning of the polity. Scholars like Solzhenitsyn have also meditated on the constitutional arrangements that are likely to suit the traditional community-based organisation of Russia.

We need to study and comprehensively examine these sources to begin moving towards the creation of a Constitution that shall be Indian in content and spirit and express the national resolve to restore the civilisational glory of India in the modern times. But the minimal changes suggested earlier in this paper and many other similar changes shall have to be undertaken immediately to open the path for the larger restructuring.

References

1. *This paper is a slightly updated version of an earlier note submitted for the consideration of the Justice Venkatachalaiah Commission set up by the NDA government led by Atal Behari Vajpayee in February 2000 to review the Constitution.*
2. *Indian Constitution is essentially colonial because it retains the colonial administrative and bureaucratic structures entirely intact. But there is also another sense in which the Indian Constitution is colonial. This Constitution has evolved out of the historical unfolding of the colonial design for India. The history of this unfolding is described in scholarly detail in Bharatiya Samvidhan ki Aupaniveshik Prishthabhumi by Devendra Swarup (Centre for Policy Studies, Chennai, 2014).*
3. *For details of the membership of the Constituent Assembly, see, Granville Austin, The Indian Constitution: The Cornerstone of a Nation, OUP, New Delhi, 1966, paperback reprint, 1999, particularly p.10 and p.19-21. The primacy of professional expertise was emphasised in an unusually candid note sent by N.G. Ayyangar, one of the 21 key people involved in the making of the Constitution, to B.N. Rau, who as the constitutional advisor at the centre of the exercise. As early as March 1947, before the Constituent Assembly began any serious work, Ayyangar wrote to Rau, "I believe... in preliminary decisions on these issues (concerning the basic principles of the Constitution) being taken*

by small numbers of selected people including party chiefs after those issues have been investigated from all points of view with the help of informed people like you... Public opinion in such matters requires both a firm lead and skilled guidance." (Granville Austin, above, p.314) Incidentally, both Ayyangar and Rau were career administrators and their concern for keeping 'public opinion' out of the expert task of making the Constitution is indeed understandable.

4. *The Constitution of the People's Republic of China, adopted on December 4, 1982, Foreign Language Press, Beijing, 1983, p.1 and p.6.*
5. *See, Carol Gluck, Japan's Modern Myths: Ideology in the Late Meiji Period, Princeton University Press, Princeton, 1985, p.42-45.*
6. *See, Carol Gluck, 1985, cited earlier, p.120-127 and p.146-148. The official translation of the Imperial Rescript reproduced by Gluck (p.121) reads: Know ye, Our Subjects: Our imperial Ancestors have founded Our Empire on a basis broad and everlasting and have deeply and firmly planted virtue; Our subjects ever united in loyalty and filial piety have from generation to generation illustrated the beauty thereof. This is the glory of the fundamental character of Our Empire, and herein also lies the source of Our education. Ye, Our subjects, be filial to your parents, affectionate to your brothers and sisters; as husbands and wives be harmonious, as friends true; bear yourself in modesty and moderation; extend your benevolence to all; pursue learning and cultivate arts, and thereby develop intellectual faculties and perfect moral powers; furthermore advance public good and promote common interests; always respect the Constitution and observe the laws; should emergency arise, offer yourselves courageously to the State; and thus guard and maintain the prosperity of Our Imperial Throne coeval with heaven and earth. So shall ye not only be Our good and faithful subjects, but render illustrious the best traditions of your forefathers.The Way here set forth is indeed the teaching bequeathed by Our Imperial Ancestors, to be observed alike by Their Descendants and the subjects, infallible for all ages and true in all places. It is our wish to lay it to heart in all reverence, in common with you, Our subjects, that we may all thus attain to the same virtue. The 30th day of the 10th month of the 23rd year of Meiji (1890).*
7. *The Collected Works of Mahatma Gandhi, The Publication Division, Government of India, Vol.19, Delhi, 1966, p.191.*
8. *A particularly drastic application of the Parliament's authority to alter the boundaries of the states was seen in the bifurcation of the Telugu-speaking state of Andhra Pradesh. Telugu people had undergone great sacrifices to achieve a unified Andhra Pradesh in 1956, which was undone by the Parliament in February 2014.*

That bifurcation also finally lay to rest the cherished principle of linguistic unity and integrity enunciated by Mahatma Gandhi. For an analysis of this event, see: http://cpsindia.org/index.php/current-articles/703-telangana-federalism-violated, http://cpsindia.org/index.php/current-articles/709-telangana-deed-is-done, and http://cpsindia.org/index.php/current-articles/710-telangana-linguistic-provinces.

9. *Incidentally, the 1982 Constitution of the People's Republic of China, cited earlier, makes just such provisions regarding religious freedom. See Article 36, p.32.*
10. *Constituent Assembly Debates, VII, i.38.*
11. *Speech to the Scheduled Caste Federation, May 6, 1945. Quoted from Austin, cited earlier, p.3.*
12. *See, Granville Austin, Working a Democratic Constitution: The Indian Experience, OUP, Delhi, 1999, p.40-50.*
13. *Granville Austin, above.*
14. *For the history of this Article in the Constituent Assembly, see Dharampal, Panchayat Raj as the Basis of Indian Polity: An Exploration into the Proceedings of the Constituent Assembly, AVARD, New Delhi, 1962.*

□

Political Parties, the Constitution and the Election Commission

—S.Y. Quraishi

Political parties in our parliamentary system of government form the link between the mighty state machinery and the common citizens. They are central to mobilising public opinion, act as potent pressure groups and take legislative action when in power. Hence, despite all their flaws, we need political parties in a democracy.

Despite having one of the most detailed and lengthy Constitutions in the history of the world, the Constitution of India, which came into force on 26 January 1950, did not contain a word about the formation, organisation or functioning of political parties in our Westminster-style parliamentary system. This is far from unprecedented as many Constitutions in history, including that of the United States of America do not mention political parties. George Washington warned against their 'insinuation' into the democratic system, and James Madison called them 'factions', a term with a negative connotation. On the other hand, Constitutions such as that of post-war Germany do mention political parties, and also have laws in place to regulate them. In the German model of party regulation, for example, a specific law exists to make sure the ideals enlisted in Article 21 of their Constitution regarding the political parties are realised.

One possible reason for this general constitutional neglect of political parties in India can be found in the way the political situation was when we gained independence. The Indian National Congress was an umbrella organisation which accommodated a plethora of cultural, social, ethnic, linguistic and religious sections differing in their ideology and vision of the future. With the situation changing rapidly from a single-dominant party system to a multi-party one in the years following 1947, political parties grew to be individual entities, something the Constituent Assembly may or may not have predicted.

Another reason could simply be the preference for ordinary legislation. As political parties are dynamic entities, and the Constitution is a broadly fixed document, the job was best left to the Parliament to make a law on the subject. Regulation requires specifics and the Constitution can only guide in this direction rather than making relatively inflexible laws that will require repeated amendments.

Party Systems in Other Countries

As mentioned earlier, there is no specific constitutional provision in most democracies. Even if there is a mention, it is to protect their freedom of organisation and functioning. For example, in the Constitution of the Fifth Republic of France, the Constitution states that the National Assembly cannot legislate to limit the free functioning of political parties. But, in other cases, such as the German Constitution, the political parties have been institutionalised by including provisions such as the 5% clause which impede the formation of fringe parties. There are statutory provisions which have come later for regulation of political parties in many countries, such as Spain, Portugal and Canada.

Party reforms are long pending in countries, such as the US, where there has been a two-party system since centuries. The party loyalties remain loose, and the number of swing and independent voters is on the rise. As the American Constitution has aged considerably, there is no mention of political parties. The concept was itself emerging in Britain when Americans wrote their Constitution.

There is generally a high degree of factionalism within the modern political parties in federal polities, such as the US, Australia and Canada. There is also class organisation of parties as seen in Australia. In Canada, the Centre remains relatively weak unless they get support from at least some regional parties.

Role of the Election Commission

The Election Commission of India plays a central role in the story of evolution of political parties in India. The commission came into existence a day before our first Republic Day, which goes on to show its importance as one of the main pillars of post-Independence India. Article 324 provides it the crucial responsibility of supervising, directing and controlling the conduct of elections to the Parliament, state Assemblies, that of the President and the Vice president.

The SC observed in Mohinder Singh Gill v. the Chief Election Commissioner (1978) that the EC has been vested with "comprehensive responsibilities" and "this responsibility (of conducting free and fair elections) may cover powers, duties and functions of many sorts, administrative or other, depending on the circumstances." The EC is also entrusted with powers to ensure that a "proper conducive atmosphere "is maintained for the conduct of elections according to Bhim Singh vs. the Election Commission (1996). It goes on to say that "it can exercise any power which is necessary to achieve this objective even if the Conduct of Elections Act and the rules made thereunder do not confer such power specifically." This, in principle, gives vast residuary powers to the EC to act in unforeseen circumstances to ensure fair political representation and those powers have aided it through seven decades in formulation of rules for the conduct of political parties.

The EC has played its role in recognising the existence and role of political parties ever since the very first general elections were held in 1951-52. Out of the 29 political parties which claimed national status, 14 were recognised as multi-state parties in July 1951. Additionally, 59 other parties were recognised as state parties. The Election Symbols (Reservation and Allotment) Order, 1968 was enacted to enable the EC to award respective symbols to candidates for facilitating recognition for the purpose of elections under the Conduct of Election Rules, 1961. This was necessary to enable 84% of the population which was illiterate to vote at the time.

Later, with the passage of the anti-defection amendment in 1985, political parties were formally recognised as part of the parliamentary process and the people changing political memberships after getting elected from a particular party's ticket were deterred. In 1989, the Election Commission of India got the authority to register the political parties due to insertion of Section 29(A) of the Representation of People Act, 1951. There was an additional qualification attached to the registration – all parties shall have a provision for a set of bye-laws/a party Constitution which unequivocally contained "a specific provision that the association shall bear true faith and allegiance to the Constitution of India as by law established, and uphold the principles of socialism, secularism and democracy and the sovereignty, unity and integrity of India."

The recognition of a party at the state or the national level brings a lot of perks with it including free air time on Doordarshan/AIR at the time of elections and free electoral rolls for members.

Under the SC judgement in the Indian National Congress (I) vs. the Institute of Social Welfare & Others, 2002, while the EC has the power to register political parties subject to specific criterion, it has no power to de-register them. There are many who argue this power should be given and many who object to the same. The opponents think that if the EC exercises that power, that will amount to politicisation of the commission as it will get to decide whose conduct is not in accordance with the constitutional spirit and, hence, will be taking political stands by deregistering political parties. Parties at present are by law de-recognised at the state or the national levels only based on poll performance of the percentage of seats secured in each election and when they are in violation of the Model Code of Conduct.

The Need for Reform

Most political parties in India today have become a hotbed of incompetence and dishonesty, and exhibit a lack of internal democracy. Lack of accessibility due to which the citizens don't get to interact with the individual politicians make the representatives out of touch with the general aspirations. The parties function in a very top-down manner with some people having too much power who get to decide who gets the tickets to contest elections. Hence, decision-making is highly centralised due to the cult of personality or dynasticism.

The voters who vote in the internal elections of political parties are nominated by the influential people within the party ranks. This is fundamentally undemocratic. As a result, the same candidates enter the fray and mobility within the party ranks is extremely difficult. As Jagdeep Chhokar has said, "These are sham elections." All of the prominent democracy and freedom indices in the world today use 'inner party democracy' as a heavily weighted indicator for assessing the robustness of a democracy in rankings, and this is not without reason. Unfortunately, the EC has, at present, no sanction to actually probe into the robustness of internal democracy within the political parties in India.

In 1994, the Justice V.R. Krishna Iyer Committee called for a law ensuring inner party democracy in all political parties and legal sanction audit and accounts. The Law Commission in its 170th report on 'Reform of the Electoral Laws' stated clearly that the political parties cannot be "dictatorship internally and democratic in its functioning outside." Besides, it also proposed the institution of a separate commissioner to ensure whether a political party is involved in any unconstitutional conduct or promoting any divisive agenda.

In 2002, the National Committee to Review the Working of the Constitution (NCRWC) recognised the need for regulation of party funds during election and non-election times, auditing accounts of political parties which should then be open for general inspection, the need for measures to check increasing casteism and communalism in elections, further strengthening of the anti-defection law and restoration of morality in public life in general. Violence, casteism, communalism and regionalism are being blindly used for partisan interests, and the result is the increasing violence.

Disclosure of financial statements is another area which needs reform from within and without. Disclosure by political parties is in their own self-interest as it leads to building of public confidence in the party and its candidates. The information deficit is bridged for the voter and she can take informed decisions about who to choose to best represent their interest in the corridors of power.

The EC has taken some laudable initiatives in this direction by making it mandatory for candidates to disclose their educational and financial information in an affidavit after the 2002 direction of the Supreme Court.

Just one of the examples of how resistant political parties are to the change in status quo is their response to the RTI Act and open audits. In 2006, the Association for Democratic Reforms filed an appeal to the Central Information Commission to make public the income tax returns of political parties. Even for this, a two-year struggle was waged until the CIC decided to make them public in 2008. In 2013, there was stiff resistance by political parties against the CIC declaring six national parties as 'public authorities', hence bringing them under the ambit of Section 2(H) of RTI Act. The plan was later dropped after there were threats that the RTI will itself be amended under Article 123(1).

The issue of electoral bonds is inescapable when talking about reforms related to financing of political parties. The electoral bonds have actually encouraged crony capitalism. It is a regressive reform. Crores of rupees can be paid by companies and one will not get to know who has given money to whom. The system is the complete opposite of transparency. The result of this reform will be that capitalists will run the country as probably they have been for years, and now more legalised. Now a company can donate 100% of their profits to one political party, which will, in turn, make policy conducive to them. The same system is a cause of great resentment for other democracies such as the US and so we should not follow it.

Another concern is that the expenditure incurred by political parties during propaganda is not added to the prescribed ceiling for the individual candidates running for elections. Hence, there is, at present, virtually no cap on how much they can spend as a political party. This leads to vested interests donating to political parties, which, in turn, legislate on terms favourable to those interests. This is a cause of great concern.

I have time and again talked about state funding of political parties in India. That is because monitoring the political parties is easier than monitoring money in elections. We cannot monitor how black money is put to use in bribing voters, in paid news, and other forms of transgressions, though we have been able to have some measure of success. As far back as 1990, the Dinesh Goswami Committee suggested that limited state funding in kind should begin for recognised political parties. In 1998, the Inderjeet Gupta Committee on State Funding of Elections endorsed partial state funding of recognised political parties and their candidates in elections. This will level the playing field and give all parties an equal chance to compete in elections, which is central to a healthy democratic process. But it also acknowledged that independent candidates cannot be funded in this manner and parties can be funded only in kind. I suggest a common pool funding which is the model prevalent in many European countries, where the parties get a fixed amount per votes polled in their favour in the last election. We could, for instance, agree that for every vote obtained, ₹100 be given. Why will it suffice? In the last general election, 55 crore votes were cast. So, at the rate of ₹100 per vote it comes to around ₹5,500 crores.

Is this adequate? This amount roughly corresponds to the amount raised by all political parties together in five years! This money can be distributed among the parties based on their poll performance and must be paid by cheque. Now unless their disclosures are inaccurate, this system of common pool funding is in their own economic self interest. State funding of parties will also go a long way in reducing the massive cost incurred in election campaigning, which the Inderjeet Gupta Committee also noted. A study, 'Political Finance Regulations Around the World', by the International Institute for Democracy and Electoral Assistance, Stockholm (2012), conducted in 180 countries revealed that as many as 71 nations give state funds based on votes. Hence, in 86% countries in Europe, 71% Africa, 63% of the Americas and 58% of Asia, this system is followed. So, this system by no means is unprecedented. All we need is political will.

Another issue is of tainted legislators. Section 8 of the Representation of People Act, 1951 bans convicted politicians. But those facing trial, no matter how serious the charges, are free to contest elections. The fielding of candidates is a function of their 'winnability' and so all political parties seem to be united in their opposition to any legislation on the matter. Justice Kuldeep Singh panel under the previously mentioned NCRWC of 2002 had recommended barring candidates with criminal background or those facing such charges framed by the court to be debarred for contesting. The past three Lok Sabhas have seen an increasing number of legislators with criminal background or pending cases against them — 124 in 2004, 162 in 2009 and 182 in 2014.

In its verdict in September 2018, a five-judge Bench of Supreme Court led by the then Chief Justice Dipak Misra said that the court cannot play the role of the Parliament. The Parliament is obliged to make a law on the matter according to Article 102(1) of the Constitution, but that has not happened and if history is any indication, it is highly unlikely to happen.

The judiciary has also refused to aid the Election Commission which has been crying hoarse for the past two decades in its fight against criminalisation of politics. The recent recommendations are certainly welcome, but are ridden with some impracticalities. They will risk the EC coming across as a politically motivated constitutional body, which should be avoided at all costs.

The methods of campaigning and reaching out to the voter base are getting more technologically sophisticated and the thin line between voter outreach and voter manipulation is frequently breached by the political parties. There needs to be regulation in place to ensure that the phenomenon of 'paid news' and 'fake news' as spread through biased news networks and social media does not distort political outcomes. While electoral rolls have been used over the years for voter outreach and there is nothing wrong with it, but the increasing use of social media has raised serious concerns about breach of privacy. Cambridge Analytica scandal is a recent case in point. The parties need to be responsible and ethical in their voter outreach.

It is high time that the political parties in India are regulated. There is a lot of lacuna to be removed in how they are formed, funded, audited and run. In a democracy, those at the helm of political affairs cannot run themselves like oligarchies. Many great models of regulating political parties are available throughout the world which have proved effective in countering criminalisation of politics, have increased accountability and decreased opacity in the system. There has been a consistent trend of politicians moulding the outcomes in their own favour by procedural misuse.

This is the antithesis of democracy as both an idea and a system. Rather than attempting to dilute existing laws and moulding the system to suit their own ends, all political parties should exhibit a collective political will to set aside their personal interests and come together to legislate in the interest of our democracy.

□

The Constitution and Official Language

—Brij Kishore Sharma

The Situation Prior to the Constitution

Before we consider the provisions of the Constitution regarding language, it would be worthwhile looking at which languages were being used in the administration before the Constitution came into effect.

From 1882 onwards, under the order of the Governor General, the use of Urdu along with English for the purpose of submission of applications in courts in northern India was allowed. In other words, in the territory from the North-West Frontier Province (NWFP; now the Pakhtoonkhwa province in today's Pakistan) to the eastern boundaries of Bihar and from Punjab to the southernmost parts of Madhya Pradesh, Urdu was accorded a place as the local language for use in the field of law and litigation. The actual situation though, was that Pashto in NWFP, Punjabi in Punjab and Hindi in Uttar Pradesh, Bihar and Madhya Pradesh (then the Central Provinces and Berar) were the chief languages in these provinces, respectively. It was not Urdu. The reason for depriving Hindi of its right was solely political. The Hindi-speaking states had been in the forefront in the revolt of 1857. The British wished to induce a feeling of inferiority in the people of these states, and also sow divisions on the lines of religion, caste and language.

Right after the founding of the Muslim League in 1906, Muslims began claiming that their language was Urdu. The League clearly reiterated in 1920 and again in 1940 that Urdu alone was the language of the Muslims. The reality, however, is that the Muslim of Kerala speaks Malayalam, just as the Muslim of Tamil Nadu speaks Tamil. Even the Punjabi Muslim in Pakistan speaks Punjabi. The province of Sindh in Pakistan is rife with the Jiye Sindh movement. Bengali Muslims consider Bengali as their language. It was the attempt to impose Urdu on them that led to the break-up of Pakistan and the creation of Bangladesh.

Almost all those who were involved in India's freedom struggle had come together on the Congress platform. However, the policy of Hindu-Muslim accord adopted by the Congress also dictated its course on language. The Congress' policy in this regard was that 'Hindustani' should be adopted as the language of the country. This would be neither Hindi nor Urdu, but a mixture of both. Even in the matter of its script, it was propagated that Hindustani would be written in both Devanagari and Persian scripts. This so-called Hindustani was neither a language of literature nor science, nor was it a language spoken by the masses. Hindi was used for literature; Hindi, Braj and Awadhi dominated its poetry. In the spoken form, Maithili, Bhojpuri, Marwari, Hadaiti, Bundeli, Chhattisgarhi, etc., were (and continue to be) widely used. Hindustani was an artificial and imaginary concept, one that was only given a name, but could never be born.

When the country was partitioned, political leaders perceived there was nothing to be gained by chasing this mirage. The resolution therefore, emanated from the Hindi Sahitya Sammelan under the leadership of Rajarshi Purushottamdas Tandon, Seth Govind Das, Balakrishna Sharma 'Naveen', Shri Ghanshyam Singh Gupt and others that Hindi should be declared the official language.

Hindi in the Constituent Assembly

The Constituent Assembly was to consist of 385 members, which came down to 298 following Partition. Of these, 208 members were from the Congress alone. Before any decision in the Constituent Assembly, important decisions would be made among the Congress members. On July 16, 1947, there was heated debate in the Congress Parliamentary Party on whether the official language should be Hindi or Hindustani. Nehru, Maulana Azad and Patel wanted Hindustani as the official language but the average Congressman stood firmly for Hindi. Gandhi though, favoured Hindustani. When this proposal was put to vote in the parliamentary party, 63 members voted in favour of Hindi and only 32 for Hindustani. Again, there were 63 votes in favour of the Devanagari script as against a mere 18 against it. Thus, the politicians lost in the parliamentary party; the people triumphed.

The outcome of this voting was that the draft of the Constitution issued in February 1948 contained 'Hindi' in place of'Hindustani (Hindi or Urdu)'.

The portion concerning the official language was passed in the Constituent Assembly on September 14, 1949. It was decided in the meeting of the parliamentary party that a special committee would be constituted for the drafting of this portion. This task was accomplished mainly by Gopalaswamy Aiyangar and Kanhaiyalal Maniklal Munshi.

The provision regarding the official language (part 17) was thus passed in the Constituent Assembly unanimously. But, it was unfortunately propagated that there being equal number of votes for and against Hindi, it could become the official language only because of the decisive vote of Dr. Rajendra Prasad, who was the President of the Constituent Assembly. The misconception was also been created that there was only one extra vote in favour of Hindi.

What is sadder is the fact that it is scholars of Hindi who teach in universities themselves propagating this misconception . The proceedings of the Constituent Assembly have been published in both English and Hindi. A scrutiny of the same will reveal the actual position that Hindi was unanimously made the official language.

Difference of opinion in the Constituent Assembly was not over Hindi, but on how long English would continue and whether Devanagari numerals should be used or not. Finally, it was decided that English would continue for a period of 15 years and in place of Devanagari numerals those numerals would be used which are written in the Roman script.

Provisions for Hindi in the Constituent Assembly

There are four portions in Part 17 of the Constitution (1) the official language of the Union; (2) regional languages; (3) languages of the Supreme Court; and High Courts and (4) special directives.

Article 343 declares that the language of the Union shall be

Hindi and it shall be written in Devanagari script. As far as the matter of numerals is concerned, Indian numerals shall be used in international form and the President can authorise for the Devanagari numerals. The parliament can provision by law that for which purposes Devanagari numerals shall be used.

Article 343(2) contains the provision that English shall be used for a period of 15 years from the commencement of the Constitution for all the purposes it was being used earlier.

It is stated in Article 343(3) that after 15 years, English shall be used for those purposes which Parliament shall specify by law.

Parliament enacted the Official Language Act 1963, which was amended in 1967. Complete consent for the use of English for all purposes was provided in Clause 3 of the Act. No restriction was done away with. This was the joint consequence of Article 343 and the Official Language Act of 1963.

The Official Language Commission

Article 344 contains the provision for a commission to be set up 5 years after the Constitution coming into force and again after a period of 10 years. This commission would recommend

a. Progressively increased use of Hindi
b. Restriction of the use of English
c. Use of language for the provisions of Article 348; and
d. Form of numerals.

A commission was set up in 1955 under the chairmanship of B.G. Kher. A second commission was to be set up in 1960, but it could not be constituted.

Parliamentary Committee

There is also a provision for constituting a parliamentary committee under the same Article 344. This committee, after considering the recommendations of the Official Language Commission, would present its report to the President of India.

A parliamentary committee was set up under the chairmanship of the then Home Minister Pt. Gobind Vallabh Pant. 20 of the members of this committee were from the Lok Sabha and 10 from the Rajya Sabha.

Presidential Decree

This Article contains an injunction that the President after considering the report of the parliamentary committee will issue a directive through a decree. The first Presidential order was issued on April 27, 1960. Seven more of such orders followed after the first one.

The Aim of the Constitution and Actual Situation

The aim of the Constitution was that the place of English should gradually be taken by Hindi and other Indian languages. But the Official Language Act of 1963 (and its amendment in 1967) lays down a provision to maintain the use of English for an indefinite period. English continues to be used as before in the functions of the Union. Hindi is used only to the extent it is mandatory under the Official Language Act or the rules framed thereunder.

This is an example of how politicians have failed the aims of the Constitution. While the language of the people is different, that of the ruling class is English. India is a democratic republic, in which the administration is conducted in a language of those foreign rulers of whom we were slaves.

Regional Languages

The Constitution does not declare what the official languages of various states will be. Article 345 confers on the states the power to make any one or more of the languages prevalent in those respective states, or Hindi their official language. This can be brought about by law. Many large states have declared the main language of their state to be their official language. For example, Maharashtra has chosen Marathi, Tamil Nadu Tamil and Uttar Pradesh, Bihar and Madhya Pradesh Hindi as their official languages. Punjab has adopted Hindi along with Punjabi. Similarly, Gujarat too has accorded Hindi an official status along with Gujarati. The states of the northeast like Nagaland, Meghalaya, Mizoram and Arunachal Pradesh have made English their official language.

In 1989, Uttar Pradesh passed the second Official Language Act to make Urdu its second official language.

The official language of the Union shall be the language of correspondence between (a) one state and another; and (b) between one state and the Union. This language is Hindi, but the use of English is permissible.

Language of the Courts, Bills and Acts

It is stated in Article 348 that till Parliament by law or otherwise makes a provision, all work in the Supreme Court and High Courts shall be conducted in English. Considering the fact that time would be needed to change the medium, the decision was left to Parliament. Anyway, it was not to be implemented for a period of 15 years.

There is also a provision in Clause 7 of the Official Language Act of 1963 that the decisions, decrees and orders of High Courts can be issued in Hindi or the official language of any state, with the prior consent of the President of India.

Till 2018, only four High Courts had sought consent in this regard. These four states happen to be Bihar, Madhya Pradesh, Rajasthan and Uttar Pradesh. The successor High Courts of these states, i.e., Jharkhand, Uttarakhand and Chhattisgarh have inherited this consent. The rules applicable to the High Court of Madhya Pradesh are automatically applicable to the state of Chhattisgarh, which has emerged from Madhya Pradesh. The same applies to Jharkhand and Uttarakhand.

Clause 7 of the Official Language Act concerns the language of the decisions, decrees and orders of the High Courts. Article 348(2) confers on the Governors of states the power of authorizing the use of Hindi or the official language of the respective state in the functions of the High Court, with prior consent of the President of India. In this context, functions of the High Court mean petitions, orders, appeals, oral and written presentations and documents to be filed.

The Union government did not permit the use of Tamil in the High Court of Tamil Nadu. The reason given was that the Chief Justice of India did not consent to this. The grounds for such refusal are totally unacceptable. Nowhere has the Chief Justice of India been assigned any advisory role in the Constitution or the Official Language Act. This is yet another example of how the executive shirks the discharge of its duty and then complains that the judiciary is exceeding its boundaries and usurping the functions of the executive.

Following table will reveal when the said permission was issued.

For actions under Article 348(2) of the Constitution	For decisions, decrees and orders under Clause 7 of the Official Language Act
Rajasthan 14.02.1950	17.02.1971
UP 05.09.1969	28.10.1970
MP 18.09.1971	24.09.1973
Bihar 09.05.1972	09.05.1972

The High Courts of Chhattisgarh, Uttarakhand and Jharkhand have the consent for the use of Hindi on the basis of their States Reorganisation Act which their parent High Courts use at the time of their coming into existence. Therefore, the consent for the use of Hindi in these three High Courts for decisions, decrees, etc., and all functions is there since the time of their establishment.

The Language of the Supreme Court

The Parliament so far has not enacted any law by which Hindi can be used in the Supreme Court. In the Madhu Limaye vs. Vedamurti case, the Supreme Court had refused to hear the complainant in Hindi (AIR 1971 SC 2608).

Authoritative Copy of Bills and Acts

There has been a great deal of confusion as to the meaning of Article 348 (3).

This paragraph contains the provision that if any language other than English is used for any enactment, ordinance or regulation in any state, an English translation in the gazette with the authority of the Governor of that state and such translation shall be considered the authoritative draft in English.

A conclusion was sought to be drawn in some decisions that if there is a discrepancy between the English and Hindi drafts, it is the English draft that ought to be the authoritative one.

But a full bench of the Allahabad High Court had in the Matabadal Pandey II case (AIR 1976 Alla.420) and the Madhya Pradesh High Court in the Chief Municipal Officer vs. Hindustan Copper Ltd [2018(2) JA21] had made it clear that when the official language of the state is Hindi, enactments passed in Hindi would prevail. The English translation published in the gazette cannot diminish the effect of the Hindi draft. The Hindi draft is the primary document that expresses the intent of the legislative body. If the English translation were to be considered as the authoritative one, it would mean that the translator would become the lawmaker, not the legislative body. The legislative body uses Hindi terminology.

The draft of the law or statute is in Hindi and it is only through that draft that the intent of the legislative body can be discerned.

The High Court of Himachal Pradesh too has expressed the same opinion, stating that the authorised draft in English cannot be accorded a place higher than the original enactment itself. This opinion was stated in the Gauri Devi vs. State of Himachal Pradesh case (Civil Writ Petition No.393/2002).

Special Directives

Part 4 of the Constitution contains the Directive Principles of State Policy. Article 351 contains directives for the development of the Hindi language. It is stated in the said Article that it shall be the duty of the Union to enhance the spread of Hindi and work for its development. For increasing the vocabulary of Hindi, words are to be drawn mainly from Sanskrit and secondarily from other languages. In the course of its development, the forms, style and words of Hindustani and other languages of the Eighth Schedule in use may be absorbed.

The Eighth Schedule

Directives concerning the Eighth Schedule are to be found in Article 344(1) and Article 351 of the Constitution.

Article 344 contains the provision for the setting up of an Official Languages Commission. Members of this Commission shall be representatives of the languages in the Eight Schedule.

Article 351 contains the directive for the development of Hindi and the drawing of words from the languages in the Eighth Schedule for the development of Hindi.

The Official Languages Commission was set up in 1955 and expired after it submitted its report. The task of the development of vocabulary has been accomplished by the Scientific and Technical Vocabulary Commission and the Ministry of Law.

This Schedule has no further utility from the point of view of the Constitution. When the Constitution came into force, there were 14 languages in the Eighth Schedule. Following the 92nd Constitutional Amendment, the Schedule now has 22 languages.

However, without paying any attention to this fact, the protagonists of many dialects and languages are demanding that their languages be included in the Eighth Schedule. The surprising thing is that the government simply accepts these demands and goes on amending the Constitution.

The Home Ministry in 2003 had set up a committee under the chairmanship of Sitakant Mahapatra to look into the Eighth Schedule. The committee had unanimously recommended that there is no need to make any fresh entry in the Eighth Schedule.

□

The First Copy of the Constitution: An Artistic Introduction

—Jawaharlal Kaul

When Nandalal Bose was requested to decorate the first copy of our Constitution, it was not merely a government or semi-government order. Certainly someone among our national leaders, who have played significant role in the freedom movement as well as framing of Indian Constitution, would have requested him. They also would have discussed the aspirations and prospects of our arriving democracy along with the adornment of the draft regarding our rights and duties. Both would have offered some suggestions and have been mutually agreed on some points. And, then, an artist like Bose would not have behaved like a dumb listener. He had developed his own art style and the concept behind it by deeply studying many creative forms from the primeval period of Indian history to the Rigvedic era, Mauryan and Buddhist art, from the delicacy of the illustrations in the caves of Ajanta and Bagh. He made all possible efforts to invigorate the fading colours of the drawings in the caves. He nourished his art-style through roving into many art galleries that fell into the limits of cultural India. So, when one commissions such an Acharya to decorate the first copy of the Constitution of a newborn republic, he does not simply commission a professional to embellish an ordinary publication. It was a moral bond of a great nation with its most prestigious art institute Vishwa Vidya Tirth Prangan namely Santi Niketan. Nandalal Bose accepted this assignment after consent from his master Abanindranath. Kala Bhawan spontaneously grew into a workshop of talented artists under the proper guidance of Nandalal Bose.

Our Constitution got framed by hundreds of mass leaders from different walks of life, who were masters of different genres after deeply assaying each and every point of it. So, its decoration too was done by a number of art experts using all their talent. Nandalal went reeving all that in one strand. Many of Nandalal's students, who accompanied him during many journeys of art, were contributing their best along with him. They had joined him during significant works like rejuvenation of the Ajanta illustrations. Among them those artists too were included who had been the students of his guru Abanindranath Bose. It was not only those 22 illustrations, but also the border which was representing a unique Indian art-style. The first copy of our Constitution was also engrossed by an embellishing calligraphy. The proper portrayal of the symbols was significant not only to the point of view of engrossing of the Constitution nay a number of those figures took the place of standards later.

Much before drafting and passing the Constitution, the decision of its decoration has been taken. At the same time, a young artist, born in a small town of Betul District of Madhya Pradesh, left for Calcutta (now Kolkata). He loved to draw different species of animals. He believed that his experience and understanding about drawing gestures and ambulation of the animal world was something that he could proud of. He arrived to evince his talent to the great art master Nandalal Bose. Nandalal got impressed by the talent of the young man but not satisfied. He picked one of the drawings of the artist. It was of the four lions atop the Ashokan Pillar in Sarnath and asked him,"Can you infuse life into these?" Nandalal wanted to see the lions in an animate form and not captivated in the stone. Young artist looked directly into the eyes of Acharya and realised that he was not kidding, but serious. The young artist replied with the same sincerity, "Yes sir." Dinanath Bhargawa of Betul took it as a challenge and set out to find a real lion. He found a couple in the local zoo. The zoo became his new pathashala. He would leave his residence early in the morning for his vintage point in front of the lions and watch the couple till the evening when the zoo got closed for the day. He watched them in every position and mood, studied the changes that took place in their bodies with the change of mood and the time, change of colours of eyes, contortion in the ears, tip of the neck, blow in the nostrils and even the whiskers. In the evening, Dinanath used to draw different gestures of the lions engraved in the stone. Whatever he could do in three-four days, took it to the Acharya, but got no change in the expression of Bose's face. Dinanath yet continued to go regularly to his pathshala, the zoo. It was perhaps his fourth effort when his drawing drew a smile on the face of Acharya. Dinanath was assigned to redraw the symbol of Sarnath which later was accepted as our national symbol and graces the first page of our Constitution.

The first copy of our Constitution is not a printed book decorated with illustrations. It's a historic artwork, written by pen and decorated by brush. It is handwritten by Prem Behari Narain Raizada from Delhi, who had learnt calligraphy from his grandfather and adopted it as his family profession since then. When he was asked to write the first copy of the Constitution by his hands, he replied that he could not do this job as a professional. I cannot accept money for it but would like to have remunerations in an alternate way. I shall do this job for my own pleasure. I would like to put my signature at each page and my grandpa will sign on the last one. Actually, it was his way to express gratitude to the guru. His wish got granted and Raizada wrote the first copy of the Constitution in Italics style.

We start our Constitution with words, "We, the people of India..." What exactly did they mean by "We, the people of India?" Who are these, the people of India? Is it any caste, creed or race? Or, we the Indians, who were the subjects of British empire in just past; or the people who were the residents of at least two-thirds of the severed Indian peninsula, which was under the British paramountcy; or did the makers of our Constitution have a certain idea of the natives of India? It is clear that what we term as Nation State had never been during the course of our history. This idea is purely western. Originally it is based on race. Yes, they have a common history, but that too is actually racial. Centuries past after the making of such human nations though, even today one needs to discretely recognise a unique race or human group, he used the same standards on the basis of which the human groups were got identified. In US or Canada, natives were called Red Indians or

Indians for two centuries. Now officially they invented a substitute for this name. In Canada, they are identified as 'first nation' now. Actually, 'nation' is synonymous to the 'tribes' here. Yet, those who made the Constitution of India, they would have some different and comprehensive picture of India than this; one which is made of its age-old history, one which does not include kings alone but ideas and cultural conceptions as well. It also includes the philosophical journey which does not only looks at the world as a family, rather believes that the whole universe is just an expansion of one absolute power. If one flips through our Independence movement, he finds that it sprouted from the womb of an enormous churning of various streams of thought which were going on in India during latter-half of the nineteenth and early twentieth centuries. Swami Vivekananda was presenting a new image of Indian philosophy and dharma. On the other hand, Tilak, who had converted Ganeshotsava from a mere religious festival into a festival of mass mobilisation, was declaring that 'Freedom is our birthright'. Arvind was assigning a new interpretation to the Indian Philosophy and Gandhi was experimenting with his concept of Satyagraha along with dreaming of Ramrajya. The movement dedicated to the awakening was also underway in the realm of literature. It was Bankim's *Anand Muth* that gifted us a song like Vandemataram that rejuvenated our sanskar of worshipping motherland like a goddess. Bankim is the person who advised for the first time to adopt Hindi as the medium of communication with every person of the country. In the south, Subrahmanian Bharati was doing the same that Jayshankar Prasad and Bhartendu Harishchandra was doing in Hindi. Artists could not remain indifferent like spectators during this multi-dimensional awakening. Abanindranath Tagore and Nandalal Bose were refining the mood of Indian Art and busy in discovering the original Indian Art-style.

Born in Munger in Bihar, Nandalal Bose was an artist by nature. He started drawing and sketching since his childhood days, when he was in school. He wanted to join some reputed art college to pursue his ambition when he was studying in Calcutta, but he could not manage to get admitted in such an institute because of some family reasons. But Nandalal continued his experiments with various types of art forms without a proper guru. Only this passion for art took him to the Art school of Abanidranath Tagore. Abanindranath's art classes were different from the ordinary. Here they hadn't used to breed art in a routine manner, instead first they made their students familiar to the sources, sense of which was the base of art in their view. It is not possible to understand the relationship between a text and an illustration without going through the source treatises of folk literature, mythology and history. Recitation of the treatises like Ramayan or Mahabharat or many fiction books like Katha Saritsagar or Brihatkatha Manjari, was a regular part of his art-classes. Nandalal, who already had been painting the episodes of Ramayan and Mahabharat and even themes of the folk narratives, set out to the historic journey of Indian Art. After holding on the responsibilities of the Chief Teacher in the Santi Niketan, established by Gurudev Shri Rabindranath Tagore, he got exposure to and practical experience of the ancient murals an the cave architecture. The illustrations which were painted on the walls of Ajanta caves during Buddhist period were started to decay, colours too got faded. It had become a reason for worry to the art-lovers. Actually, they feared to lose it forever.

So, they voiced their demand internationally to rejuvenate it. Nandalal Bose along with many of his supporters joined it. The murals of Ajanta proved to be a great inspiration for him. The stone-art in the Bagh caves of Vindhyachal mountain range along with Ajanta also added new dimensions to his creativity. His auto-education though did never finish. He felt that without having without having sense of the art of those neighbouring oriental countries with whom India had cultural exchange, one cannot have the complete sense of Indian art. He believed China and Japan to be important to this point of view. It was this period only when Okakura Kakuzo joined his admirers' list.

In his Introduction for Christies Catalogue, noted Art critic and Historian R. Shiv Shankar writes, "Nandalal Bose occupies a place in the history of Modern Indian art that combines those of Raphael and Durer in the history of the Renaissance. Like Raphael, Nandalal was a great synthesizer, his originality lay in his ability to marshal discrete ideas drawn from Abanindranatha Tagore, Rabindranath Tagore, E.B. Havell, Ananda Coomaraswamy, Okakura Kakuzo and

Mahatma Gandhi into a unique and unified programme for the creation of a new art movement in India." It is this from which the new Indian Art-style came into being. It was the reason that when Mahatma Gandhi suggested to emblazing the Constitution of India, he didn't mean to the commercial design like of an ordinary book, but to create an art-work. Undoubtedly, he was asking Nandalal Bose to create an introduction to the newly framed Indian Constitution through his art. He needed an explanation of the sub-text of the text through illustrations and images. Naturally, it was the reason that they picked 22 illustrations in a way that it could signify the different stages of the history and development of us, the natives of India. R. Shivkumar says Nandalal a synthesizer. This is, actually, the nature of Indian knowledge tradition. The *Gita*, that Vyasa had narrated through Vasudeva, he didn't claim of any originality in it and nor Shankaracharya do so for his works. An eminent Shaiva scholar Abhinav Gupta, introducing his Trik Phiolosphy, says that I could touch this height only by stepping up the stairs carved my preceding masters. Nandalal Bose too was a master from the same tradition who strived to propound the accumulated knowledge and not of his own alone.

The Constitution of India is the largest Constitution in the world. It is perhaps because of being a collection of laws and code of conduct for the country which is multidimensional, not only to the point of view of people, but also culture and thought. It is multidimensional to the point of view of faiths and beliefs as well as geography. It is obvious that the Constitution, which compiles concerns of every class and community in such a broad-based country, would be large one. Some people though complain that there is no originality in the rules and laws compiled in it. Most of the thoughts are borrowed from the Constitutions of alien countries. Actually, we need to give a thought to the recent history of India to understand this matter. We lost most of our wealth and also forgot something when got enslaved to the British. We could not find an opportunity to synchronise our tradition. Later, after a long period of two centuries when our eyes saw the light of Independence, we didn't have an example to set to carry out our home-rule. It became a need for us to look towards experiences and achievements of other independent countries. Whatever we felt suitable, we picked. Different countries of the world have different experience because they went through different circumstances. We could not move with setting one country as our ideal. On one hand we liked European knowledge and science, on the other the Asian spirituality, for many times we saw the image of African tribes in our own forest-dwellers though sometimes American openness too attracted us. So, it is natural that we find the marks of all these in our Constitution. It is also asked that are the illustrations of which we are discussing, a part of the Constitution. A Constitution can be looked from two angles — one, what is written in it and the second what are the feeling embedded in it. Whatever we wrote in the Constitution can alter in the changed circumstances. We have made changes in it for hundred times till now. It has happened because no one Constitution can imagine all types of circumstances all along. Circumstances keep changing many times automatically or due to external reasons. But, can we say that we change the feeling behind the creation of our Constitution? It is possible only in one condition that if we, the people of India, be no more the same in our mind that were at the time of the framing of the Constitution.

The illustration of the Constitution is a documentation of the perpetuity of that, the people of India. Thus, may it be true that we have borrowed much from others in our Constitution, but one thing which is borrowed from nowhere is the history of the people of India, their culture and their civilisation, which is inscribed in the illustrations. Can an independent Constitution refuse its own roots?

□

Indian Constitution and Mahatma Gandhi

—Dr. Ramesh Bharadwaj

It was after the struggle of many centuries that India got established as an independent constitutional state. But this Constitution could not actualise the dreams of the inspiring icons of the freedom movement. It specifically was contrary to the idea of India that Gandhi had visualised. But, it cannot be denied that the basic character of the Constitution clearly reflects the influence of Gandhian thought. The 1931 Karachi Session of Congress, in which resolutions about the matters such as the Constituent Assembly, the structure of the Constitution, the Fundamental Rights of the citizens, security of the minorities and the economic progress of the rural population were passed, became the milestone in the process of framing of Indian Constitution. The subjects such as Fundamental Rights and security of the minorities, approved by the Constitution we have today are similar to the resolutions passed by the Karachi Congress. Besides, the subjects like freedom from bonded labour, women's security, the right to form labour unions, abolishing child labour and adult franchise have been taken from there only. The constitutional provisions for the solution of inhuman problem of untouchability, too, are the representations of the Gandhian vision. But the creators of the Constitution, not only ignored Gandhiji's insistence on granting the 'village' the constitutional status of being the basic unit of the state, but did not even bother to take the idea for discussion in the Constsituent Assembly. Why the Gandhian Concept of reconstructing the nation on the principle of 'village self-rule' was not made a part of the Constitution is a question worth pondering over.

The topmost leader of the Indian freedom movement Mahatma Gandhi, from the very beginning, did not want any interference from the British government regarding the framing of the Constitution that was going to provide guidelines for the future of the Indian society. Gandhiji wanted the representatives elected through direct franchise by the Indian people as the members of the Constituent Assembly. His wish was respected to the extent that all members were Indians but as per the Cabinet Mission Plan. All members were chosen through indirect franchise by the provincial assemblies. These provincial assemblies also were elected under The Government of India Act, 1935 and were chosen through just 11% of the people of the Indian society. This makes it clear that our Constitution was framed by a group of elite and powerful people of British India.

In the backdrop of the first and second world wars, Indian freedom movement was at its peak. As the topmost leader of that movement, Gandhiji could see very clearly that at the core of these disastrous wars lies the western way of thinking due to which the capitalist forces turn fascist in the name of democracy and the high-pitch slogans of Nationalism blunt the overall possibilities of development of man. This fascist capitalism makes the four basic constituting elements of democracy the legislative, the judiciary, the executive and the media, mere instruments to achieve its selfish goals.

We witness the same scenario when we look at the history of the past seventy years that our polity having the foundations of the western civilisation under it has travelled through. After our country achieved independence, it adopted an admixture of the western parliamentary political system with a tinge of communist ideal and socialist slogan, that has transformed into corporate capitalism from fascist capitalism and stands internationalised today with the aim to earn profit only through the establishment of humans as mere consumers in the market. That is what results in making the rich richer and the poor poorer.

In his book 'Hind Swarajya' written in 1908, Mahatma Gandhi has given a vivid description of the monster, that is western civilisation. He makes it clear that the future of India does not lie in the bloody path of the western civilisation, but we have to tread the non-violent path of simple dharmic life to ensure a future full of peace and tranquility. He underlined the fact that India faced the danger of losing her soul.[1]

What is the 'Soul of India'? What are its perpetual determining elements? What are those constituting elements which from times immemorial make this Indian society pulsate with an unceasing, perennial enthusiasm. Gandhiji saw India as a spirituality-centric society, that in its continuity through many millennia, reached the pinnacle of contemplating ultimate human welfare. It is the society with truth and non-violence as its determining factors. So, when Gandhiji uses the word 'Swaraj', he does not take it in the usual meaning of 'Independence', the autocratic freedom devoid of human dignity and principle, but means by it the Indian cultural endeavour of Vedic 'Swaraj'. He means by it the governance of Bharatvarsha that goes by the voice of the people...The true Swaraj does not come through the attainment of power by few, but is ascertained when the misuse of power is resisted by all.[2] My Swaraj is to keep the soul of our civilisation intact.[3]

Gandhiji did not want just political self-rule. He was for a decentralised system taken from the Indian tradition in social, economic and every sphere of life. So, in any future Constitution of India, he wanted to see the reflection of the soul of India. He said that he would try to make them frame such a Constitution that could break the shackles of any kind of dependence and slavery.

He expressed his resolve to work for such India where the poorest of the poor could feel that this was their country and their voice has got a meaning when it comes to building up the country. When the road for the freedom of India was becoming clear and the country was eager to give a shape to its concept of a bright future a Gandhian Shriman Narayan Aggarwal, understanding the bent of mind of the nation, wrote a book based on the Gandhian thought. The book was titled Gandhian Constitution for Free India. Gandhiji wrote in the foreword of the book, "The framework is really Principal Aggarwal's based on his study of my writings. He has been interpreting them for a number of years... He has made it perfectly clear in the beginning pages that he has only laid down broad lines to indicate what a Constitution of my conception could be."

The Gandhian thought advocated a Cultural Renaissance in India. So, in Gandhiji's view, the concept of a Constitution for India is not just a political matter as it has developed in the west. As he led the Indian freedom movement, he always underlined the importance of Indian culture and civilisation. He was of the firm view that while going for any social, political, and economic changes in India, the Indian tradition cannot be ignored.

This very feeling of Gandhiji has been expressed in the introductory note by Sriman Narayan, "The question naturally arises: 'what kind of Constitution shall free India have? Shall we imitate some of the western Constitutions like those of Switzerland, the United States or Russia? Or shall we try to evolve a Swadeshi Constitution based on our national genius, culture and traditions?'... India is a very ancient land. A study of her past constitutional development would indicate that she had enjoyed almost all the varieties of political organisation many years before Christ. At a time when Europe and the New World had not come within the pale of civilisation, India had experimented with monarchy, autocracy, democracy, republicanism and even anarchy... Let me not be misunderstood. I do not mean to suggest that we should be blind to the experiences of other nations and develop a kind of narrow nationalism. Far from it. But it is high time for us to realise that our sense of 'inferiority complex' must go, and instead of looking always to the west, we should cultivate the habit of looking within. We have aped the west for long. Let us now be proud of our Indian Culture and institutions in the right spirit."

To substantiate his argument, not only did Sriman Narayan quote India thinkers like K.P. Jaiswal, Mukerjee, Majumdar and the researchers of ancient India, he referred to western thinkers as well.[4] According to all these, no nation can have the Constitution as an imported entity.[5]

In light of Gandhian thought, Sriman Narayan Agarwal gave the concept of a Constitution with the following basic elements:

Non-Violence

Gandhi visualised democracy as a system where the weakest get everything that is available to the mightiest. It is impossible to achieve through violence.[6] The modus operandi of the democracy we see in the world today leads us to Nazism and Fascism. So democracy, and violence cannot co-exist. If they want genuine democracy they have to accept non violence.[7] This makes it clear that non-violence is indispensable for the development of democracy.

Decentralisation

For non-violence-based democracy decentralisation is the primary requisite. Gandhiji considered a self-sufficient and self-governed village the first unit of a government that could lead us to decentralisation of economic and political power. The reason for the unceasing continuity of the Indian society was that it stood on the strong foundations of 'village self-rule'. Gandhiji did not want to restore the villages of the olden times, but aimed at re-establishing them in accordance with the needs of the modern times.

Indian Village Republic

Quoting from ancient works such as ***Vedas***, ***Manusmriti***, ***Mahabharat***, ***Ramayan***. ***Arthshastra***, etc., Sriman Narayan makes the point that from times immemorial, India has been a country of village republics. Since Vedic era, 'the village' has been the basic unit of government and this phenomenon continued till the arrival of East India Company. This political tradition was rooted in our culture. But Britishers replaced it with their own system and destroyed it. This political tradition must be re-established in the new system and the Constitution.

Decentralised Economy

The intellectuals involved in the framing of Constitution were overwhelmed with the imperialist concepts of Capitalism and Communism. Gandhiji wants them to adopt the economy based on village industries, cottage industries and small industries which are the products of the Indian tradition. This decentralised economy can ensure work to every hand and guarantee freedom from exploitation.

The Philosophy of Decentralisation

Gandhiji was not for economic and political decentralisation only, but wanted to re-establish spiritual and cultural philosophy of India. Physical labour is essential to establish harmony between body and mind. So, it is the basic element of decentralisation. Gandhiji favoured village-based decentralised economy which is a spontaneous manifestation of co-operation without any exploitation.[8]

Decentralised Village and Society

In a decentralised village system, clean air is available that can save us from the diseases of urban overcrowding. This clearly implies that a village base system must be adopted to ensure a healthy country. This only can guarantee social harmony and security.

Joy of life, Art and Beauty

Old traditions are still intact in villages. The society can attain more joy in a folk tradition. Art has never been for art's sake in Indian tradition, but has always been there to serve life.

National Security

Not only do decentralisation and ruralisation save us from foreign invasions, but keep us insulated against the influences of modern wars. The basic amenities of life bread, clothing and other things will be available at the local level and there will be no dependence on far away markets. So, there will be no trouble for the people in times of any emergency situations.

International Co-ordination

The basic aim behind fighting wars is economic exploitation and capturing the world market. The economy based on cottage industry leaves no room for imperialist greedy mindset. So, with military disarmament, economic disarmament is also required. This can eliminate the possibilities of war and establish international harmony.

International Vs. Universal

As per Sriman Narayan, the 'Village Self-rule' of Gandhi takes the man from internationalism to universalism. The Indian tradition makes available to us a world view where man has to live his life in unison with animate and inanimate creation. As the torch-bearer of this very tradition, Gandhiji says that our worldly existence can find its meaning only in a village and from cultural and spiritual points of view this whole creation is our home. So, I find myself one with everything animate and inanimate.[9]

A New Civilisation

Gandhiji's 'Village Self-rule', in fact, is not a recurrence of the Middle Ages, but is the dawn of a new civilisation. It is not at all imaginary, but practically possible.

After this, Srimanji discusses fundamental rights and duties. It needs to be mentioned here that in our Constitution, the provisions regarding rights and duties are the same which were laid down by Gandhiji along with Nehru in the Lahore session of Congress. Whatever is Gandhian in the Indian Constitution, this aspect stands out as a very important aspect out of that all.

In the sixth chapter of the book, village a is taken as the basic unit and Gandhi's five levels of state philosophy are underlined, the basic points of which are as under:

Village Panchayat

1. All adults of a village will choose at least five representatives called Panchs. These Panchs will choose a chief panch called Sarpanch. If there is no agreement over electing the chief, then all adult voters will elect one of the panchs as the chief through direct election. In the event of no confidence 75% votes are required to remove the elected official.
2. Regarding all matters of a village, such as economic, political or social, the village Panchayat will be sovereign. Its main jobs will be in the fields of education, entertainment, security, agriculture, industry, trade and

commerce, health and hygiene, justice, economy and taxation.

Taluka Panchayat

The Sarpanchs of all villages of a Tehsil will be the members of the Taluka Panchayat and one of them will be the head of that Panchayat. The rules for a Taluka Panchayat will be the same as a village Panchayat. The work entrusted to a Taluka Panchayat will be:

1. Guidance in the matters of Village Panchayat, cooperation with the Panchayats and auditing their accounts,
2. To make arrangements for secondary education,
3. Administration of a big hospital and maternity centres,
4. Management of Taluka Co-operative Bank and markets, etc.

District Panchayat

The heads of all Taluka Panchayats will be the members of the District Panchayat and they will choose one of them as the head of this Panchayat. It will facilitate the execution of the work of Taluka Panchayat at the district level. Its primary focuss will be on college education.

Urban Municipality

Municipalities on the lines of District Panchayat will be constituted.

State-Level Administration

The heads of district panchayats and urban municipalities will be the members of the state-level Panchayat.

The Central Administration

The heads of the state-level Panchayats will constitute a Panchayat on all India level.

Gandhian Constitution: Practical Applications

Gandhiji's view of the Constitution for our country, penned down by Sriman Narayan was not just an imaginary play of words. An example of its practical application was already seen in 1938 in Oundh state of Maharashtra. Raja Bhagwandas Pant, the representative of this small state of 72 villages made an agreement of democratic system with his subjects. A month after this, he met Gandhiji in Vardha and conveyed his decision. Gandhiji even prepared a draft for the prospective Constitution of his state. Gandhiji said that the ruler of Oundh had a clear view of the needs of the people and their social development. The fundamental rights of the people must be ascertained and everybody must be equal in the eyes of law, untouchability should be eradicated and the freedom of expression must be ensured. Gandhiji expressed the hope that other rulers will follow this ideal.[10]

In the schedule of Oundh state, many significant rights were included. The people had to be moral and non-violent in their attitude. The right to live was granted and they were free to express themselves. They had the right to peaceful assembly, right to worship, the right to be equal before law, the right to basic education, job guarantee and the right to minimum wages. All these rights were the fundamental rights.

Every village will have a village Panchayat which will choose a Sarpanch through direct election. Education, social welfare, management of pastures and markets, water supply, sanitation, roads, maintenance of public places, etc., will be the responsibility of the Panchayat. A state will be divided in four Talukas and the Sarpanchs of the villages will be the members of the Taluka Panchayat. The heads of four Talukas and two elected members from every Taluka will be the members of the state legislative assembly. The legislative assembly will never remain completely vacant as every year one-third of the members will retire and new ones will be elected. The Speaker and the Deputy Speaker of the Assembly will be chosen from the members of the Assembly. The rules passed by the Assembly will become laws after the approval of the King of the state. The ruler will choose a Prime Minister and two ministers from the members. The King will be the first servant of the people.

This system came into effect on 21 January, 1939 after the approval from the Legislative Assembly of Oundh and, in this way the first-ever constitutional State as per the dreams of Gandhiji became a reality and remained operative for nine years.

Gandhiji was not a Political Scientist but he certainly had his sociological sense. His view of constitutional rights and duties, state power and democracy was that all these were inseparable from the individual and through the individual were associated with the society, while as in western state-philosophy, all these subjects are related to the state and the citizen. Gandhiji says that we have always accepted that the power emanates from the Legislative Council which is totally wrong. The truth is that the power is inherent in the people. It is this plain and simple truth that I have been trying to make you understand for the last twenty-one years.[11]

With this basic distinction, this also needs to be noted that according to Gandhiji, the relationship of the individual and the society is not limited to physical levels. This relationship stands on the solid ground of morality and mutualness. This age-old experienced fact is the essence of the Indian cultural tradition. Gandhiji says that he does not mean that we should remain aloof from the rest of the world and erect solid walls around us. This is a big deviation from my line of thought. But I do want to make it clear that we should learn to respect our culture and internalise it. Respecting other cultures, understanding their specifications and accepting them comes after that and never before that. Gandhiji was of the firm view that the invaluable things we have in our culture have no match in any other culture. The problem is that we have not recognized those things. We have been taught to be disdainful towards their study, to undermine those vital elements. He further adds that his Dharma commands him to learn about his culture, to receive it from the core of being and act according to that, otherwise cut off from our culture, we shall commit social suicide.[12]

It was unfortunate that the Congress-oriented experts, who framed the Indian Constitution, did not care a fig about the cultural institutions of ancient India. All experts belonged to the English-educated elite class and favoured western political system. Some of them had no association at all with the freedom movement. Some progressive intellectuals were such that in spite of being nationalists, they never had any role in the Indian freedom movement and subscribed to the British parliamentary system. And the rest of the people were those who had accepted the leadership of Gandhiji in the freedom movement, but never had their heart in the Gandhian concept of new India.

So, the Constitution that was framed had no concept of India that could flourish on the solid substratum of Indian culture and traditions as per the dreams of Mahatma Gandhi.

References

1. *Hindi Navjeevan, October 7, 1926*
2. *Ibid*
3. *Ibid*
4. *Cited on p.11*
5. *Constitutions are not exportable commodities. Each nation has its unique culture and civilisation which may be called its 'soul'. Sir John Marriott, Dictatorship and Democracy, p-9*
6. *Harijan, May 18, 1940*
7. *Ibid, November 12, 1938*
8. *Ibid, November 4, 1939*
9. *Wisdom of Gandhi by Roy Walker, p-55*
10. *Harijan, November 12, 1938*
11. *CWMG, Vol. lxxv, pp.146-6*
12. *Young India, September 1, 1921: from the Cover Page of Mangal Prabhat*

□

Constituent Assembly and Indian Socialists

—Dr. Anand Kumar

The Constituent Assembly created the Constitution of India, which became the basis of decolonisation and democratic nation-building in post-colonial India. The work for it started in July 1946 and the draft of the Constitution was completed on 26 November 1949 after lengthy deliberations for over a period of 40 months. But, it was boycotted by Congress Socialist Party, which was then the main organisation of the Indian socialists within the Indian National Congress since 1934. They left Congress after Independence and assassination of Mahatma Gandhi in 1948 and established Socialist Party and played the role of Opposition. They were highly critical of the draft Constitution circulated by the Drafting Committee for public responses. What were the main objections of the socialists? Why did the socialists not participate in the making of the Constitution of the Republic of India? Do they consider the boycott as a 'lost opportunity'?

Socialist Critique of Constitution of India

The socialist criticism was not an insignificant phenomenon. It was properly acknowledged, reported and responded at the highest level of the Constituent Assembly by the chairman of the Drafting Committee Dr B.R. Ambedkar. It was not summary rejection. There was invitation to adopt a 'futuristic' – or Jeffersonian – approach.

In his last speech before the Constituent Assembly on 25 November 1949, Dr. Ambedkar said: "The condemnation of the Constitution largely comes from two quarters – the Communist Party and the Socialist Party. Is it because it is really a bad Constitution? I venture to say 'no'. The Communist Party wants a

Constitution based upon the principle of the 'dictatorship of the proletariat'. They condemn the Constitution because it is based on 'parliamentary democracy'. The Socialists want two things. The first thing they want is that if they come to power, the Constitution must give them freedom to nationalise or socialise all private property without payment of compensation. The second thing the Socialists want is that the Fundamental Rights mentioned in the Constitution must be absolute and without any limitations so that if their party fails to come to power, they would have the unfettered freedom not merely to criticise, but also to overthrow the state. These are the main grounds on which the Constitution is being condemned."

Dr. Ambedkar did not ignore the philosophical or political aspects of these objections. He responded to these objections in a constructive and conceptual way. According to him, "I do not say that the principle of parliamentary democracy is the only ideal form of political democracy. I do not say that the principle of no acquisition of private property without compensation is so sacrosanct that there can be no departure from it. I do not say that Fundamental Right can never be absolute, and the limitations set upon them can never be lifted. What I do say is that the principles embodied in the Constitution are the views of the present generation. Or, if you think this to be an overstatement, I say they are the views of the Constituent Assembly. Why blame the Drafting Committee for embodying them in the Constitution? I say, why blame even the Members of the Constituent Assembly? Jefferson, the great American statesman who played so great a part in the making of the American Constitution, has expressed some weighty views which makers of the Constitution can never afford to ignore. In one place, he has said, We may consider each generation a distinct nation, with a right, by the will of the majority, to bind themselves, but none to bind the succeeding generation, more than the inhabitants of another country."

Why Socialists boycotted Constituent Assembly?

There were several reasons for the boycott of the Constituent Assembly by the Socialists. First, it was not elected by the people of India based on universal adult franchise. The Congress committed to participate in a Constituent assembly where members were elected indirectly by the provincial assemblies, which, in turn, were elected under the Government of India Act of 1935 by no more than 15 percent of the people. Nehru had deviated from his earlier stand about the formation of the Constituent Assembly as he had been an advocate of a body elected based on adult franchise. His acceptance of the pattern prescribed by the British government was a shock for the Socialists. Second, the representation from the princely states was quite defective and arbitrary. Out of a total of 69 members from the princely states, 28 were the nominees of rulers and 41 were nominees of the Congress leaders who dominated the All India States Peoples' Conference. Three, they saw the proposal of the Constituent Assembly as a part of the conspiracy of the British government in alliance with the Muslim League. Fourth, they found it intriguing that the Congress Working Committee accepted the Cabinet Mission proposal while Gandhiji went on insisting that he would not accept a truncated India. The resolution was approved in the Bombay session of All India Congress Committee held in July 1946 by 204 to 51. Four, they were not prepared to take oath of loyalty to the British government which was an essential part of the nomination form for entering the contest for the membership of the Constituent Assembly.

According to Congress Socialist Party general secretary Jayaprakash Narayan aka JP: "The Constituent Assembly is the creation of the British and it can never bring us the freedom that we have been fighting for years. It is not an outcome of the strength of the people."[1] Jayaprakash pleaded for preparing the Congress and the country for a decisive struggle for independence. He moved a resolution on Congress manifesto at the AICC session at Meerut (November 23-24, 1946) arguing that the All India Congress Committee rather than the Congress members of the Constituent Assembly were competent to decide the shape of swaraj (self-rule) in the light of the Congress manifesto. He said, "Swaraj cannot be real for the masses unless it makes possible the achievement of a society in which democracy extends from the political to the social and economic spheres, and in which there would be no opportunity for privileged classes to exploit the bulk of the people, not for gross inequalities such as exist at present. Such a society would ensure individual liberty, equality of opportunity and the fullest scope for every citizen for development of his personality."[2]

Acharya Narendra Dev, who was the senior-most Socialist leader of the country, moved a resolution in the Constituent Assembly which was seconded by Rao Saheb Patwardhan (an influential social reformer and mass leader of Maharashtra). The resolution stated: "This Congress declares that it stands for an independent sovereign republic wherein all powers and authorities are deprived from the people, and for a Constitution wherein social objectives are laid down to promote freedom, progress and equal opportunity for all the people of India, so that this ancient land may attain its rightful and honourable place in the world and make its full contribution to the promotion of world peace and the progress and welfare of mankind, and directs all Congressmen to work to this end."[3]

Warning of Achyut Patwardhan and protest by JP

Achyut Patwardhan, a founder leader of Congress Socialist Party (a hero of the August Revolution of 1942 who led the liberation of Satara in Maharashtra and the British forces failed to arrest him between 1942 and 1946), joined Jayaprakash in opposing the Congress Working Committee decision about joining the Constituent Assembly. Patwardhan said, "How could the Congress having agreed to enter the Constituent Assembly, say that it did not wish to participate in grouping? The Congress Working Committee had said that they had accepted the clause relating to grouping with their own interpretation. Jinnah had his own interpretation which was opposed to the interpretation of the Congress. The correspondence published so far does not contain any evidence of the Cabinet delegation accepting the Congress interpretation of the grouping clause. On the contrary, the Cabinet Mission has made it clear that the Congress interpretation of the clause was not in accordance with the intentions of the Cabinet Mission... The Congress leaders by their participation in the Interim Government, were trading on a slippery ground. At the AICC meeting of Bombay, the president and other leaders assured the committee that the Congress was entering the Constituent

Assembly without any commitment. But later on they had to declare that they accepted the Cabinet Mission's statements in its entirety."[4]

Patwardhan gave a timely warning that the administration of India should not be carried on with the help of alien troops who must be withdrawn. He would prefer Hindus and Muslims to fight among themselves rather than keep foreign troops in India to maintain order. On 27 July 1946, the Muslim League withdrew its acceptance of the long-term plan of the Cabinet Mission and called on 16 August for 'direct action' to achieve Pakistan. For the subsequent 18 months, the sub-continent was plunged into bloodshed and riots. The orgy of violence reached unprecedented heights and spread from Calcutta to Noakhali and from there to Bihar. It ultimately reached Punjab and North West Frontier Province.

The British Cabinet released a statement on 6 December 1946, saying: "There has never been any prospect of success of the Constituent Assembly except upon the basis of an agreed procedure. Should a Constitution come to be framed by a Constituent Assembly in which a large section of the Indian population had not been represented (i.e., the Muslim League), His Majesty's Government could not of course contemplate – as the Congress have stated they would not contemplate – forcing such a Constitution upon any unwilling parts of the country." This declaration gave a new lease of life to the demand for Pakistan. Nehru moved a resolution in AICC on 6 January 1947, advising acceptance of the 6 December declaration of the British Cabinet. Jaiprakash opposed the resolution. He even offered resignation from the Committee. He held the view that the declaration would push the situation one more step forward to the ultimate acceptance of Pakistan.[5]

Any regrets about the boycott of the Constituent Assembly?

What was the immediate self-assessment of the socialists about boycotting the Constituent Assembly? Responding to the suggestion that the socialists were sorry about being "left out of the picture having boycotted the Constituent Assembly", Jayaprakash has stated that "So far as we are concerned, we do not at all regret having boycotted the Constituent Assembly. We were anxious by doing so to make it clear to the country that the whole basis of compromise with the British was wrong and should be rejected in toto. To attempt of the compromise and reject the whole would have been height of political opportunism." [6]

He further pointed out: "As events developed, and the Muslim League walked out of the Constituent Assembly, it was clear that what remained of a body was no longer capable of drafting the Constitution of free India. The only thing remained to be done then was, as I have stated above, to tear up the whole agreement with the British, to get out of the Interim Government, and the Constituent Assembly, and to call finally a real Constituent assembly elected by the people. The Constituent Assembly would then have become the centre of revolutionary power and challenged the British authority to a final showdown. The Socialist Party would have heartily cooperated with such an assembly and taken full responsibility for enforcing its decisions.

We were told that such a course of action would have led to civil war, which the acceptance of Pakistan would avoid. We replied that in the first place the risk should be taken, and in the second place, acceptance of Pakistan would not remove but accentuate the risk. Easily gained power, however, was too much of a temptation to be resisted, with what tragic result history has already shown."

References

1. *Press statement of July 12, 1946. The Indian Annual Register, Vol. II, 1946*
2. *Ibid, p. 121*
3. *Ibid*
4. *Ibid*
5. *Brahmanand (1974)– 'Editors introduction' in Nationbuilding in India (Varanasi, Navchetna Prakashan) p. 66-67*
6. *From a speech at the Sixth Annual Conference of the Socialist Party, Nasik 1948. See: Jayaprakash Narayan (1974) Nationbuilding in India (Ed. Bahmanand) (Varanasi, Navchetana Prakashan) 125-128*
7. *Ibid*

□

Dr. B.R. Ambedkar and Constitution—Some Aspects

—Prof. Vijay K. Kayat

Dr. B.R. Ambedkar, known as the main architect of the Indian Constitution, was a great jurist. Born in a poor family, he experienced the sufferings of the members of the downtrodden. He was an advocate of high repute and possessed extraordinary skills. As token of recognition of his extraordinary talents, he was elected chairman of the Drafting Committee for preparing a Constitution for Independent India.

Dr. Bhimrao Ambedkar was great in his time, he continues to great in stature after his demise in 1956. This is explained not so much by his singular contribution in the drafting of the Indian Constitution, as by the fact of his deep and abiding empathy with the cause of the Dalits, his uncompromising political stance and untiring efforts for the amelioration of their lot – a class which has by now attained not only a political identity of their own, but also the capability to substantially (if not decisively) influence the electoral politics of the country. The more the empowerment of the Dalits, the greater would be the stature and relevance of Dr. Ambedkar. His observations too, regarding the action, reaction and interaction of social, economic and political pulls and pressures operating in the country and ways of channelising them along democratic and egalitarian lines, are coming true with the passage of time. This too adds to the relevance of his thoughts.

Dr. Ambedkar's contribution in the making of the Constituent of India is truly remarkable. His role will be remembered so long as the Constitution lasts and continues to control the destiny of this nation.

On November 4, 1948 Dr. Ambedkar introduced the Draft Constitution prepared by the Drafting Committee in the Constituent

Assembly. He said that a Constitution is merely a mechanism for the purpose of regulating the work of various organs of the state.

Introducing the Draft Constitution before the Constitution Assembly, Ambedkar lucidly explained the main features of the presidential and parliamentary forms of government. He thought, inter alia, that American Presidential system offers more stability but less responsibility, on the other hand, in the British Parliamentary system assessment of the responsibility of the executive is both daily and periodic. This principle of daily assessment of responsibility of the government is necessary and suited to Indian Conditions. That is why, the draft Constitution had envisaged Parliamentary System of Government.

India's struggle for freedom from the foreign rule was by and large a constitutional war in which Indians gradually advanced towards self-governance till the British rulers, forced by circumstances, decided to surrender and quit. Dr. Bhimrao Ramji Ambedkar's role in this constitutional struggle was second to none in importance.

Although he remained outside the orbit of Indian National Congress, Ambedkar was one of the few national leaders who actively participated in all the major constitutional events of pre-independence period, and with his stupendous knowledge, forensic brilliance, fiery speeches and disarming logic influenced their outcome. A few politicians could match his meticulous evaluation of governmental structures, his deep understanding of federal system and his thorough knowledge of political economy.

Dr. Ambedkar was a valiant fighter for human rights and a social visionary. Throughout his life, he fought against inequality, injustice and oppression. The depressed classes of India found in him a crusader for their cause. His relentless struggle to secure justice for them and his able advocacy before the Southborough Committee on Franchise secured for depressed classes for the first time representation by nomination in legislatures under the Government of India Act of 1919. He appeared as a witness before the Simon Commission and Suggested amendments to the Act of 1919. Ambedkar had very clear ideas about federalism, fundamental rights and rights of the minorities. He was opposed to separate electorate for Hindus and Muslims because he thought that would be detrimental to communal harmony.[1] Besides Gandhiji, Ambedkar was the only Indian leader who foresaw that the western model of democracy would not be suitable for India.[2]

Ambedkar was a radical in his social thinking as well as in his political ideas. He was the first Indian leader to raise the demand of equal work without discrimination of sex. As a law member of Governor General's executive council, he suggested such amendments in the labour laws which the Governor General found too radical to accept. Many of these suggestions were later incorporated in labour laws of independent India.

Coming from the untouchable Mahar Community of Maharashtra, Ambedkar in his early life suffered the worst kind of humiliation at the hands of caste Hindus which made him bitter and belligerent. Little wonder that this crusade against inequality and injustice carried a ring of vindictiveness against the high castes. His defiant public postures were unpalatable to the Congress leadership by the Congressmen of that period who did not hesitate in labelling him a stooge of British Empire.

Ambedkar clung steadfastly to the principles of liberty, equality and fraternity. He applied them to all spheres of life, in his speeches and writings, religious thinking, politics, annihilation of caste and other social and economic goals, as well as the whole range of human relations. He was such an ardent adherent of this trinity of principles that he observed: "Equality is the main principle of public morality. To apply the principle of equality in political, religious, social and economic sphere means structuring the society on the basis of morality." He continues to argue, "... Equality will be of no value without fraternity or liberty."[3] He, therefore, perceived Marxism as inadequate since it could pursue only equality. Buddhism, he thought, consisted of all the three principles.[4]

He was not interested in the mere formalistic of these principles, but made every effort to restructure society on the basis of these principles. As regards, liberty, for example, he was more interested in providing a mechanism which could create the capacity amongst the individuals to exercise their rights. He considered it meaningless to prepare a list of negative rights – as mere constraints on the powers of the state. For Ambedkar, liberty for the oppressed meant security against oppression and exploitation. Similarly, it was a total programme of societal transformation which constituted his conception of Swaraj.

According to him, the concept of liberty is inseparable from that of equality. Therefore, while discussing liberty, he implies equal opportunity; and replacing the 'one man one vote' principle he places emphasis on the principle of 'one man one value'.[5]

Most of his discussion on equality appears by way of his analysis of inequality existing in Hindu society. He felt rightly that caste was the major impediment in the establishment of liberty and equality. He was as much opposed to extreme individualism as to collectivist notions of equality denying all individuality to members of a society. He was quite conscious that absolute equality or uniformity is a fallacious ideal; he, therefore, preferred equity or justice to mere equality. In the matter of caste hierarchy, however, it was uncompromisingly in favour of equality.

Fraternity alone, he felt, could forestall attacks on liberty and equality. It encompasses compassion and a sense of brotherhood for human beings around us – an attitude of mind and heart which promotes dialogue and cooperation in any society. Society cannot be made up of different goals. A society requires human association; it requires a common point of reference. Fraternity creates an inner force which pushes different sections into unity. The term 'maître' used by him appropriately encompasses the meaning of fraternity. Love for living beings and empathy/communion with respect to human beings are the hallmarks of fraternity. He emphasised equal sharing on the basis of equal status rather than accommodation. He believed that 'fraternity' could be achieved only by the fulfilment of just rights.[6]

Another contribution of Dr. Ambedkar was to reserve seats in Parliament and State Legislatures for the Scheduled Castes and Scheduled Tribes. At one stage in his life, he had insisted upon separate electorates, he reconciled to the idea of joint electorates. Separate electorates tend to separate the different groups in the society. However, he felt that for some time, it is necessary to give some preferential representation to these classes in the legislatives; hence, Article 334. While pleading for such reservation, his speech is extremely apologetic as he believed that with political equality being established, all are equal and all must join the mainstream of the public and national life. Hence, he felt reservation should be for a limited period and all classes would be united in the fabric of national life.[7] Only ten years, therefore, were proposed initially in the Constitution. It is now 68 years that we have continued the reservation by amending Article 334 from time to time and still the end of reservation is not in sight. One more suggestion of his was extremely important to which, it appears, and our politicians have not paid serious and adequate attention to it. He wanted healthy conventions to be developed during the course of the working of the Constitution. He had the British model in view. To him a written Constitution may tend to be rigid at times and growth of healthy conventions would go a long way in avoiding rigidity. In the matter of selection and appointment of judges of High Court and the Supreme Court, such conventions were being gradually established during the regime of Pandit Jawaharlal Nehru. However, during the time of Mrs. Indira Gandhi as Prime Minister, there was gradual erosion in such conventions. Particularly after the Allahabad High Court judgement against her and after her re-election, after a brief gap of two and a half years, she was bent upon destroying all conventions in that behalf, with vengeance. Unfortunately, some Supreme Court judgements assisted her in giving complete set back to those conventions. When this happens, the sufferer is the nation.

The last point, I would like to mention, is the reply given by Dr. Ambedkar regarding the provisions of Directive Principles of State Policy incorporated in Part IV of the Constitution. A question was raised during the debate about the propriety of incorporating the provisions of Part IV in the Constitution, if those provisions were not enforceable in the courts of law. Dr. Ambedkar pointed out that the Constitution should incorporate the philosophy and the dream of Indian people as to what they want to achieve. It is not possible to bring into existence all improvements we want as there are bound to be economic and historical constraints. Hence, it was wise to include the entire dream of the people within the Constitution by way of the ultimate goal to be achieved, but at the same time, it was impossible to make them enforceable through courts of law. However, these principles would be nevertheless fundamental in the Governance of the country and it shall be the duty of the State to apply these principles in making laws. Dr. Ambedkar was, thus, believed in classifying provisions into two parts, i.e., enforceable and unenforceable. If we just have a cursory look at the provisions of Part IV of the Constitution, it would be obvious that most of the provisions are beyond the reach of attending them for various reasons, the principle being economic constraints. This was the most pragmatic view of life to take. There may be an occasion when the Supreme court can and should consider a wider proposition for the sake of interpretation of the Constitution, and by fetching at times indirectly bring under Part III (Fundamental rights), provisions which are expressly incorporated by the founding fathers in Part IV. Perhaps Dr. Ambedkar knew the practical difficulties as against the emotional approach. He thus, justified the inclusion of those provisions in the Constitution to represent the ultimate goal to be achieved, but not to make them enforceable due to pragmatic and down to earth consideration. On the whole, he has succeeded in handing over to us a very workable and equally flexible Constitution. It seems to be suited to serve all times and all situations. However, for its successful working, Dr. Ambedkar assumed that the provisions of the Constitution would be implemented faithfully and in the spirit in which they have been framed. If that is done, I believe that the Constitution would serve us well and Dr. Ambedkar's expectation would come true.

References

1. *Kusum Sharma, Ambedkar and Indian Constitution, 1992, New Delhi: Ashish Publishing House, preface, p.v.*
2. *Ibid.*
3. *K.I. Vibhute (ed.), Dr. Ambedkar and Empowerment: Constitutional Vicissitudes, 1953, Pune: University of Poona, p. xxv, para no. 2.02.*
4. *Golwalkar, Dr. B.R. Ambedkar and India's Constitutiion: Some Glimpses, p. 28.*
5. *Ibid, p. xxvi.*
6. *Ibid, p. xxvi.*
7. *K.I. Vibhute (ed.), op.cit., Justice B.N. Deshmukh, Dr. Ambedkar and the Constitution, Punme: University of Poona, p.20.*

□

Constitution of India and Dr. Rammanohar Lohia

—Raghu Thakur

The Constitution of India came into being through a long process during the Indian freedom movement. Since the beginning of the 19th century, it began to be debated that a Constitution for India ought to be formed by a Constituent assembly elected by the people of India. The Indian National Congress in its 1934 Bombay session passed a resolution on an elected Constituent assembly. The charge of this Congress session, its 48th, was in the hands of Dr. Rajendra Prasad. He mentions in his autobiography: "There was much debate in amendment to the statute as well. A committee was set up, which prepared the draft of the amendment. It had the particular role of Gandhiji and the newly formed Socialist Party."[1]

Dr. Rammanohar Lohia was one of the founder-members of this very Congress Socialist Party.[2] Born in Uttar Pradesh's Akbarpur in 1910, Dr. Lohia had by 1934 become a part of active politics. Till then, the policies and programmes pertained to the role of being a catalyst while remaining within the Congress. The Cabinet Mission comprising British officials arrived in India a little before Independence. It was based on the report of this mission that indirect voting took place in 1946 to elect a Constituent Assembly. The members of this Assembly were not elected directly by the people but by the members of the central and provincial legislatures. The first meeting of the Constituent Assembly took place on December 9, 1946. Only 207 of the Assembly's members took part in this meeting that day as the Muslim League had boycotted it. Dr. Rajendra Prasad was chosen as its president and Dr. Ambedkar the chairman of its Draft Committee.

Four Socialists from the country were elected to the Constituent Assembly.[3] It was doubtlessly decided in the formation of the Constituent Assembly that decisions would be made not by majority, but by taking everyone along. J.B. Kripalani wanted the functioning of the process to draft the Constitution to adhere to a common way in which all segments could be included. His idea of a common approach was supported by Dr. Suresh Banerjee with one amendment, which the Constituent Assembly accepted.[4]

After the transfer of power by the British rulers, debate continued over who would form a Constitution. Would it be the representatives elected by the people or the overall representative party – the Congress or any other party? Of the leaders of the Congress Socialist Party, Acharya Narendra Dev, Dr. Lohia and Jayaprakash Narayan decided on the grounds of principle to stay out of the Constituent Assembly which was not elected by adult franchise. The Socialists had created a special identity in the minds of the people in the nationwide Quit India Movement of 1942 called for by Mahatma Gandhi. For this reason, Gandhi wished that the Socialist leaders should be included in the Constituent Assembly.

Owing to the tension and hatred in the country's environment following Partition, Mahatma Gandhi was in favour of a Constituent assembly that would be set up on the basis of consensus. He even made efforts to mediate with and convince the Socialists. However, despite their respect for him, the Socialists did not agree to this role. In a public meeting in 1946 in Calcutta, Dr. Lohia did urge the Socialists to accept the membership of the Constituent Assembly. He was of the opinion that the British wouldn't free India so easily. There was still the need for a broader struggle, one that would be decisive. In his view, the Congress entry into the Constituent Assembly was an act of surrender and shameless compromise.[5]

All the country's Socialists gathered in Kanpur in January 1948 after nine years and elected Dr. Lohia as their president. The name 'Congress' was erased from the Congress Socialist Party, although Lohia opposed setting up a new political party. He was of the view that till Mahatma Gandhi was alive and provided leadership to the country, this should not be done. Dr. Lohia was in constant touch with Gandhi since 1939. His politics almost entirely dovetailed with Gandhi after Partition[6] Gandhi would regularly write to Dr. Lohia and call him to meet him (Gandhi). Once he sent a letter through Humayun Kabir, that said, "I am convinced that we shall soon meet some time at mutual convenience."[7]

There were some important issues in the process of setting up of the Constituent Assembly on which no firm decision was made then. Mahatma Gandhi conceived of Gram Swaraj and, for this, it was essential to strengthen the gram panchayat system. The panchayats had not been empowered to any extent till then. Dr. Lohia thought about a four-pillared system in which the centre, states, district and the village would be the four pillars on which the administration would rest.

He explained this concept in detail at the Hind Kisan Panchayat organised at Rewa, where he said that supreme power must not vest in the centre and its affiliated organs alone. Such power must be disseminated among smaller regions wherever groups of men and women reside. Dr. Lohia considered this to be essential to safeguard the Constitution. He did not consider this scheme to be merely the management of administration. It wouldn't be that Parliament and state assemblies would make laws, which had to be adhered to by the lower zones and village institutions. This would be a way of life that would be connected to all aspects of human life—like production, ownership, the system, planning, education, etc.[8]

In Mahatma Gandhi's view, Dr. Lohia was a learned man.[9] However, the governing system of the country could not take shape in accordance with the ideas of either individual. The Constitution accorded place only to a centralised system of governance in which all powers were given to the centre and provincial governments. Local institutions, districts and the gram panchayats were reduced to the position of elected beggars. Had Mahatma Gandhi not been assassinated on January 30, 1948, it was possible that effective provisions that would empower the panchayats might have been included in the Constitution. Dr. Lohia would say that if we wished to establish a people's government, it would have be done from the villages. A lot of work pertaining to villages would have to be done through the village panchayats.[10] Rajiv Gandhi upon becoming the prime minister brought in an amendment to the Constitution introducing provisions to strengthen the panchayat system. He had paved the way for providing financial and administrative powers to the panchayats. However, this effort is not adequate in the context of the present time and needs.

Dr. Lohia was in favour of smaller machines that would utilise less capital and generate greater employment. He called this small unit technology. But, such an approach to technology in order to generate employment could not find a place in the Indian Constitution along with the notion of development. This idea of his and Mahatma Gandhi's concept of gram swaraj and village and cottage industry was supported by the Bharatiya Jana Sangh too. Deendayal Upadhyaya said in Amritsar that no economic plan can be successful without making village, cottage and small industry its base.[11]

The fundamental commitment of both Mahatma Gandhi and Dr. Lohia could not find a place in the Constitution of India. In actual terms, it is these ideas that are realistic and idealistic, as well as in complete accordance with Indian conditions. One often feels that those individuals whom the political class declares to be its ideal or policy guides are put on a pedestal to be worshipped and then converted into images of stone. The irony is that this class regards them as untouchable when it comes to acting on their ideals. One such instance was the non-inclusion of any provision in the Constitution that would make employment a fundamental right. Gauging the state of unemployment in the country and feeling deeply about it, Dr. Lohia would remark pithily that if he could, he would change the country's flag to depict a creature that was half man and half animal.

Mahatma Gandhi conceived of value-based and employment-oriented education, which he called *buniyadi talim* (basic education).[12] Dr. Lohia forcefully made the case for equitable education for all. His slogan was: "President or peon, everyone must have the same education." But an equitable and free education system could not be implemented in the country after independence. The portion regarding education as a fundamental right was incorporated in the Constitution, but it remains no more than an ineffective provision. As long as the government does not accept the responsibility of making college, i.e., postgraduate education available to all and free of charge, this right to education will have no meaning.

There have to be constitutional initiatives for introducing provisions in the Constitution for a four-pillared and people-oriented polity of decentralisation, employment, education and healthcare. The Constitution has entrusted the Supreme Court with the responsibility of being the highest interpreter of the Constitution. The honourable court too has made a clear decision that the basic structure of the Constitution, which includes fundamental rights, secularism and directive principles of state policy, is unalterable. These are the country's permanent objectives which are perennial. It is only when these are altered that the abovementioned elements can be changed or amended. The people along with the governments will have to awaken in this regard. Only then can the pious objectives of the Constitution be attained.

The final draft of the Constitution was passed only with unanimity. Pakistan, which along with Independence was declared a separate country on August 14, 1947, could create its own Constitution only nine years later in 1956, and that too was a document which was formulated by legal experts. The people's opinion or elected representation had no role in it. This may perhaps have been the reason why Pakistan had to create a new Constitution only two years later in 1958 and then again four years later in 1962.

Viewed in this light, the Constitution of India must be regarded as successful in that there have been only three or four major amendments to it. One was the abolition of the fundamental right to property. Another was the 73rd and 74th amendments, under which panchayats were empowered.

References

1. *Rajendra Prasad; Autobiography; Sahitya Sansar: Patna, 1947; page 416*
2. *The Congress Socialist Party was founded in Patna in May 1934*
3. *Girish Mishra and Brajkumar Pandey; Dr. Rammanohar Lohia Vyakti aur Vichar, Vani Prakashan, New Delhi; page 40*
4. *Working of the Constituent Assembly, Volume 1; Speeches of J.B.*

Kripalani; December 10, 1946

5. *Girish Mishra and Brajkumar Pandey; Dr. Rammanohar Lohia Vyakti aur Vichar, Vani Prakashan, New Delhi; page 40*
6. *Omprakash Deepak; Lohia—Asamaapt Jeevani, Samata Adhyayan Nyas, Bombay, 1978; page 72*
7. *Collected Works of Mahatma Gandhi; Volume 90, page 265 (Gandhi's Letters to Lohia, April 17, 1946)*
8. *Surendra Pratap Yadav and Shyam Prasad Yadav, Dr. Lohia–Virasat Ka Sawal; Neeraj Books; Delhi, 1993, page74*
9. *Collected Works of Mahatma Gandhi; Volume 92, page 276 (Speeches during his prayer meetings, October 2, 1946)*
10. *Surendra Pratap Yadav and Shyam Prasad Yadav, Dr. Lohia–Virasat Ka Sawal; Neeraj Books; Delhi, 1993, page 73*
11. *Organiser, November 29, 1954*
12. *This is also known as the Wardha Plan, Nayee Taleem, Buniyadee Taleem and Basic Education. Gandhi formulated the Nayee Taleem plan on October 23, 1937 which was given a practical nationwide form.*

□

The Making of Indian Constitution and Deendayal Upadhyaya

—Dr. Mahesh Chandra Sharma

"The biggest flaw in the laws framed by the British Parliament was that these were the laws made by a foreign power. Contrary to that, the Constitution that governs India today possesses the greatest virtue that it is created by some people who were Indians to the core, and that makes it the duty of every patriot to accept this Constitution in letter and spirit."

—Deendayal Upadhyaya

Deendayal Upadhyaya entered Indian politics in 1950 when Bharatiya Jana Sangh was being established. Before this he was active in Rashtriya Swayamsewak Sangh for a decade. His writings during the period are focussed on the cultural concept of Nationalism. From this very point of view, he was writing about the Constitution when it was being framed. His writings during the period from 1948 to 1950 are relevant in this context. The first write-up *Swatantra Bharat ka Prastavit Samvidhan* (Proposed Constitution for Free India) was published in *Panchjanya*, November 18, 1948. The same magazine published his second write up titled *Bhartiya Samvidhan: Ek Drishti* (An Overview of Indian Constitution) on November 24, 1949. The third one *Bhartiya Rajniti ki Maulik Bhool* (The Fundamental Flaw in Indian Politics) was published in *Rashtradharma*, December 5, 1949. In the same year, he wrote his fourth article again in *Panchjanya*. It was titled *Laukik, Dharmik, Dharmarahit, Dharmanirapeksha, Adharmik, Adharmi Athwa Asampradayik* (Worldly, religious, irreligious, secular, non-righteous or non-communal). When the Constituent Assembly approved the whole draft and the Constitution became operative, he wrote his fifth article in *Rashtradharma*, February 2, 1950. It was titled *Samvidhan ka Kya Karen?* (What to do with the Constitution?)[1]

The first article has a wide sphere of implications. In it, Deendayalji analyses the structure of the Constituent Assembly. In 1946, the Constituent Assembly sat for the creation of a Constitution for an undivided India, but after the 'India Independence Act' of the British Parliament, it became the sovereign Constituent Assembly of a divided India. The draft put forth by this Constituent Assembly was established on the basis of 'Cabinet Mission Plan' and the Act of 1935. Deendayal Upadhyaya visualises imperialist mischief behind this establishment.

"The British left but through their political tactics, they divided India into pieces. With this division, they left for us the problems of princely states, communal representation and provincial self-rule that led to regionalism. Abundance of disruptive forces, fifth columnists and predominance of party interests remains a continual crisis for the national life."[2]

This establishment compelled India to adopt an unwanted federality. Deendayal Upadhyaya is a bitter critic of the federality of the Constitution. When we read the text of the discussion in the Constituent Assembly, it becomes clear that it was not Deendayal Upadhyaya only who thought like that. Pandit Jawaharlal Nehru moved the first resolution on 13 December 1946, it is Aims and Objective, which contains the provision of that federalism. This resolution is also referred to as 'the Manifesto of the Freedom of India'. It is an elaborate resolution. It was supported by Rajarishi Purushottam Das Tandon. Regarding this, Mr. Tandon said, "Residuary powers and political rights, which may conduce to unity and progress in our country, should lie with the Central or Union Government. The Resolution, however, gives residuary powers to the provinces so that the Muslim League may not say that we have done in their absence in an arbitrary way. Moreover, the *State Paper* published by the British Cabinet, which is the base of this Assembly, also said that the residuary powers should go to the provinces. We accepted it in the hope that the Muslim League will agree to work with us. To have the Muslim League with us, we have, actually, crossed the limits. Nay, I would rather say, we went farther than was needed, because the Muslim League aims at certain objectives which are absolutely against our objectives and this will cause a lot of trouble in the future. For the sake of securing Muslim League's co-operation, we have been accepting many things against our ideals. We should now put a stop to that and should not ignore our fundamental principles for the sake of coming to an agreement with the Muslim League.[3]

Tandonji deals with the subject in detail and speaks with much intensity.

After the resolution was moved and adopted, Srikrishna Sinha was the first to speak. He said, "I know sir, there are members in this Assembly—and I must confess that I am one of them,who believe that—there has arisen in India a nation, an Indian nation with an Indian culture and Indian civilisation. Such men certainly are only too anxious to have a republic of the unitary type in this country. There has been such a tremendous increase in the economic forces of production in the world that if full use is to be made of these forces in this world, it is necessary that we should have still larger political units which will transgress the national boundaries of national states. It is a realisation of this truth which makes many Indians feel that India must have a Unitary Republic. But inspite of that, if we want to have a republic in India which will be democratic and, at the same time, federal republic, it is because the framers of this resolution have taken care to take into account the feelings of our Muslim League friends."[4]

These two examples are symbolic only. The hypothesis of multinationalism inherent in federalism was the operative force behind the Cabinet Mission. It had to face strong opposition and the situation changed only after the partition was accepted. The result was that the federal structure remained intact but setting aside the idea of a weak centre, the rights of provinces regarding separate laws and residuary powers. The provisions regarding a strong centre and residuary powers for the center got passed. But Pandit Deendayal Upadhyaya was opposed to the very concept of federalism that had its roots in 'multinationalism'. He opposed this federalism till the end.

This is a large write-up. He raises questions over the sidelining of the Panchayati concept and calls upon the members of the Constituent Assembly:

"Each of the provisions of the proposed Constitution is about to be accepted. The members of the Constituent Assembly have a sacred duty to perform. Whatever they create today will make them accountable to the next generations. Therefore, it is necessary to bear the following issues in mind while finally accepting the Constitution:

1. The soul of India must not be suppressed.
2. We must not be trapped in intellectual slavery in the process of emulating others.
3. Fundamental human rights and the four freedoms must be protected. The path of all-round development for the Indian people must be kept open.
4. The endeavour should be to make India powerful in every way.
5. The forces of fragmentation must be destroyed. Indian unity must be furthered.[5] (*Panchjanya*, November 18, 1948).

The Constituent Assembly approved the Draft Constitution on 26 November 1949. Deendayalji wrote an article *Bharatiya Samvidhan Par Ek Dristhi* (An Overview of Indian Constitution) at the same time on 24 November 1949. He was writing it when the third reading of the Draft was being done in the Constitutent Assembly. He expresses his disapproval but the amendments in the basic draft fill him with hope.

"These few examples pertaining to the proposed Constitution make it amply clear that the Draft and the form of the Constitution is changing along with the ongoing changes in the political, economic and social changes taking place in the country and in the thinking of the members of the Constituent Assembly. We must admit that our Constitution is undergoing the process of development. This also happens to be the reason the Draft Committee introduces new resolutions in every session of the Constituent Assembly. This is natural as our country after attaining its independence is gradually coming into its natural state and recognising its form and soul."[6]

The three articles written after this, namely *Bharatiya Rajneeti Kee Maulik Bhool, Laukik aur Asampradayik* and *Samvidhan Ka Kya Karen* are full of incisive analysis. These articles written immediately after the framing of the Constitution go for a fundamental debate over various issues. But he himself demarcates the limits to the debate:

"Should we, therefore, boycott the Constitution? This is a question that would naturally arise. How can one endorse a Constitution which is going to cause harm to the country in the future? But, then, one has also to consider the fact that if we were to boycott a Constitution prepared by the people of our own country, this would set a wrong precedent. This would lay the grounds for cold, heartless thinking instead of emotional thought and reaction or action. Should we, therefore, endorse the Draft of the Constitution but work for its demise, as the Mahatmaji had done in the context of the Act of 1935? But endorsing anything for its eventual boycott is improper, and it can also be argued that a future Constituent Assembly can draft only a comprehensive Constitution, as no Constitution can be complete or perfect. In such a situation, there remains only one way out. That is to endorse the Constitution with intent to reform it."[7]

According to Deendayalji, only a government, whose power is limited to the constitutional discipline, is the *Dharma-rajya* or the Rule of Law. After the Constitution was framed, he remained active regarding its refinement. In this context, he kept propagating the five-fold spiral integral government that is decentralised from a profound centre to Panchayats and districts.

While visualising this concept of ancient governance, Upadhyaya refers to the concept of 'Integral Government' as 'District and Panchayat self-rule'. These Districts or Panchayats put together do not form the Indian Union, but all these are the constitutional units and the parts of the Indian Integral state. He does not consider it sensible to separate these units in the beginning and then artificially put them together into a federal union.

While replying to a question posed by *The Organiser,* he puts a counter question:

"Q. Jana Sangh has accepted the idea of unitary state that aims at the centralisation of power, then why in the manifesto the idea of democratic decentralisation has been relied on?

A. Unitary state is not synonymous with the centralisation

of power. The comparison between centralisation and decentralisation has nothing to do with integral or federal systems. If we decentralise power down to district councils, does that mean India is going to be a union of districts?"

That means, according to him, a federal system also can have the centralisation of powers, just like our present structure that stands on administrative bureaucratisation, and the unitary structure will provide democratic autonomy to all constitutional units which stand as its parts, thus providing an appropriate expression to decentralisation of political power.

Nowhere has Upadhyaya put forth his idea of unitary governance in a sequential manner. We, however, can draw inferences from the analysis he has done in different contexts:

1. The constitutional government of India will not be as a 'Union of Provinces', but as a 'unitary state' constituted as one country, one culture and one nation.
2. A 'unitary state' shall not be a union of units, but the units will be its integral parts.
3. All integral units shall have constitutional autonomy and administrative powers.
4. Panchayats and Districts shall have constitutional autonomy with their elected representative councils.
5. The central Parliament shall have the right to frame laws for the whole country. The representative councils of Districts and Panchayats shall frame the regional byelaws and the Parliament shall have the right to frame special laws.
6. Development blocks and provinces shall have their administrative powers. The provinces shall acquire power from the centre and the Development block from the District.
7. In this way, it will be a five-fold spiral administrative system—three constitutional and two administrative.
8. Power and sources of administration shall be regulated in such a way that every fold should be self-sufficient and enjoy its own responsible autonomy.

In the wide expanse of his ruminations over the Constitution Deendayal also includes so-called secularism, language, National anthem, etc., alongwith federalism and he expressed his thoughts from time to time through his articles. Besides being inspirational for the future, these views are full of possibilities for future research.

References

1. *Rashtradharma, February 2, 1950*
2. *Panchajanya, Margashirsh Krishna 2, 2005 (November 18, 1948)*
3. *Constituent Assembly of India Debates (Proceedings)–Voume-1, Book No. 1, (December 13, 1946, P.17)*
4. *Constituent Assembly of India Debates (Proceedings)–Voume-1, Book No. 5, (December 16, 1946, P.33)*
5. *Panchajanya, Margashirsh Krishna 2, 2005 (November 18, 1948)*
6. *Panchajanya, Margashirsh Shukla 4, 2006 (November 24, 1949)*
7. *Rashtradharma, Magha Shukla Purnima, 2006 (February 2, 1950)*

□

Elections are Important but not Enough

How India has learnt from Experiences of Other Countries

—Dr. Vinay Sahasrabuddhe

With the passage of time, connotations of concepts change, without much of a change in the core of the idea. What was luxury yesterday has become comfort today and comfort almost necessity. Individualism today also connotes yearning for personal space while the concept of Human Rights in modern times has covered recognition for personal choices as well. Similarly, due to the wider realisation that changing traditional male mindset is a pre-requisite for real gender equality, the issue has gained prominence in the entire gamut of issues concerning gender today.

On the one hand, while concepts are becoming more and more broad, wide enough to accommodate multiple shades of meanings they are also acquiring a more practical dimension. Modern-day popular thinking has shaped a trend to abhor anything that is just theoretical. Today, unless concepts manifest in practise, their impact remains limited and relevance, questionable at least in the eyes of the younger generation.

All this compels one to have a relook at the traditional vision of democracy. While the talk about deepening and widening of democracy continues to dominate democratic discourse, the reasons for the lack of ability to deliver on the part of democracy gets lesser attention than it deserves.

What distinguished Prime Minister Narendra Modi when he took over in 2014, among other factors was the fact he had an experience of over 13 years as Chief Minister at his command.

Acutely conscious of the factors of our Governance infrastructure that requires a relook, Modi courageously took risks even at the cost of some political losses. But one thing was very clear, he was here not to be lured by the comforts of status quo! The name of Prime Minister Narendra Modi invites sharp and polarized responses. He has braved huge criticism and he has also earned appreciations and laurels from within India and abroad too. But one factor – even his arch detractors would not be able to contest – is the fact that he is a disruptor, a creative disruptor. All along he has courageously fought against what could rightly be described as Status-quo-ism. Organisations like Association of Democratic Reforms also had some compliments to be offered to PM Modi. It said, "On the regulatory front, the record has been better. Early in its tenure, the government passed the Arbitration and Conciliation (Amendment) Act that smoothened out the wrinkles and established a time-bound mechanism for binding arbitration. It followed that up with a Central-level Real Estate (Regulation & Development) Act, or RERA. RERA needs to be notified in each state (since land is a state subject). So, this is still a bit of a work in progress. Paving the way for the GST with a constitutional amendment and a complex set of other steps and establishing a new Insolvency and Bankruptcy Code (IBC) must count as the two biggest legislative accomplishments. Overall, grade A."

It was, therefore, natural for him to make a fervent appeal for a nationwide debate on electoral reforms. That he chose the occasion of the celebrations of the Birth Centenary of Pt. Deendayal Upadhyaya in September 2016 at Kozikode in Kerala was also natural. In Deendayalji there was a strong advocate of democratic reforms in general and electoral reforms in particular. Deendayal Upadhyaya, ideologue and one of the founding fathers of the Jana Sangh, had similar views. He had stressed that parties should be giving importance to qualities like devotion and discipline, besides being 'wedded to certain ideals', with all their policies 'framed with a view to realising these ideals'. He was of the firm view that democracy is not just about elections, but also well-organised people, well-built parties and well-established conventions of political conduct.

In the present-day context, discourse on democratic reforms demands further strengthening for multiple reasons. True, democracy is widening. There is absolutely no doubt that the global community has marched towards making democracy a universally accepted model of governance. Nobody disputes that of all the available options, democracy is the 'available best' model. As pointed out by many, liberal representative democracy has emerged as the dominant system of national rule across the globe – at least in a formal sense. And yet, the gap between reasonable popular expectations from democratic governance and the actual performance of elected rulers seems to be widening more and more. Professor of International Relations at the University of Southampton, Anthony McGrew[1] is right in observing "While public disenchantment with elected politicians and the capacity of democratic governments to deal with many of the enduring problems – from inequality to pollution – confronted by modern societies suggest that all is not well within the old democracies."

When it comes to concepts like democracy and good governance, things become all the more complicated. This is because at least at the conceptual level, the idea of Good Governance was rightly considered as is inherent to the concept of Democracy. "When elected representatives of the people, supported by a majority are at the helm of affairs; the governance will naturally be people-oriented and, hence, 'Good'" – was the simple logic behind this consideration. But, in the last century, all over the world, while the acceptability and preference for democracy has increased manifold, efficacy of democracy in the specific context of making the lives of the principal stakeholders, i.e. the people – easier and qualitatively better has largely remained a chimera. It would not be an exaggeration to say that democracies have sustained not because of the overwhelming popular support, much less because they have developed a strong conviction about democratic values. Democracies have sustained because – regardless of the fact whether they are sham democracies or genuine – simply because they seemingly provide at least some window of opportunity for the people to have some say in selecting their rulers.

This certainly is a potentially dangerous situation! It does not effectively negate the possibility of any autocratic regime providing Good Governance being seen as acceptable to the people, who are fed up of a democracy that has failed to deliver. The most significant factor in such a scenario is the all-pervading cynicism. When people appear to be more than convinced about the inability of democratic governance to deliver anything significant, the atmosphere of cynicism deepens further. The only way to effectively overrule emergence of this situation is to make democracies – both established, as well as emerging or recently reformed – deliver!

Democracy and State Building

But, for democracy to deliver, first of all it must take a proper birth where it is non-existent, must be groomed and cultivated where it is a new born infant and must undergo a process of structured overhaul where people perceive it as ineffective on governance count. In all the three categories, what is essential is the consideration of what Pippa Norris calls as the Unified Theory where liberal democracy has to go hand in hand with State building. This Unified Theory has been elaborately explained later in this article.

Rose Revolution in Georgia, Arab Spring in Egypt and Jantar Mantar upsurge in India present before us three distinct cases, happened within the last decade. In Georgia, State Building was stressed to such an extent that democratic liberalism itself came under a dark cloud. In Egypt, neither liberal democracy could find its roots nor State Building was paid any proper attention. In India, the popular upsurges of 2013 remained extempore and short-lived besides being highly unstructured. In effect, the full-blown popular upsurge did reflect relatively strong credentials of liberal democracy, making political establishment sound irrelevant. However, in the process, the objective of ensuring reforms in State apparatus bringing greater accountability and transparency under the then leadership at the helm just remained unachieved. In a way, all the three examples offer us great learnings. In all the three cases, the outer structure of representative democracy was present all along, but the mandate failed in articulating, much less translating into reality; the popular yearning for bettering their lives.

In a way, recent happenings in all the three countries provide copybook lessons on two distinct counts. Firstly, they tell us how not to handle popular upsurges and cause shaking of popular confidence in mass movements. Secondly, they also tell us that mere conduct of elections – even if truly free and fair – is far from enough for responding to democratic aspirations of the people as the generation next expects democracies to go beyond elections. One can say with reasonable evidence at hand that Prime Minister Modi has proved that he has understood the yearnings of the Gen Next and has effectively worked to deliver the 'second-generation democracy'.

Responsive and Effective

From Georgia or Egypt and also India, events underscore what has been effectively theorised by Pippa Norris[2] as the combination of democratic responsiveness and state effectiveness. According to her, regardless of whatever the theory suggests, in practice, liberal democracies often prove imperfect on the count of accountability and good governance-related procedures "particularly where party competition is limited, electoral systems are manipulated, or channels of participation are skewed towards money votes over people votes." Norris further argues that "the institutions in liberal democracy can limit the abuse of power, but curbing Leviathan does not ensure that leaders will necessarily have the capability to implement effective public policies addressing social needs."

Norris further points out: "Moreover the initial move from autocracy, and the rhetorical promises commonly made by leaders during transitional elections, often encourages rising expectations among ordinary citizens. If these cannot be met by elected officials, due to limited state capacity, this can be a recipe for frustration."[3]

The Arab Spring brings to the fore the fault lines of as well as recent anti-corruption movements in India makes us keep our fingers crossed as nothing could be conclusively stated about the success or otherwise of these movements. Although some measures by the governments in some Arab countries as well as India and some of its State governments leave a scope for hope, popular turbulence in both these countries leave a lot to be desired.

Senior American journalist and political commentator, David Broder once pointed out that there is a widening gap between acceptance and effectiveness of democracy.[4] Analysing the reasons for the same, he says that death of ideology, decline of state, decline of religion, low esteem of politics as a profession, and the irresponsible role of media in general, are the causes behind democracy becoming less effective.

On the performance count, new and emerging democratic governments all over the world have, more often than not, met with failures. Even countries where democracy was supposed to be already well established, such as Venezuela and Columbia, became "destabilised and seriously threatened in the past decade by economic mismanagement, corruption, and state decay as established parties and politicians grew complacent and distant from popular concerns."[5] Many countries in South America, suffered a deep crisis of governance that inevitably resulted in sharp erosion in the authority and capacity of the state as also public confidence in democratic institutions. Similar is the case with some of the former Soviet countries. Even after a decade of democratisation, here, power is wielded with the same old style that smacks of authoritarianism, elections are still less fair and rule of law continues to be fragile.

Learnings

What Pippa Norris has analysed is significant in the context of India and Brazil too. Venomous statements of the likes of civil society leader, Arvind Kejriwal in India will come always under flack, and rightly so. But the emergence of the likes of Kejriwal in India and Marina Silva, also a non-traditional politician in Brazil has a lesson for all those traditional politicians. And happily, politicians like PM Narendra Modi understand this very well. No wonder, both, his politics and governance too stand apart.

The most distinguishing factor in the case of PM Narendra Modi's success is the organisational support structure that he had in the form of a well-knit Bharatiya Janata Party. BJP is now a cadre based party with a mass following. And here again, the way party was built and is being strengthened, reflects what Pt. Deendayal Upadhyaya had said. According to him, a Party is "not simply a collection of individuals but (is) a body corporate with a distinctive purposeful existence different from its desire to capture power. Political power should be a means rather than an end to members of such a Party." Presumably, in the context of governance as well, he had further said, "It is necessary that the Philosophy of the Party is not confined to the pages of party manifesto. Members should understand it and devote themselves to translating it into action."

Understandably, PM Modi's world view as well as his policies are influenced by Pt. Deendayal Upadhyaya's thinking. Deendayal Upadhyaya had his own opinion about Nationalism, Democracy and Socialism. About Deendayal Upadhyaya's approach to these concepts, Walter K Anderson has said, "Nationalism, democracy and socialism, in his opinion, were uncritically accepted by many Indians. Each had a certain merit, but taken alone each provided only a partial solution to the human quest for the good life. Nationalism posed a threat to world peace. Democracy, when linked with capitalism, gave free reign to exploitation. Socialism, the reaction to the linked concept of democracy-capitalism, robbed the individual of dignity and freedom. Each of these political concepts, he asserted, exacerbated material acquisitiveness, and, thus, stimulated greed, class antagonism, exploitation and social anarchy. If this is the case, what are the guiding political principles suitable to India?" Happily, PM Modi has found answers to this question where he has, through three conceptual mainstays of his governance-philosophy, successfully tried to make a difference to the lives of the people at large. These three mainstays include : Good Governance and Development, *Sab ka sath – sab ka vikas*, (all together, for development of all) and *Ek Bharat-Shreshtha Bharat* (one India, great India). The first, 'Good Governance and Development' has provided a robust sense of purpose to his idea of democratic governance. The second is his version of social justice where he underscores the idea of participative governance as well. The third is his definition of what is normally described as Nationalism.

The apparent choice that democracy as a theory offers has unfortunately – been negated by the principal vehicles of given democratic system; parties, electoral systems, media and now even the civil society. This has given rise to the feeling of having been trapped. Interestingly, the liberators in the form of democratic system have themselves apparently become chains.

Notably, PM Modi was able to grasp the insightful message of popular risings – whether in Latin America, Middle East, Eastern Europe or South Asia – before he took over as PM some five years before. Students of democracy need to understand the simple, yet powerful, message of the popular unrests in parts of the democratic world. This unambiguous message was that for any democracy to be successful, elections are important but not enough!

Five years before, even the democratic world appeared flat. Factors like strong visionary leadership with organisational skills; strategic thinking and ability to balance strong capacity to enforce reforms while ensuring greater public participation in a strategic manner were seen as in short supply on the banks of all, Kura (on the banks of which Tbilisi is located), or Nile in Egypt and Yamuna in India. But thanks to the dexterity shown by PM Modi, India now stands apart. In India, we traditionally believe in Raja or the ruler Kalasya Karanam, meaning the leader or the ruler decides the shape of the things to come. PM Modi has lived up to this notion quite remarkably.

References

1. *http://www.polity.co.uk/global/transnational-democracy-theories-and-prospects.asp*
2. *http://www.hks.harvard.edu/fs/pnorris/Acrobat/WhyDemocraticGovernance/Chapter%201.pdf*
3. *ibid*
4. *David Broder, Lecture at the Salzburg Seminar session 384, on Democracy. June 13, 2001*
5. *Larry Diamond, 'The Global State of Democracy', in 'Current History' December 2000, Vol. 99, No. 641 p. 416*

□

Historic Speeches in the Constituent Assembly

The Constitution of India is one of the most comprehensive Constitutions of the world. Despite being such well-thought, well-organised and even large it is unable to fulfil the wishes of many people, but their disappointment doesn't lessen its importance and relevance. Actually, our Constitution doesn't make a promise like fulfilling all the wishes of everyone and for always. Instead, it facilitates us to amend and enlarge itself in accordance with our future requirements and expectations. In a meeting of the Drafting Committee, Dr. Bhimrao Ramji Ambedkar himself said that the principles embodied in the Constitution are the views of the present generation. If coming generations will not agree with it, they would amend it according to their requirements. All the issues that have been raised during entire tenure of our Constituent Assembly, the replies came in forth to those and even the debates that took place, all are of the historic importance. Here is the text of some of the most important speeches.

A Free India can be Nothing but a Republic

—Pandit Jawaharlal Nehru

December 13th, 1946

In the Constituent Assembly of India Pandit, Jawaharlal Nehru moved the first Resolution in a session. It was regarding Aims and Objectives. Here is the text of speech.

Mr. Chairman, this Constituent Assembly has not been in session for some days. It has done much formal business, but more is yet to be done. We have been cutting our way and clearing the ground on which we intend to erect the edifice of a Constitution. It, however, seems proper that before we proceed further we should clearly understand where we are going and what we intend building. It is apparent that on such occasions details are unnecessary. In building, you will, no doubt, use each brick after mature consideration. Usually, when one desires to construct a building, one must have a plan for the structure that one wishes to erect and then collect the material required. For a long time, we have been having various plans for a free India in our minds, but now, when we are beginning the actual work, I hope, you will be at one with me when I say, that we should present a clear picture of this plan to ourselves, to the people of India and to the world at large. The Resolution that I am placing before you defines our aims, describes an outline of the plan and points the way which we are going to tread.

You all know that this Constituent Assembly is not what many of us wished it to be. It has come into being under particular conditions and the British Government has a hand in its birth. They have attached to it certain conditions. We accepted the State Paper, which may be called the foundation of this Assembly, after serious deliberations and we shall endeavour to work within its limits. But, you must not ignore the source from which this Assembly derives its strength. Governments do not come into being by State Papers. Governments are, in fact, the expression of the will of the people. We have met here today because of the strength of the people behind us and we shall go as far as the people not of any party or group, but the people as a whole – shall wish us to go. We should, therefore, always keep in mind the passions that lie in the hearts of the masses of the Indian people and try to fulfil them.

I am sorry there are so many absentees. Many members who have a right to come and attend the meeting are not here today. This, in one sense, increases our responsibility. We shall have to be careful that we do nothing which may cause uneasiness in others or goes against any principle. We do hope that those who have abstained will soon join us in our deliberations, since this Constitution can only go as far as the strength behind it can push it. It has ever been and shall always be our ardent desire to see the people of India united together so that we may frame a Constitution which will be acceptable to the masses of the Indian people. It is, at the same time, manifest that when a great country starts to advance, no party or group can stop it. This House, although it has met in the absence of some of its members, will continue functioning and try to carry out its work at all costs.

The Resolution that I am placing before you is in the nature of a pledge. It has been drafted after mature deliberation and efforts have been made to avoid controversy. A great country is sure to have a lot of controversial issues, but we have tried to avoid controversy as much as possible. The Resolution deals with fundamentals which are commonly held and have been accepted by the people. I do not think this Resolution contains anything which was outside the limitations laid down by the British Cabinet or anything which may be disagreeable to any Indian, no matter to what party or group he belongs. Unfortunately, our country is full of differences, but no one, except perhaps a few, would dispute the fundamentals which this Resolution lays down. The Resolution states that it is our firm and solemn resolve to have a sovereign Indian republic. We have not mentioned the word 'republic' till this time, but you will well understand that a free India can be nothing but a republic.

On this occasion, when the representatives of the Indian States are not present, I desire to make it clear how this Resolution will affect the Indian States. It has also been suggested, and the suggestion may take the form of an amendment lying down that since certain sections of the House are not present, the consideration of the Resolution may be postponed. In my opinion, such an amendment is not in keeping with the spirit of the times, because if we do not approve the first objective that we are placing before ourselves, before our country and before the world at large, our deliberations will become meaningless and lifeless, and the people will have no interest in our work. Our intention regarding the States must be clearly understood. We do desire that all sections of India should willingly participate in the future Indian Union, but in what way and with what sort of government, rests with them. The Resolution does not go into these details. It contains only the fundamentals. It imposes nothing on the States against their will. The point to be considered is how they will join us and what sort of administration they will have. I do not wish to express my personal opinion on the matter. Nevertheless I must say that no State can have an administration which goes against our fundamental principles or gives less freedom than obtaining in other parts of India. The Resolution does not concern itself with what form of government they will have or whether the present Rajas and Nawabs will continue or not. These things concern the people of the States. It is quite possible that the people may like to have their Rajas. The decision will rest with them. Our republic shall include the whole of India. If a part within it desires to have its own type of administration, it will be at liberty to have it.

I do not wish that anything should be added to or subtracted from the Resolution. It is my hope that this House will do nothing that may appear in Papers, so that, at no time, should people, who are concerned with these problems, but who are not present here, be able to say that this House indulged in irregular talk.

I desire to make it clear that this Resolution does not go into details. It only seeks to show how we shall lead India to gain the objectives laid down in it. You will take into consideration its words and I hope you will accept them, but the main thing is the spirit behind it. Laws are made of words, but this Resolution is something higher than the law. If you examine its words like lawyers, you will produce only a lifeless thing. We are, at present, standing midway between two ears; the old order is fast changing, yielding place to the new. At such a juncture, we have to give a live message to India and to the world at large. Later on, we can frame our Constitution in whatever words we please. At present, we have to send out a message to show what we have resolved to attempt to do. As to what form or shape this Resolution, this declaration will ultimately take, we shall see later. But, one thing is, however, certain, it is not a law, but is something that breathes life in human minds.

I hope the House will pass the Resolution which is of a special nature. It is an undertaking with ourselves and with the millions of our brothers and sisters who live in this great country. If it is passed, it will be a sort of pledge that we shall have to carry out. With this expectation and in this form, I place it before you. You have copies of it in Hindustani with you. I will, therefore, not take more of your time to read it one way, or, I will, however, read it in English and speak further on it in that language.

I beg to move

"1. This Constituent Assembly declares its firm and solemn resolve to proclaim India as an Independent Sovereign Republic and to draw up for her future governance a Constitution;

2. WHEREIN the territories that now comprise British India, the territories that now form the Indian States, and such other parts of India as are outside British India and the States as well as such other territories as are willing to be constituted into the Independent Sovereign India, shall be a Union of them all; and

3. WHEREIN the said territories, whether with their present boundaries or with such others as may be determined by the Constituent Assembly and, thereafter, according to the Law of the Constitution, shall possess and retain the status of autonomous Units, together with residuary powers, and exercise all powers and functions of government and administration, save and except such

powers and functions as are vested in or assigned to the Union, or as are inherent or implied in the Union or resulting therefrom; and

4. WHEREIN all power and authority of the Sovereign Independent India, its Constituent parts and organs of government, are derived from the people;
5. WHEREIN shall be guaranteed and secured to all the people of India justice, social, economic and political; equality of status, of opportunity, and before the law; freedom of thought, expression, belief, faith worship, vocation, association and action, subject to law and public morality;
6. WHEREIN adequate safeguards shall be provided for minorities, backward and tribal areas, and depressed and other backward classes;
7. WHEREBY shall be maintained the integrity of the territory of the Republic and its sovereign rights on land, sea, and air according to Justice and the law of civilised nations; and
8. This ancient land attains its rightful and honoured place in the world and makes its full and willing contribution to the promotion of world peace and the welfare of mankind."

"Sir, this is the fifth day of this first session of the Constituent Assembly. Thus far we have laboured on certain provisional and procedural matters which are essential. We have a clear field to work upon; we have to prepare the ground and we have been doing that these few days. We have still much to do. We have to pass our Rules of Procedure and to appoint Committees and the like, before we can proceed to the real step, to the real work of this Constituent Assembly, that is, the high adventure of giving shape, in the printed and written word, to a Nation's dream and aspiration. But even now, at this stage, it is surely desirable that we should give some indication to ourselves, to those who look to this Assembly, to those millions in this country who are looking up to us and to the world at large, as to what we may do, what we seek to achieve, whither we are going. It is with this purpose that I have placed this Resolution before this House. It is a Resolution and yet, it is something much more than a resolution. It is a Declaration. It is a firm resolve. It is a pledge and an undertaking and it is for all of us I hope a dedication. And I wish this House, if I may say so respectfully, should consider this Resolution not in a spirit of narrow legal wording, but rather to look at the spirit behind that Resolution. Words are magic things often enough, but even the magic of words sometimes cannot convey the magic of the human spirit and of a Nation's passion. And so, I cannot say that this Resolution at all conveys the passion that lies in the hearts and the minds of the Indian people today. It seeks very feebly to tell the world of what we have thought or dreamt of so long, and what we now hope to achieve in the near future. It is in that spirit that I venture to place this Resolution before the House and it is in that spirit that I trust the House will receive it and ultimately pass it. And may I, Sir, also, with all respect, suggest to you and to the House that when the time comes for the passing of this Resolution let it be not done in the formal way by the raising of hands, but much more solemnly, by all of us standing up and, thus taking this pledge anew.

The House knows that there are many absentees here and many members, who have a right to come here, have not come. We regret that fact because we should have liked to associate with ourselves as many people, as many representatives from different parts of India and different groups as possible. We have undertaken a tremendous task and we seek the co-operation of all people in that task, because the future of India that we have envisaged is not confined to any group or section or province or other, but it comprises all the four hundred million people of India, and it is with deep regret that we find some benches empty and some colleagues, who might have been here, absent. I do feel I do hope that they will come and that this House, in its future stages, will have the benefit of the co-operation of all. Meanwhile, there is a duty cast upon us and that is to bear the absentees in mind, to remember always that we are here not to function for one party or one group, but always to think of India as a whole and always to think of the welfare of the four hundred millions that comprise India. We are all now, in our respective spheres, party men, belonging to this or that group and presumably we shall continue to act in our respective parties. Nevertheless, the time comes when we have to rise above party and think of the Nation, think sometimes of even the world at large of which our Nation is a great part. And when I think of the work of this Constituent Assembly, it seems to me, the time has come when we should, so far as we are capable of it, rise above our ordinary selves and party disputes and think of the great problem before us in the widest and most tolerant and most effective manner so that whatever we may produce, should be worthy of India as a whole and should be such that the world should recognise that we have functioned, as we should have functioned, in this high adventure.

There is another person who is absent here and who must be in the minds of many of us today – the great leader of our people, the Father of our Nation (applause) – who has been the architect of this Assembly and all that has gone before it and possibly of much that will follow. He is not here because, in pursuit of his ideals, he is ceaselessly working in a far corner of India. But I have no doubt that his spirit hovers over this place and blesses our undertaking.

As I stand here, Sir, I feel the weight of all manner of things crowding around me. We are at the end of an era and possibly very soon we shall embark upon a new age; and my mind goes back to the great past of India to the 5,000 years of India's history, from the very dawn of that history which might be considered almost the dawn of human history, till today. All that past crowds around me and exhilarates me and, at the same time, somewhat oppresses me. Am I worthy of that past? When I think also of the future, the greater future I hope, standing on this sword's edge of the present between this mighty past and the mightier future, I tremble a little and feel overwhelmed by this mighty task. We have come here at a strange moment in India's history. I do not know but I do feel that there is some magic in this moment of transition from the old to the new, something of that magic which one sees when the night turns into day and even though the day may be a cloudy one, it is day after and for when the clouds move away, we can see the sun later on. Because of all this, I find a little difficulty in addressing this House and putting all my ideas before it and I feel also that in this long succession of thousands of years, I see the mighty figures that have come and gone and I see also the long succession of our comrades who have laboured for the freedom of India. And now we stand on the verge of this passing age, trying, labouring, to usher in the new. I am sure the House will feel the solemnity of this moment and will endeavour to treat this Resolution which it is my proud privilege to place before it in that solemn manner. I believe there are a large number of amendments coming before the House. I have not seen most of them. It is open to the House, to any member of this House, to move any amendment and it is for the House to accept it or reject it, but I would, with all respect, suggest that this is not a moment for us to be technical and legal about small matters when we have big things to face, big things to say and big things to do, and, therefore, I would hope that the House would consider this Resolution in this big manner and not lose itself in wordy quarrels and squabbles.

I think also of the various Constituent Assemblies that have gone before and of what took place at the making of the great American nation when the fathers of that nation met and fashioned out a Constitution which has stood the test of so many years, more than a century and a half, and of the great nation which has resulted, which has been built up on the basis of that Constitution. My mind goes back to that mighty revolution which took place also over 150 years ago and to that Constituent Assembly that met in that gracious and lovely city of Paris which has fought so many battles for freedom, to the difficulties that Constituent Assembly had and to how the King and other authorities came in its way, and still it continued. The House will remember that when these difficulties came and even the room for a meeting was denied to the then Constituent Assembly, they took themselves to an open tennis court and met there and took the oath, which is called the Oath of the Tennis Court, that they continued meeting in spite of Kings, in spite of the others, and did not disperse till they had finished the task they had undertaken. Well, I trust that it is in that solemn spirit that we too are meeting here and that we, too, whether we meet in this chamber or other Chambers, or in the fields or in the market-place, will go on meeting and continue our work till we have finished it.

Then my mind goes back to a more recent revolution which gave rise to a new type of State, the revolution that took place in Russia and out of which has arisen the Union of the Soviet Socialist Republics, another mighty country which is playing a tremendous part in the world, not only a mighty country, but for us in India, a neighbouring country.

So, our mind goes back to these great examples and we seek to, learn from their success and to avoid their failures. Perhaps we may not be able to avoid failures because some measure of failure is inherent in human effort. Nevertheless, we shall advance, I am certain in spite of obstructions and difficulties, and achieve and realise the dream that we have dreamt so long. In this Resolution which the House knows, has been drafted with exceeding care, we have tried to avoid saying too much or too little. It is difficult to frame a resolution of this kind. If you say too little, it becomes just a pious resolution and nothing more. If you say too much, it encroaches on the functions of those who are going to draw up a Constitution, that is, on the functions of this House. This Resolution is not a part of the Constitution we are going to draw up and it must not be looked at as such. This House has perfect freedom to draw up that Constitution and when others come into this House, they will have perfect freedom too to fashion that Constitution. This Resolution therefore steers between these two extremes and lays down only certain fundamentals which I do believe, no group or party and hardly any individual in India can dispute. We say that it is our firm and solemn resolve to have an Independent sovereign republic. India is bound to be sovereign, it is bound to be independent and it is bound to be a republic. I will not go into the arguments about monarchy and the rest, but obviously we cannot produce monarchy in India out of nothing. It is not there. If it is to be an independent and sovereign State, we are not going to have an external monarchy and we cannot have a research for some local monarchies. It must inevitably be a republic. Now, some friends have raised the question: "Why have you not put in the word 'democratic' here? Well, I told them that it is conceivable, of course, that a republic may not be democratic, but the whole of our past is witness to this fact that we stand for democratic institutions. Obviously, we are aiming at democracy and nothing less than a democracy. What form of democracy, what shape it might take is another matter? The democracies of the present day, many of them in Europe and elsewhere, have played a great part in the world's progress. Yet it may be doubtful if those democracies may not have to change their shape somewhat before long if they have to remain completely democratic. We are not going just to copy, I hope, a certain democratic procedure or an institution of a so-called democratic country. We may improve upon it. In any event whatever system of Government we may establish here must fit in with the temper of our people and be acceptable to them. We stand for democracy, It will be for this House to determine what shape to give to that democracy, the fullest democracy, I hope. The House will notice that in this Resolution, although we have not used the word 'democratic' because we thought it is obvious that the word 'republic' contains that word and we did not want to use unnecessary words and redundant words, but we have done something must more than using the word. We have given the content of democracy in this Resolution and not only the content of democracy but the content, if I may say so, of economic democracy in this Resolution. Others might take objection to this Resolution on the ground that we have not said that it should be a Socialist State. Well, I stand for Socialism and, I hope, India will stand for Socialism and that India will go towards the Constitution of a Socialist State and I do believe that the whole world will have to go that way. What form of Socialism again is another matter for your considerations? But the main thing is that in such a Resolution, if, in accordance with my own desire, I had put in, that we want a Socialist State, we would have put in something which may be agreeable to many and may not be agreeable to some and we wanted this Resolution not to be controversial in regard to such matters. Therefore, we have laid down, not theoretical words and formulae, but rather the content of the thing we desire. This is important and I take it there can be no dispute about it. Some people have pointed out to me that our mentioning a republic may somewhat displease the Rulers of Indian States. It is possible that this may displease them. But I want to make it clear personally and the House knows. That I do not believe in the monarchical system anywhere and that in the world today monarchy is a fast disappearing institution. Nevertheless it is not a question of my personal belief in this matter. Our view in regard to these Indian States has been, for many years, first of all that the people of those States must share completely in the freedom to come. It is quite inconceivable to me that there should be different standard and degrees of freedom as between the people in the States and the people outside the States. In what manner the States will be parts of that Union that is a matter for this House to consider with, the representatives of the States. And I hope in all matters relating to the States, this House will deal with the real representatives of the States. We are perfectly willing, I take it, to deal in such matters as appertain to them, with the Rulers or their representatives also, but, finally, when we make a Constitution for India, it must be through the representatives of the people of the States as with the rest of India. Who are present here? (Applause). In any event, we may lay down or agree that the measure of freedom must' be the same in the States elsewhere. It is a possibility and personally I should like a measure of uniformity too in regard to the apparatus and machinery of Government. Nevertheless, this is a point to be considered in co-operation and in consultation with the States. I do not wish, and I imagine this Constituent Assembly will not like, to impose anything on the States against their will. If the people of a particular State desire to have a certain form of administration, even though it might be monarchical, it is open to them to have it. The House will remember that even in the British Commonwealth of Nations today, Eire is a Republic and yet in many ways it is a member of the British Commonwealth. So, it is a conceivable thing. What will happen, I do not know because that is partly for this House and partly for others to decide. There is no incongruity or impossibility about a certain definite form of administration in the States, provided there is complete freedom and responsible Government there and the people really are in charge. If monarchical figure-heads are approved by the people of the State, of a particular State, whether I like it or not, I certainly will not like to interfere. So I wish to make it clear that so far as this Resolution or Declaration is concerned, it does not interfere in any way with any future work that this Constituent Assembly may do, with any future negotiations that it may undertake. Only in one sense, if you like, it limits our work, if you call that a limitation, i.e., we adhere to certain fundamental propositions which are laid down in the Declaration. Those fundamental propositions, I submit, are not controversial in any real sense of the word. Nobody challenges them in India and nobody ought to challenge them and if anybody does challenge, well, we accept that challenge and we hold our position. (Applause).

Well, Sir, we are going to make a Constitution for India and it is obvious that what we are going to do in India, is going to have a powerful effect on the rest of the word, not only because a new free independent nation comes out into the arena of the world, but because of the very fact that India is such a country that by virtue, not only of her large size and population, but of her enormous resources and her ability to exploit those resources, she can immediately play an important and a vital part in world affairs. Even today, on the verge of freedom as we are today, India has begun to play an important part in world affairs. Therefore, it is right that the framers of our Constitution should always bear this larger international aspect in mind.

We approach the world in a friendly way. We want to make friends with all countries. We want to make friends in spite of the long history of conflict in the past, with England also. The House knows that recently I paid a visit to England. I was reluctant to go for reasons which the House knows well. But, I went because of a personal request from the Prime Minister of Great Britain. I went and I met with courtesy everywhere. And yet at this psychological moment in India's history when we wanted, when we hungered for messages of cheer, friendship and co-operation from all over the world and more especially from England, because of the past contact and conflict between us, unfortunately, I came back without any message of cheer, but with a large measure of disappointment. I hope that the new difficulties that have arisen, as every one knows, because of the recent statements made by the British Cabinet and by others in authority there, will not come in our way and that we shall yet succeed in going ahead with the co-operation of all of us here and those who have not come. It has been a blow to me, and it has hurt me that just at the moment when we are going to stride ahead, obstructions were placed in our way, new limitations were mentioned which had not been mentioned previously and new methods of procedure were suggested. I do not wish to challenge the bona fides of any person, but I wish to say that whatever the legal aspect of the thing might be, there are moments when law is a very feeble reed to rely upon, when we have to deal with a nation which is full of the passion for freedom. Most of us here during the Past many years, for a generation or more have often taken part in the struggle for India's freedom. We have gone through the valley of the shadow. We are used to it and if necessity arises we shall go through it again. (Hear, hear). Nevertheless, through ill this long period we have thought of the time when we shall have an opportunity not merely to struggle, not merely to destroy, but to construct and create. And now when it appeared that the time was coming for constructive effort in a free India to which we looked forward with joy, fresh difficulties are placed in our way at such a moment. It shows that, whatever force might be behind all this, people who are able and clever and very intelligent somehow lack the imaginative daring which should accompany great offices. For, if you have to deal with any people, you have to understand them imaginatively; you should understand them emotionally; and 'of course, you have also to understand them intellectually. One of the unfortunate legacies of the past has been that there has been no imagination in the understanding of the Indian problem. People have often indulged in, or have presumed to give us advice, not realising that India, as she is constituted today, wants no one's advice and no one's imposition upon her. The only, way to influence India is through friendship and co-operation and goodwill any attempt at imposition, the slightest trace of patronage, is resented and will be resented. (Applause). We have tried, I think honestly, in the last few months, in spite of the difficulties that have faced us, to create an atmosphere of co-operation. We shall continue that endeavour. But I do very much fear that that atmosphere will be impaired if there is not sufficient and adequate response from others. Nevertheless, because we are bent on great tasks, I hope and trust, that we shall continue that endeavour and I do hope that if we continue, that we shall succeed. Where we have to deal with our own countrymen, we must continue that endeavour even though in our opinion some countrymen of ours take a wrong path. For, after all, we have to work together in this country and we have inevitably to co-operate, if not today, tomorrow or the day after. Therefore, we have to avoid in the present anything which might create a new difficulty in the creation of that future which we are working for. Therefore, so far as our own countrymen are concerned, we must try our utmost to gain their co-operation in the largest measure. But, co-operation cannot mean the giving up of the fundamental deals on which we have stood and on which we should stand. It is not co-operation to surrender everything that has given meaning to our lives. Apart from that, as I said, we seek the co-operation of England even at this stage which is full of suspicion of each other. We feel that if that co-operative is denied, that will be injurious to India, certainly too some extent probably more so to England, and to some extent, to the world at large. We have just come out of the World War and People talk vaguely and rather wildly of new wars to come. At such a moment, this New India is taking birth-renascent, vital and fearless. Perhaps it is a suitable moment for this new birth to take place out of this turmoil in the world. But we have to be cleared at this moment, we, who have this heavy task of Constitution building. We have to think of this tremendous prospect of the present and the greater prospect of the future and not get lost in seeking small gains for this group or that. In this Constituent Assembly, we are functioning on a world stage and the eyes of the world are upon us and the eyes of our entire past are upon us. Our past is witness to what we are doing here and though the future is still unborn, the future too somehow looks at us, I think, and so, I would beg of this House to consider this Resolution in this mighty prospect of our past, of the turmoil of the present and of the great and unborn future that is going to take place soon. Sir, I beg to move.

Source: *http://164.100.47.194/Loksabha/Debates/Result_Nw_15.aspx?dbsl=13*

□

Revolutionary Changes Possible

—Dr. Sarvapalli Radhakrishnan

January 20, 1947

The second round of the debates in the Constituent Assembly started with this speech of Dr. Radhakrishnan which took place after Pandit Jawaharlal Nehru moved the Resolution regarding Aims and Objectives.

Mr. Chairman. Sir, I have great pleasure in commending this Resolution to the acceptance of the House. From the list of amendments tabled, I see that there are three different questions raised: whether a declaration of this character is essential; whether this is the proper time for considering such a declaration; and thirdly, whether the objectives included in this Resolution are matters of general agreement or they require modification or Amendment.

I believe that such a Declaration is essential. There are people who are suspicious, who are wavering, who are hostile, who look upon the work of this Constituent Assembly with considerable misgivings. There are people who affirm that, within the Cabinet Plan, it will not be possible for us to affect either real unity in the country or true freedom or economic security. They tell us that they have seen before squirrels move round in a cage, and that within the limits of this Cabinet Statement, it will not be possible for us to effect the revolutionary changes which the country is aiming at. They argue from history that revolutionary changes are generally effected by violent action overthrowing established Governments. The British people were able to end monarchical despotism that way; the United States of America attained her primary freedom through direct action; the French, the Bolshevist, the Fascist and the Nazi revolutions were also affected by similar methods. We are told that we cannot effect revolutionary changes through peaceful methods, through negotiation and discussion in Constituent assemblies. We reply that we have similar ends; we wish to bring about a fundamental alteration in the structure of Indian society. We wish to end our political and economic dependence, but those who are strong of spirit, those who are not short of sight, take their chances – they make their chances. Here is a chance that is open to us and we wish to use this to find out whether it will be possible for us to gain the revolutionary ends by methods which are unusual so far as past history is concerned. We want to try whether it will not be possible for us to effect a smooth and rapid transition from a state of serfdom to one of freedom. That is the undertaking which this particular Assembly has on hand. We wish to tell all those who are abstaining, from this Assembly that it is not our desire to establish any sectional Government. We are not here asking anything for a particular community or a privileged class. We are here working for the establishment of Swaraj for all the Indian people. It will be our endeavour to abolish every vestige of despotism, every heir loom of inorganic tradition. We are here to bring about real satisfaction of the fundamental needs of the common man of this country, irrespective of race, religion or community. If the trumpet gives an uncertain sound, we cannot rally the people to our support. It is therefore essential that our bugle call, our trumpet sound, must be clear, must give the people a sense of exhilaration, must give the suspicious and the abstaining a sense of reassurance that we are here pledged to achieve full independence of India, where no individual will suffer from undeserved want, where no group will be thwarted in the development of its cultural life. Therefore, I believe that a declaration of objectives of this character is essential and it is not necessary for us to wait till this Assembly is fuller than it happens to be at the present moment.

Now let us turn to the objectives themselves. We resolve that India shall be an Independent, Sovereign Republic. On the question of independence, there is no difference of opinion. Premier Attlee, in his first statement, made on 15th March, said:

"I hope that the Indian people may elect to remain within the British Commonwealth. I am certain that she will find great advantages in doing so, but if she does so elect, it must be by her own free will. The British Commonwealth and Empire is not bound together by chains of external compulsion. If, on the other hand, she elects for independence, in our view, she has a right to do so."

The Muslim League and the Princes have all agreed to it. In the Memorandum on States' Treaties and Paramountcy, presented by the Cabinet Mission to the Chancellor of the Chamber of Princes on the 12th May, 1946, it is said that – "the Chamber has since confirmed that the Indian States fully share the general desire in the country for the immediate attainment by India of her full stature. His Majesty's Government have now declared that, if the Succession Government or Governments in British India declare independence, no obstacle would be placed in their way. They effect of these announcements is that all those concerned with the future of India wish her to attain a position of independence within or without the British Commonwealth."

All those concerned with the future of India, the Congress, the Muslim League, and other organisations and the Princes also, they all desire independence for India within or without the British Commonwealth.

Mr. Churchill, in the House of Commons, referring to His Majesty's Government's offer of independence, said on the 1st of July, 1946 – "However, it is another matter when we try to short-circuit the process and say 'Take independence now'. That is what the Government are going to get and they are going to get it very soon. They should not blind themselves to the idea. There is going to be no hesitation on the part of those with whom the Government is dealing in taking full and immediate independence. That is what is going to happen."

This Resolution on the objectives does not wish to disappoint Mr. Churchill. It tells him that the expected is happening. You gave us the choice to get out of the British Commonwealth. We are electing to go out of the British Commonwealth. May I say why? So far as India is concerned, it is not a mere Dominion like Australia, like New Zealand or Canada or South Africa. These latter are bound to Great Britain by ties of race, religion and culture. India has a vast population, immense natural resources, a great cultural heritage and has had an independent career for a very long time, and it is inconceivable that India can be a Dominion like the other Dominions.

Secondly, let us consider the implications of what happened at the United Nations Organisation, when the Indian Delegation, headed by our distinguished colleague, Mrs. Vijayalakshmi Pandit, so ably defended – the rights of Indians in South Africa – look at the attitude that was adopted by Great Britain. Great Britain along with Canada and Australia supported South Africa, New Zealand abstaining from voting. It shows that there is a community of ideals between Great Britain and the other Dominions in which India has no share. There is no sense of belonging in the British Commonwealth. We do not feel that we are all members, enjoying similar rights as parts of the British Commonwealth. Some of you may also have heard of the recent move launched by Mr. Churchill and Lord Templewood for a European Union under the fostering care and leadership of Great Britain. That also shows in what way the wind is blowing.

Yet, even though India may elect to quit the British Commonwealth, there are a hundred different ways of voluntary co-operation, ways of mutual collaboration, in trade, in defence, in matters of culture; but whether all these forms of mutual co-operation are going to develop in a spirit of friendship, trust and harmony, or whether they will be allowed to die out in mutual distrust and recrimination, depends entirely on the attitude which Great Britain will adopt in this crises. This Resolution about the Indian Republic seems to have irritated Mr. Churchill and his followers. Our Chairman today referred to one statement by Mr. Churchill and I will refer to some others.

When the debate on Burma took place, Mr. Churchill stated that the annexation of Burma happened during his father's Secretaryship, and that now Burma is given the liberty to get out of the British Commonwealth. He seems to look upon Burma and India as parts of his ancestral estate and now when they are passing out, he seems to be terribly disheartened.

On the debate on India, he asked His Majesty's Government to remember its obligations "to the Muslims, numbering 90 millions, who comprised the majority of the fighting elements of India" – truth is not rated high in Indian debates and international intercourse– "and of untouchables of anything from 40 to 60 millions." He refers to the representatives of the Great Congress Party as the mouthpiece "of actively organised and engineered minorities who, having seized upon power by force, or fraud or chicanery, go forward and use that power in the name of vast masses with whom they have long since lost all effective connection." A party of men who have braved the perils of life, who have suffered for their patriotism whose love of country and capacity for sacrifice are second to none in the whole world who are led by one who is today leading a lonely trek in a far off corner of India, bearing on his aging shoulders the burden of a nation's shame and sorrow, to talk of that party in the way in which Mr. Churchill has done is – I do not know how to describe it (Cries of shame). Mr. Churchill's outbursts are bereft of dignity or discretion. Provocative and irrelevant remarks, sneers of derision in regard to our communal divisions, have punctuated his speech on that occasion and on other occasions. I shall only say here that such speeches and such statements cannot prevent the end, but can only postpone it and thus, prolong the agony. The British connection will end, it must end. Whether it ends in friendship and goodwill or in convulsions and agony, depends upon the way in which the British people treat this great problem.

Republic is a word which has disturbed some of the representatives of the States in this country. We have said from this platform that a Republican India does not mean the abolition of Princely rule. Princes may continue; Princes will be there so long as they make themselves constitutional so long as they make themselves responsible to the people of the States. If the great paramount power which is sovereign in this country by conquest is now transferring responsibility to the representatives of the people, it goes without saying that those who depend on that paramount power should do what the British have done. They must also transfer responsibility to the representatives of the people.

We cannot say that the republican tradition is foreign to the genius of this country. We have had it from the beginning of our history. When a few merchants from the north went down to the south, one of the Princes of the Deccan asked the question. "Who is your King?" The answer was, "Some of us are governed by assemblies, some of us by kings."

Kechid desho ganadhina kechid rajadhina.

Panini, Megasthenes and Kautilya refer to the Republics of Ancient India. The Great Buddha belonged to the Republic of Kapilavastu.

Much has been said about the sovereignty of the people. We have held that the ultimate sovereignty rests with the moral law, with the conscience of humanity. People as well as kings are subordinate to that. Dharma, righteousness, is the king of kings.

Dharmam Kshatrasya Kshatram.

It is the ruler of both the people and the rulers themselves. It is the sovereignty of the law which we have asserted. The Princes– I count many of them amongst my personal friends – have agreed with the Cabinet Statement and wished to take their share in the future development of this country, and I do hope that they will realise that it is their duty to take notice of the surging hopes of their peoples and make themselves responsible. If they do so, they will play a notable part in the shaping of our country. We have no ill-will towards the Princes. The assertion of republicanism, the assertion of the sovereignty of the people, do not in any manner indicate any antagonism to the Princely rule itself. They do not refer to the present facts of past history of the Indian States but they indicate the future aspirations of the peoples of the States.

The next thing that we find in this Resolution is about the Union of India. The Cabinet Statement has ruled out the partition of India. Geography is against it. Military strategy is against it. The aspirations of Hindus, Muslims and Sikhs from the very beginning have been against it. The present tendency is for larger and larger aggregations. Look at what has happened in America, in Canada and Switzerland. Egypt wishes to be connected with Sudan, South Ireland wishes to be connected with North Ireland. Palestine is protesting against any division. Again nationalism, not religion, is the basis of modern life. Allenby's liberating campaigns in Egypt, Lawrence's adventures in Arabia, Kemal Pasha's defiant creation of a secular Turkey, point out that the days of religious States are over. These are the days of nationalism. The Hindus and Muslims have lived together in this country for over a thousand years. They belong to the same land, speak the same language. They have the same racial ancestry. They have a common destiny to work for. They interpenetrate one another. It is not a kind of Ulster, which we can separate; but our Ulster is a ubiquitous one. Even if we have two States, there will be large minorities and these minorities, whether really oppressed or not, will look across their frontiers and ask for protection. This will be a source of continual strife which will go on, as long as we do not have a United India. We realise that while a strong Centre is essential to mould all the people into one united whole, on account of the grievances real or imaginary, we have to be satisfied with a Centre which is limited to the three subjects, which the Cabinet Plan has put before us. Therefore, we are proceeding on the principle of Provincial Autonomy, with the residuary powers to the Provinces themselves. Events that have happened in Bihar and Bengal, tell us that there is an urgent need for a strong Centre. Yet as there are these difficulties, we propose to develop a multinational State which will give adequate scope for the play of variations among the different cultures themselves.

Grouping has given us a lot of trouble. But grouping is subject to two essential factors – which are the integral parts of the Cabinet Plan, a Union Centre and residuary powers in the Provinces; and in these Groups also we will have large minorities. Those who are insistent on the rights of minorities will have to concede these rights to others who happen to be included in the Groups. In a statement made by Sir Stafford Cripps on July 18, 1946, he said:

"A fear was expressed that somehow or other the new Provincial Constitutions might be so manoeuvred as to make it impossible for the Provinces afterwards to opt out. I do not myself see how such a thing would be possible, but if anything of that kind were to be attempted, it would be a clear breach of the basic understanding of this Scheme."

That is what Sir Stafford Cripps said. If any attempt is made to so manipulate electorates as to make it difficult for the Provinces to opt out, then that would be, in the words of Sir Stafford Cripps, "a clear breach of the basic understanding of this Scheme."

After all we have to live together and it is impossible to impose any Constitution against the wishes of the people who are to be governed by that Constitution.

There is also a reference to fundamental rights in this Resolution. It is a socio-economic revolution that we are attempting to bring about. It is therefore necessary that we must re-make the material conditions; but apart from re-making the material conditions, we have to safeguard the liberty of the human spirit. It is no good creating conditions of freedom without producing a sense of freedom. The mind of man must have fall liberty to flower and mature and to grow to its fullest Stature. The progress of man is due to the play of his mind, now creating now destroying, always transmuting. We must safeguard the liberty of the human spirit against the encroachments of the State. While State regulation is necessary to improve economic conditions, it should not be done at the expense of the human spirit.

We are actors today in a great historical drama. We are involved in it and therefore we are unable to perceive the large contours of it. This declaration, which we make today, is of the nature of a pledge to our own people and a pact with the civilised world.

The question was put by Mr. Churchill to Mr. Alexander whether this Assembly is functioning validly. Mr. Alexander said:

"I repeat the scheme for elections for the Constituent Assembly was carried out. If the Muslim League abstained from going there, how can you prevent a duly elected Assembly from going on to do its business?"

That is what Mr. Alexander said. There was some difficulty about the interpretation of the grouping. Much against its will, the Congress has accepted His Majesty's Government's interpretation. The only two clauses that remain are adequate safeguards for minorities, and a treaty on the problems which arise out of transfer of power. The Constituent Assembly is legally functioning. Every part of the State Paper has been completely accepted and if we are able to frame adequate safeguards for minorities, safeguards which will satisfy not so much the British or our own people, but the civilised conscience of the world, then while yet the British have the power to put it into action, they must give this

Constitution the force of law. It is essential that they should do so If after all these conditions are satisfied, if some excuse is invented for postponing the independence of India, it would be the most callous betrayal of history. If, on the other hand, the British argue that the Constituent Assembly has started functioning on the basis of the Cabinet Plan and they have accepted every clause of the State Paper of May 16, and have provided adequate safeguards for all minorities and, therefore, they should implement it, then it will be an achievement of history which will secure the co-operation and goodwill of two great peoples.

In that very speech which Mr. Attlee made as the Prime Minister on March 15th, he said:

"In the mass of Asia, an Asia ravaged by war., we have here the one country that has been seeking to apply the principles of democracy. I have always felt myself that political India might be the light of Asia..." Nay, the light of the world giving to its distracted mind an integral vision and to its bewildered will an upward direction.

Here are the two alternatives. Accept the Constituent Assembly. Take its findings. Find out whether there are adequate safeguards for minorities or not. If they are there, give them the force of law and you may get cooperation. If, after all these conditions are fulfilled, you still try to make out that something is lacking, the British will be understood as violating the spirit of the whole State Paper, and the dark possibilities which will lie ahead of us in the present world conditions, I do not wish to contemplate.

Source: *http://164.100.47.194/Loksabha/Debates/Result_Nw_15.aspx?dbsl=46*

□

No Reference to Our Culture

—Dr. Raghu Vira
January 20, 1947

A speech by Dr. Raghu Vira during debate on the Draft Constitution in the Constituent Assembly of India:

Mr. President, we the people of this country have secured our independence and freedom—We are going to have a Republic of our own as also a Democratic State. We have been assured that during our present life we shall be provided with economic prosperity and social progress. But, Sir, a question yet remains unsolved. I do not find in this Constitution any reference to the position of our ancient culture. Whenever any nation, such as British in India sought to consolidate their rule by striking deeper the roots of their domination into the heart of the subject nation, struck at the very cultural bonds of that nation and thereby enfeebled it altogether. They take three steps to reach this objective – an attack on the language, an attack on the religion and an attack on the historic ideals of the subject nation. This was what England also did with us. It brought our religion into contempt. But, I need not go here into the question of how it was done. But, it is sufficient to say that they gave no place to religion in the sphere of the State. Moreover, this significant word of the Sanskrit language was equated by them the Englishmen and their camp bearers to religion which is much narrower and restricted than the former. The fact is that Dharma never meant and can never mean religion. I think the word Panth may properly be translated as Religion but, I do not think that Religion can ever be taken to connote Dharma. But the Englishmen made a deliberate use of this for their own ulterior purposes.

The Englishmen imposed their language on us in place of our language. In order that our language be restored its due place and the Constitution be framed in it we felt necessary that all the things which the English people had deliberately destroyed in order to consolidate their rule here should be restored, so that our country may recover its soul again. But, I say with regret that the word 'Dharma' does not find any mention in this Constitution. When I raised this point with a friend here he replied that the Constitution was a law and it could contain only those matters which could be subjects of interpretation in law courts. But, Sir, my submission is that this country is not eager to have new laws alone, it wants earnestly to rise to higher planes than that of the laws.

There was a time, Sir, when our country had glorious place of its own and had a Dharma of its own. At that time Sir, we were high in the scale of nations – as a matter of fact we were the teachers of the world. But the Englishmen reduced that glory of ours to dust and ashes. The Englishmen, specially the English members of the Indian Civil Service wrote histories of India in which they showed our countrymen to have been primitive and insignificant, to have always been victims of division and dissension and to have always been defeated in battle. It was all the more necessary, that we should have made some effort to provide avenues for the expression and development of genius in the sphere of culture. But, this has not been done. I think, Sir, that it was absolutely necessary for us to have put this glorious word in our Preamble. We have the phrase the glorious triplet of words-Liberty, Equality and Fraternity from the political slogans of the French Revolution, but it is my submission, Sir, that these words have or never had a revolutionary appeal in this country, and so far I can judge these words would not be able to promote a revolution in this country. I do not suggest that we should not take anything from other countries. We can borrow from other countries but only those things which are likely to prove of use for our country. But, when we could give a place to these three words in our Constitution, could we not have given a place also to some of the ancient words of our own country. Could we not for example, use the expression Ram Rajiya in this Constitution – an expression which even our children in villages understand and appreciate. Again we have in our literature the expression '*Matsa Nyaya*' which suggests that the bigger fish should not swallow a smaller fish. It was a duty laid on the King that the rich should not be permitted to exploit the poor – that is to say there should not be exploitation of the people, nor the exploitation of the poor by the rich nor even the exploitation of the weak by the strong. But this significant word *Matsya Nyaya* – this ancient word which has come down to us since thousand of years – which connotes all these has not found a place in our Constitution. I may refer here to a suggestion which I made during the course of my conversation with the President of the League of Nations which I visited to in the year 1931. I told him that the motto of the League of Nations should be '*Ma Gradhat*' (do not covet) which is to be found in the *Ishopanishad* and the *Yajur Veda*. But such expressions and others which stand for ideals regarding the conduct and spiritual upliftment of men and which satisfy their physical and spiritual needs do not find and place in this Constitution. This country was the originator of the Republican system of government. Again it was this country which spread this system to the other parts of the world. Besides it had the biggest democratic organisation which was engaged in a system propagation of a new ideal. Its principal mottos were '*Dharma Sharnam Gacchaimi*' (I submit to the commands of Dharma) and '*Sangham Sharnam Gachami*' (I surrender myself to the Samgha or Order). These in effect that I dedicate myself to my duty and that I shall not and cannot run away from it. I ask 'should not such a motto have been included in the Constitution of this country?" It is my submission that this motto is to be found in our country from the Rigvedic time down to the present age. I feel that we have suffered from the malady of division and dissensions – the malady of internecine conflicts. I think that it is regrettable that in view of this malady the ideal of *San Gachaodhwam 'Sam Baddivam San Vo Manausi Jantam'* march together bound together are consciousness of Jantam has not been placed before us here. Another ideals we find in the assertion of King Ashwapati. He said:

namaste no janpade nakadaryo namadyapah nana hitagni no vidwanah

Which means that there is not thief or robber, no coward, and no drunkard nor any ignorant person in my State. But these ideals do not find any place in our Constitution. I therefore ask you, Sir, whether the mere fact that a statement is made in Hindi or in our language robes it of dignity and gravity, when we say in Hindi that two plus two are equal to four we lose their mathematical significance and we can retain the mathematical significance by expressing this idea in English. If not, I fail to see why we could not have expressed in our language the ideals which we have put in this Constitution in terms of English language, of an alien history and a foreign syntax.

There was another ideal, Sir, which was also followed in our country. It is contained in the verse which says:

karshayanang bhaved dandeyo yatranyah prakrito janah
tatra shriman bhaved dandaya sahasramiti dharana

It meant that where a common person could be fined for an offence one hundred Rupees, a king or a rich person should be fined for the same offence one thousand Rupees. The offence committed by a rich man was thus decided by a fine which may be a hundred times or even one thousand times than that awarded on a common man. But, I do not find any such thing in this Constitution. If the facts I place before you from the history of our country are not to your tastes you may not accept them. But, I do ask that if Sir B.N. Rau our constitutional adviser could go to Ireland, Switzerland or America to find out how the people of those countries are running their governmental system, could you not find a single person in this who was well read in the political lore of this country who could have told you that this country has also something to contribute, that there was a political philosophy in this country which had permeated the entire being of the people of this country and which could be used beneficially in preparing a Constitution for India. It is a matter of deep regret to me that this aspect of thought was not considered at all by us.

My time is running short and I would, therefore, conclude my speech after making three points. I am very glad that in the matter of language, which always is the repository of civilisation, a decision has been taken in favour of Hindi. All the friends here and all the provinces have voted for its adoption. I am very glad that some one of our languages has been adopted as the official language of the Union. I, however, feel sorry that even in accepting it, it has been provided that it will become the official language only after fifteen years. It is not only I who had felt sorry for this, but also several other friends also have felt the same. My sorrow and humiliation, however, folded hundred times when I come to have a talk with a few foreign ambassadors and diplomatic representatives in our country. They twitted me by remarking that for many years, the Imperial sway of English will continue in your country. I would appeal, therefore, friends here not to forget that Englishmen are still having their hold in this country. I know that not a single diplomatic representative of any other country liked this decision of ours for they know well the deep inter-relationship between language and Politics. The decision with regard to nationalities in Europe is always on the basis of language, and, therefore, they are well aware of the political significance of a language in the life of a country. When you give a place to English in your country you come logically to be bound up with the English People. Some French Friends, who came to this country, often asked my why there was no arrangement for teaching French or Spanish in the Universities of this country. I am sure that if there had been arrangement for the teaching of French and Russian in our Universities that would have given considerable satisfaction to our French and Russian friends because then they could have been sure that you would study their literature and value their friendship. I, therefore submit Sir, that it has not been desirable for us to have retained English for another fifteen years. The fact is that Hindi had been kept so far away out of fear that it may not enter the seat of government. As against this, English has been given a position in our Constitution which it did not have even during the British regime so much that not only the rule to be made by the Parliament would be in English, but even a rule made by the Delhi Electric power Authority to the effect that their tram service would function from 5 A.M. to 11 P.M. that would also have to be made in English under the provisions of this Constitution. This injustice to Hindi was not considered sufficient in itself. Even the alien form of numerals has been imposed on it. The fact is that we are being treated even worse than children. We are told that the form used that the form used in Roman is the international form of the Indian numerals. This is, in fact, adding insult to injury. I am sure that if Gandhiji had been alive he would never have accepted the retention of English by a provision in our Constitution for another fifteen years.

Besides, I find that real masters of this country still continue to be the Bureaucrats who should as a matter of policy be its servants only. Nor have we made any effort to eliminate litigation from this country. I am afraid that in the next fifteen years the roots of English influence in this country would have become twice as strong as the English people were able to make in their rule extending over a period of hundred and fifty years. The effect of all this is that the reins of power would remain in the hands of the English knowing classes. I am however hoping that after elections on the basis of adult franchise many people who do not know English would be returned to the Parliament and they would certainly dethrone English from its ruling position. I am convinced that that boycott of English is absolutely necessary for the progress of the country.

I would also like to say a few words about the boundaries of India. We have absorbed and assimilated the Indian States of the country. But we had permitted the division of our country and I do not find any limit in this Constitution that this country would become one again. Those who have been students of the culture and history of India know fully well that the natural boundaries of our country were on the Vakshu which in greek is termed Dkhum and which the Englishmen termed as the Oxus. But that boundary has now received back to the Ravi. Even in the days of Moghuls, Afghanistan was a part of India. Besides, a big slice has been cut from our heart – I refer to East Bengal being cut off from the midst of Bengal and Assam. I ask you, Sir, could we not strive to unite these again. I do not know how this unity would be brought about-whether by means of war or by peaceful means. Future will reveal the means to be adopted. But, I am afraid this is not an objective today. We do not dream that India that is now partitioned and fragmented would become one again, and that it shall not be further divided.

I feel that our indifference to our duty to the nation has been much greater in the matter of Kashmir. The Maharaja of Kashmir offered to accede to India. The people of Kashmir also desire to accede to India. More particularly, the people of Jammu Province of that state want to accede to India unconditionally. Again the people of Ladakh desire that they should be permitted to accede to India irrespective of the decision taken with regard to Kashmir. But, in spite of all this, we find that in this Constitution our Parliament still have no power to make any laws for that State. Our soldiers went to Kashmir to drive the invaders from there. They have shed their blood there and have undergone untold sufferings and hardships. Even then the flag of India does not fly in Kashmir. Side by side with it and their flag has to be kept flying there. But, I fail to see the reason for flying another flag there. It is a matter of deep regret to me that even after having spent so much money and shed so much blood we have not yet succeeded in making Kashmir our own. Even today in our politics Englishmen continue to wield great influence. We have no doubt sent the Englishmen away from our country but they continue to rule over our minds even now. I am reminded Sir, of the famous words of Lord Macaulay, which he had recorded when the education began to be imparted in English. He had said that as a result of western education a race of persons would arise in India who would be English in every thing except their skin. Alas the proof of the truth of the prophecy is before our eyes today. It is only foreign ideals that have been incorporated in this Constitution. It has nothing Indian about it. I, however, hope that some years hence this Constitution would not remain in the form in which it has been passed and that it will come to acquire a genuine Indian character, and would fulfil the basic and fundamental requirements of the people of this country.

Source: *http://164.100.47.194/Loksabha/Debates/Result_Nw_15.aspx?dbsl=492*

□

Constitution Embodies the Views of the Present Generation

—Dr. B.R. Ambedkar
November 25, 1949

The Chairman of the Draft Committee of the Constitution of India, Dr. Ambedkar answered the debates on the draft of the Constitution, which took place in the Constituent Assembly. His speech:

Sir, looking back on the work of the Constituent Assembly, it will now be two years, eleven months and seventeen days since it first met on the 9th of December 1946. During this period, the Constituent Assembly has altogether held eleven sessions. Out of these eleven sessions the first six were spent in passing the Objectives Resolution and the consideration of the Reports of Committees on Fundamental Rights, on Union Constitution, on Union Powers, on Provincial Constitution, on Minorities and on the Scheduled Areas and Scheduled Tribes. The seventh, eighth, ninth, tenth and eleventh sessions were devoted to the consideration of the Draft Constitution. These eleven sessions of the Constituent Assembly have consumed 165 days. Out of these, the Assembly spent 114 days for the consideration of the Draft Constitution.

Coming to the Drafting Committee, it was elected by the Constituent Assembly on 29th August 1947. It held its first meeting on 30th August. Since August 30th, it sat for 141 days during which it was engaged in the preparation of the Draft Constitution. The Draft Constitution as prepared by the Constitutional Adviser as a text for the Drafting Committee to work upon, consisted of 243 articles and 13 Schedules. The first Draft Constitution as presented by the Drafting Committee to the Constituent Assembly contained 315 articles and 8 Schedules. At the end of the consideration stage, the number of articles in the Draft Constitution increased to 386. In its final form, the Draft Constitution contains 395 articles and 8 Schedules. The total number of amendments to the Draft Constitution tabled was approximately 7,635. Of them, the total number of amendments actually moved in the House were 2,473.

I mention these facts because at one stage, it was being said that the Assembly had taken too long a time to finish its work, that it was going on leisurely and wasting public money. It was said to be a case of Nero fiddling while Rome was burning. Is there any justification for this complaint? Let us note the time consumed by Constituent Assemblies in other countries appointed for framing their Constitutions. To take a few illustrations, the American Convention met on 25th May, 1787 and completed its work on, 17th September 1787 i.e., within four months. The Constitutional Convention of Canada met on the 10th October 1864 and the Constitution was passed into law in March 1867 involving a period of two years and five months. The Australian Constitutional Convention assembled in March 1891 and the Constitution became law on the 9th July 1900, consuming a period of nine years. The South African Convention met in October, 1908 and the Constitution became law on 20th September 1909 involving one year's labour. It is true that we have taken more time than what the American or South African Conventions did. But we have not taken more time than the Canadian Convention and much less than the Australian Convention. In making comparisons on the basis of time consumed, two things must be remembered. One is that the Constitutions of America, Canada, South Africa and Australia are much smaller than ours. Our Constitution as I said contains 395 articles while the American has just seven articles, the first four of which are divided into sections which total up to 21, the Canadian has 147, Australian 128 and South African 153 sections. The second thing to be remembered is that the makers of the Constitutions of America, Canada, Australia and South Africa did not have to face the problem of amendments. They were passed as moved. On the other hand, this Constituent Assembly had to deal with as many as 2,473 amendments. Having regard to these facts the charge of dilatoriness seems to me quite unfounded and this

Assembly may well congratulate itself for having accomplished so formidable a task in so short a time.

Turning to the quality of the work done by the Drafting Committee, Mr. Naziruddin Ahmed felt it his duty to condemn it outright. In his opinion, the work done by the Drafting Committee is not only not worthy of commendation, but is positively below par. Everybody has a right to have his opinion about the work done by the Drafting Committee and Mr. Naziruddin is welcome to have his own. Mr. Naziruddin Ahmed thinks he is a man of greater talents than any member of the Drafting Committee. The Drafting Committee does not wish to challenge his claim. On the other hand, the Drafting Committee would have welcomed him in their midst if the Assembly had thought him worthy of being appointed to it. If he had no place in the making of the Constitution, it is certainly not the fault of the Drafting Committee.

Mr. Naziruddin Ahmed has coined a new name for the Drafting Committee evidently to show his contempt for it. He calls it a Drifting Committee. Mr. Naziruddin must no doubt be pleased with his hit. But he evidently does not know that there is a difference between drift without mastery and drift with mastery. If the Drafting Committee was drifting, it was never without mastery over the situation. It was not merely angling with the off chance of catching a fish. It was searching in known waters to find the fish it was after. To be in search of something better is not the same as drifting. Although, Mr. Naziruddin Ahmed did not mean it as a compliment to the Drafting Committee. I take it as a compliment to the Drafting Committee. The Drafting Committee would have been guilty of gross dereliction of duty and of a false sense of dignity if had not shown the honesty and the courage to withdraw the amendments which it thought faulty and substitute what it thought was better. If it is a mistake, I am glad the Drafting Committee did not fight shy of admitting such mistakes and coming forward to correct them.

I am glad to find that with the exception of a solitary member, there is a general consensus of appreciation from the members of the Constituent Assembly of the work done by the Drafting Committee. I am sure the Drafting Committee feels happy to find this spontaneous recognition of its labours expressed in such generous terms. As to the compliments that have been showered upon me, both by the members of the Assembly as well as by my colleagues of the Drafting Committee, I feel so overwhelmed that I cannot find adequate words to express fully my gratitude to them. I came into the Constituent Assembly with no greater aspiration than to safeguard the interests of the Scheduled Castes. I had not the remotest idea that I would be called upon to undertake more responsible functions. I was therefore greatly surprised when the Assembly elected me to the Drafting Committee. I was more than surprised when the Drafting Committee elected me to be its Chairman. There were in the Drafting Committee men bigger, better and more competent than myself, such as my friend Sir Alladi Krishnaswami Ayyar. I am grateful to the Constituent Assembly and the Drafting Committee for reposing in me so much trust and confidence and to have chosen me as their instrument and given me this opportunity of serving the country. (Cheers)

The credit that is given to me does not really belong to me. It belongs partly to Sir B.N. Rau, the Constitutional Adviser to the Constituent Assembly, who prepared a rough draft of the Constitution for the consideration of the Drafting Committee. A part of the credit must go to the members of the Drafting Committee who, as I have said, have sat for 141 days and without whose ingenuity of devise new formulae and capacity to tolerate and to accommodate different points of view, the task of framing the Constitution could not have come to so successful a conclusion. Much greater, share of the credit must go to Mr. S.N. Mookerjee, the Chief Draftsman of the Constitution. His ability to put the most intricate proposals in the simplest and clearest legal form can rarely be equalled, nor his capacity for hard work. He has been as acquisition to the Assembly. Without his help, this Assembly would have taken many more years to finalise the Constitution. I must not omit to mention the members of the staff working under Mr. Mookerjee. For, I know how hard they have worked and how long they have toiled sometimes even beyond midnight. I want to thank them all for their effort and their co-operation. (Cheers)

The task of the Drafting Committee would have been a very difficult one if this Constituent Assembly has been merely a motley crowd, a tessellated pavement without cement, a black stone here and a white stone there is which each member or each group was a law unto itself. There would have been nothing but chaos. This possibility of chaos was reduced to nil by the existence of the Congress Party inside the Assembly which brought into its proceedings a sense of order and discipline. It is because of the discipline of the Congress Party that the Drafting Committee was able to pilot the Constitution in the Assembly with the sure knowledge as to the fate of each article and each amendment. The Congress Party is, therefore, entitled to all the credit for the smooth sailing of the Draft Constitution in the Assembly.

The proceedings of this Constituent Assembly would have been very dull if all members had yielded to the rule of party discipline. Party discipline, in all its rigidity, would have converted this Assembly into a gathering of yes' men. Fortunately, there were rebels. They were Mr. Kamath, Dr. P.S. Deshmukh, Mr. Sidhva, Prof Sexena and Pandit Thakur Das Bhargava. Along with them I must mention Prof. K.T. Shah and Pandit Hirday Nath Kunzru. The points they raised were mostly ideological. That I was not prepared to accept their suggestions does not diminish the value of their suggestions nor lessen the service they have rendered to the Assembly in enlivening its proceedings. I am grateful to them. But, for them, I would not have had the opportunity which I got for expounding the principles underlying the Constitution which was more important than the mere mechanical work of passing the Constitution.

Finally, I must thank you Mr. President for the way in which you have conducted the proceedings of this Assembly. The courtesy and the consideration which you have shown to the Members of the Assembly can never be forgotten by those who have taken part in the proceedings of this Assembly. There were occasions when the amendments of the Drafting Committee were sought to be barred on grounds purely technical in their nature. Those were very anxious moments for me. I am, therefore, especially grateful to you for not permitting legalism to defeat the work of Constitution making.

As much defence as could be offered to the Constitution has been offered by my friends Sir Alladi Krishnaswami Ayyar and Mr. T.T. Krishnamachari. I shall not, therefore, enter into the merits of the Constitution. Because I feel, however good a Constitution may be, it is sure to turn out bad because those who are called to work it, happen to be a bad lot. However bad a Constitution may be, it may turn out to be good if those who are called to work it, happen to be a good lot. The working of a Constitution does not depend wholly upon the nature of the Constitution. The Constitution can provide only the organs of State such as the Legislature, the Executive and the Judiciary. The factors on which the working of those organs of the State depends are the people and the political parties they will set up as their instruments to carry out their wishes and their politics. Who can say how the people of India and their purposes or will they prefer revolutionary methods of achieving them? If they adopt the prophet to say that it will fail, it is, therefore, futile to pass any judgement upon the Constitution without reference to the part which the people and their parties are likely to pay.

The condemnation of the Constitution largely comes from two quarters, the Communist Party and the Socialist Party. Why do they condemn the Constitution? Is it because it is really a bad Constitution? I venture to say 'no'. The Communist Party wants a Constitution based upon the principle of the Dictatorship of the Proletariat. They condemn the Constitution because it is based upon parliamentary democracy. The Socialists want two things. The first thing they want is that if they come in power, the Constitution must give them the freedom to nationalise or socialise all private property without payment of compensation. The second thing that the Socialists want is that the Fundamental Rights mentioned in the Constitution must be absolute and without any limitations so that if their Party fails to come into power, they would have the unfettered freedom not merely to criticise, but also to overthrow the State.

These are the main grounds on which the Constitution is being condemned. I do not say that the principle of parliamentary democracy is the only ideal form of political democracy. I do not say that the principle of no acquisition of private property without compensation is so sacrosanct that there can be no departure from it. I do not say that Fundamental Rights can never be absolute and the limitations set upon them can never be lifted. What I do say is that the principles embodied in the Constitution are the views of the present generation or if you think this to be an overstatement, I say they are the views of the members of the Constituent Assembly. Why blame the Drafting Committee for embodying them in the Constitution? I say why blame even the Members of the Constituent Assembly? Jefferson, the great American statesman, who played so great a part in the making of the American Constitution, has expressed some very weighty views which makers of Constitution, can never afford to ignore. In one place, he has said, "We may consider each generation as a distinct nation, with a right, by the will of the majority, to bind themselves, but none to bind the succeeding generation, more than the inhabitants of another country."

In another place, he has said, "The idea that institutions established for the use of the national cannot be touched or modified, even to make them answer their end, because of rights gratuitously supposed in those employed to manage them in the trust for the public, may perhaps be a salutary provision against the abuses of a monarch, but is most absurd against the nation itself. Yet our lawyers and priests generally inculcate this doctrine, and suppose that preceding generations held the earth more freely than we do; had a right to impose laws on us, unalterable by ourselves, and that we, in the like manner, can make laws and impose burdens on future generations, which they will have no right to alter; in fine, that the earth belongs to the dead and not the living."

I admit that what Jefferson has said is not merely true, but is absolutely true. There can be no question about it. Had the Constituent Assembly departed from this principle laid down by Jefferson, it would certainly be liable to blame, even to condemnation. But I ask, has it? Quite the contrary. One has only to examine the provision relating to the amendment of the Constitution. The Assembly has not only refrained from putting a seal of finality and infallibility upon this Constitution by denying to the people the right to amend the Constitution as in Canada or by making the amendment of the Constitution subject to the fulfilment of extraordinary terms and conditions as in America or Australia, but has provided a most facile procedure for amending the Constitution. I challenge any of the critics of the Constitution to prove that any Constituent Assembly anywhere in the world has, in the circumstances in which this country finds itself, provided such a facile procedure for the amendment of the Constitution. If those who are dissatisfied with the Constitution have only to obtain a 2/3 majority and if they cannot obtain even a two-thirds majority in the parliament elected on adult franchise in their favour, their dissatisfaction with the Constitution cannot be deemed to be shared by the general public.

There is only one point of constitutional import to which I propose to make a reference. A serious complaint is made on the ground that there is too much of centralisation and that the States have been reduced to Municipalities. It is clear that this view is not only an exaggeration, but is also founded on a misunderstanding of what exactly the Constitution contrives to do. As to the relation between the Centre and the States, it is necessary to bear in mind the fundamental principle on which it rests. The basic principle of Federalism is that the Legislative and Executive authority is partitioned between the Centre and the States not by any law to be made by the Centre but by the Constitution itself. This is what Constitution does. The States under our Constitution are in no way dependent upon the Centre for their legislative or executive authority. The Centre and the States are co-equal in this matter. It is difficult to see how such a Constitution can be called centralism. It may be that the Constitution assigns to the Centre too large field for the operation of its legislative and executive authority than is to be found in any other federal Constitution. It may be that the residuary powers are given to the Centre and not to the States. But, these features do not form the essence of federalism. The chief mark of federalism as I said lies in the partition of the legislative and executive authority between the Centre and the Units by the Constitution. This is the principle embodied in our Constitution. There can be no mistake about it. It is, therefore, wrong to say that the States have been placed under the Centre. Centre cannot by its own will alter the boundary of that partition. Nor can the Judiciary. For as has been well said, "Courts may modify, they cannot replace, they can revise earlier interpretations as new arguments, new points of view are presented, they can shift the dividing line in marginal cases, but there are barriers they cannot pass, definite assignments of power they cannot reallocate. They can give a broadening construction of existing powers, but they cannot assign to one authority powers explicitly granted to another."

The first charge of centralisation defeating federalism must therefore fall. The second charge is that the Centre has been given the power to override the States. This charge must be admitted. But before condemning the Constitution for containing such overriding powers, certain considerations must be borne in mind. The first is that these overriding powers do not form the normal feature of the Constitution. Their use and operation are expressly confined to emergencies only. The second consideration is: Could we avoid giving overriding powers to the Centre when an emergency has arisen? Those who do not admit the justification for such overriding powers to the Centre even in an emergency do not seem to have a clear idea of the problem which lies at the root of the matter. The problem is so clearly set out by a writer in that well-known magazine 'The Round Table' in its issue of December 1935 that I offer no apology for quoting the following extract from it. Says the writer, "Political systems are a complex of rights and duties resting ultimately on the question, to whom, or to what authority, does the citizen owe allegiance. In normal affairs the question is not present, for the law works smoothly, and a man, goes about his business obeying one authority in this set of matters and another authority in that. But, in a moment of crisis, a conflict of claims may arise, and it is then apparent that ultimate allegiance cannot be divided. The issue of allegiance cannot be determined in the last resort by a juristic interpretation of statutes. The law must conform to the facts or so much the worse for the law. When all formalism is stripped away, the bare question is, what authority commands the residual loyalty of the citizen. Is it the Centre or the Constituent State?"

The solution of this problem depends upon one's answer to this question which is the crux of the problem. There can be no doubt that in the opinion of the vast majority of the people, the residual loyalty of the citizen in an emergency must be to the Centre and not to the Constituent States. For it is only the Centre which can work for a common end and for the general interests of the country as a whole. Herein lies the justification for giving to all Centre certain overriding powers to be used in an emergency.

And, after all, what is the obligation imposed upon the Constituent States by these emergency powers? No more than this – that in an emergency, they should take into consideration alongside their own local interests, the opinions and interests of the nation as a whole. Only those who have not understood the problem can complain against it.

Here I could have ended. But my mind is so full of the future of our country that I feel I ought to take this occasion to give expression to some of my reflections thereon. On 26th January 1950, India will be an independent country (Cheers). What would happen to her independence? Will she maintain her independence or will she lose it again? This is the first thought that comes to my mind. It is not that India was never an independent country. The point is that she once lost the independence she had. Will she lose it a second time? It is this thought which makes me most anxious for the future. What perturbs me greatly is the fact that not only India has once before lost her independence, but she lost it by the infidelity and treachery of some of her own people. In the invasion of Sind by Mahommed-Bin-Kasim, the military commanders of King Dahar accepted bribes from the agents of Mahommed-Bin-Kasim and refused to fight on the side of their King. It was Jaichand who invited Mahommed Gohri to invade India and fight against Prithvi Raj and promised him the help of himself and the Solanki Kings. When Shivaji was fighting for the liberation of Hindus, the other Maratha noblemen and the Rajput Kings were fighting the battle on the side of Moghul Emperors. When the British were trying to destroy the Sikh Rulers, Gulab Singh, their principal commander sat silent and did not help to save the Sikh Kingdom. In 1857, when a large part of India had declared a war of independence against the British, the Sikhs stood and watched the event as silent spectators.

Will history repeat itself? It is this thought which fills me with anxiety. This anxiety is deepened by the realisation of the fact that in addition to our old enemies in the form of castes and creeds we are going to have many political parties with diverse and opposing political creeds. Will Indian place the country above their creed or will they place creed above country? I do not know. But, this much is certain that if the parties place creed above country, our independence will be put in jeopardy a second time and probably be lost for ever. This eventuality we must all resolutely guard against. We must be determined to defend our independence with the last drop of our blood. (Cheers)

On the 26th of January 1950, India would be a democratic country in the sense that India from that day would have a government of the people, by the people and for the people. The same thought comes to my mind. What would happen to her democratic Constitution? Will she be able to maintain it or will she lose it again? This is the second thought that comes to my mind and makes me as anxious as the first.

It is not that India did not know what is Democracy. There was a time when India was studded with republics, and even where there were monarchies, they were either elected or limited. They were never absolute. It is not that India did not know Parliaments or Parliamentary Procedure. A study of the Buddhist Bhikshu Sanghas discloses that not only there were Parliaments-for the Sanghas were nothing but Parliaments – but the Sanghas knew and observed all the rules of Parliamentary Procedure known to modern times. They had rules regarding seating arrangements, rules regarding Motions, Resolutions, Quorum, Whip, Counting of Votes, Voting by Ballot, Censure Motion, Regularisation, Res Judicata, etc. Although these rules of Parliamentary Procedure were applied by the Buddha to the meetings of the Sanghas, he must have borrowed them from the rules of the Political Assemblies functioning in the country in his time.

This democratic system India lost. Will she lost it a second time? I do not know. But it is quite possible in a country like India – where democracy from its long disuse must be regarded as something quite new – there is danger of democracy giving place to dictatorship. It is quite possible for this new born democracy to retain its form, but give place to dictatorship in fact. If there is a landslide, the danger of the second possibility becoming actuality is much greater.

If we wish to maintain democracy not merely in form, but also in fact, what must we do? The first thing in my judgement we must do is to hold fast to constitutional methods of achieving our social and economic objectives. It means we must abandon the bloody methods of revolution. It means that we must abandon the method of civil disobedience, non-cooperation and satyagraha. When there was no way left for constitutional methods for achieving economic and social objectives, there was a great deal of justification for unconstitutional methods. But, where constitutional methods are open, there can be no justification for these unconstitutional methods. These methods are nothing but the Grammar of Anarchy and the sooner they are abandoned, the better for us.

The second thing we must do is to observe the caution which John Stuart Mill has given to all who are interested in the maintenance of democracy, namely, not "to lay their liberties at the feet of even a great man, or to trust him with powers which enable him to subvert their institutions." There is nothing wrong in being grateful to great men who have rendered life-long services to the country. But there are limits to gratefulness. As has been well said by the Irish Patriot Daniel O'Connel, no man can be grateful at the cost of his honour, no woman can be grateful at the cost of her chastity and no nation can be grateful at the cost of its liberty. This caution is far more necessary in the case of India than in the case of any other country. For, in India, Bhakti or what may be called the path of devotion or hero-worship, plays a part in its politics unequalled in magnitude by the part it plays in the politics of any other country in the world. Bhakti in religion may be a road to the salvation of the soul. But in politics, Bhakti or hero-worship is a sure road to degradation and to eventual dictatorship.

The third thing we must do is not to be content with mere political democracy. We must make our political democracy a social democracy as well. Political democracy cannot last unless there lies at the base of it social democracy. What does social democracy mean? It means a way of life which recognizes liberty, equality and fraternity as the principles of life. These principles of liberty, equality and fraternity are not to be treated as separate items in a trinity. They form a union of trinity in the sense that to divorce one from the other is to defeat the very purpose of democracy. Liberty cannot be divorced from equality; equality cannot be divorced from liberty. Nor can liberty and equality be divorced from fraternity. Without equality, liberty would produce the supremacy of the few over the many. Equality without liberty would kill individual initiative. Without fraternity, liberty equality could not become a natural course of things. It would require a constable to enforce them. We must begin by acknowledging the fact that there is complete absence of two things in Indian Society. One of these is equality. On the social plane, we have in India a society based on the principle of graded inequality which elevation for some and degradation for others. On the economic plane, we have a society in which there are some who have immense wealth as against many who live in abject poverty. On the 26th of January 1950, we are going to enter into a life of contradictions. In politics we will have equality and in social and economic life we will have inequality. In politics we will be recognizing the principle of one man one vote and one vote one value. In our social and economic life, we shall, by reason of our social and economic structure, continue to deny the principle of one man one value. How long shall we continue to live this life of contradictions? How long shall we continue to deny equality in our social and economic life? If we continue to deny it for long, we will do so only by putting our political democracy in peril. We must remove this contradiction at the earliest possible moment or else those who suffer from inequality will blow up the structure of political democracy which is Assembly has to laboriously built up.

The second thing we are wanting in is recognition of the principle of fraternity. What does fraternity mean? Fraternity means a sense of common brotherhood of all Indians– if Indians being one people. It is the principle which gives unity and solidarity to social life. It is a difficult thing to achieve. How difficult it is, can be realised from the story related by James Bryce in his volume on American Commonwealth about the United States of America.

The story is - I propose to recount it in the words of Bryce himself – that – "Some years ago the American Protestant Episcopal Church was occupied at its triennial Convention in revising its liturgy. It was thought desirable to introduce among the short sentence prayers a prayer for the whole people, and an eminent New England divine proposed the words `O Lord, bless our nation'. Accepted one afternoon, on the spur of the moment, the sentence was brought up next day for reconsideration, when so many objections were raised by the laity to the word nation' as importing too definite a recognition of national unity, that it was dropped, and instead there were adopted the words `O Lord, bless these United States."

There was so little solidarity in the U.S.A. at the time when this incident occurred that the people of America did not think that they were a nation. If the people of the United States could not feel that they were a nation, how difficult it is for Indians to think that they are a nation. I remember the days when politically minded Indians, resented the expression 'the people of India'. They preferred the expression 'the Indian nation'. I am of opinion that in believing that we are a nation, we are cherishing a great delusion. How can people divided into several thousands of castes be a nation? The sooner we realise that we are not as yet a nation in the social and psychological sense of the world, the better for us. For then only we shall realise the necessity of becoming a nation and seriously think of ways and means of realising the goal. The realisation of this goal is going to be very difficult – far more difficult than it has been in the United States. The United States has no caste problem. In India there are castes. The castes are anti-national. In the first place because they bring about separation in social life. They are antinational also because they generate jealousy and antipathy between caste and caste. But, we must overcome all these difficulties if we wish to become a nation in reality. For fraternity can be a fact only when there is a nation. Without fraternity, equality and liberty will be no deeper than coats of paint.

These are my reflections about the tasks that lie ahead of us. They may not be very pleasant to some. But, there can be no gainsaying that political power in this country has too long been the monopoly of a few and the many are only beasts of burden, but also beasts of prey. This monopoly has not merely deprived them of their chance of betterment; it has sapped them of what may be called the significance of life. These down-trodden classes are tired of being governed. They are impatient to govern themselves. This urge for self-realisation in the down-trodden classes must not be allowed to devolve into a class struggle or class war. It would lead to a division of the House. That would indeed be a day of disaster. For, as has been well said by Abraham Lincoln, a House divided against itself cannot stand very long. Therefore, the sooner, room is made for the realisation of their aspiration, the better for the few, the better for the country, the better for the maintenance for its independence and the better for the continuance of its democratic structure. This can only be done by the establishment of equality and fraternity in all spheres of life. That is why, I have laid so much stresses on them.

I do not wish to weary the House any further. Independence is no doubt a matter of joy. But let us not forget that this has thrown on us great responsibilities. By independence, we have lost the excuse of blaming the British for anything going wrong. If hereafter things go wrong, we will have nobody to blame except ourselves. There is great danger of things going wrong. Times are fast changing. People are being moved by new ideologies. They are getting tired of Government by the people. They are prepared to have Governments for the people and are indifferent whether it is Government of the people and by the people. If we wish to preserve the Constitution in which we have sought to enshrine the principle of Government of the people, for the people and by the people, let us resolve not to be tardy in the recognition of the evils that lie across our path and which induce people to prefer Government for the people to Government by the people, nor to be weak in our initiative to remove them. That is the only way to serve the country. I know of no better.

Source: *http://164.100.47.194/Loksabha/Debates/Result_Nw_15.aspx?dbsl=503*

□

A Law-giver Requires Intellectual Equipment

—Dr. Rajendra Prasad
November 26, 1949

Presidential address by Dr. Rajendra Prasad on the draft of the Constitution in the Constituent Assmebly of India. His speech:

I desire to congratulate the Assembly on accomplishing a task of such tremendous magnitude. It is not my purpose to appraise the value of the work that the Assembly has done or the merits or demerits of the Constitution which it has framed. I am content to leave that to others and to posterity. I shall attempt only to point out some of its salient features and the method which we have pursued in framing the Constitution.

Before I do that, I would like to mention some facts which will show the tremendousness of the task which we undertook some three years ago. If you consider the population with which the Assembly has had to deal, you will find that it is more than the population of the whole of Europe minus Russia, being 319 millions as against 317 millions. The countries of Europe have never been able to join together or coalesce even in a Confederacy, much less under one unitary Government. Here, in spite of the size of the population and the country, we have succeeded in framing a Constitution which covers the whole of it. Apart from the size, there were other difficulties which were inherent in the problem itself. We have got many communities living in this country. We have got many languages prevalent in different parts of it. We have got other kinds of differences dividing the people in the different parts from one another. We had to make provision not only for areas which are advanced educationally and economically; we had also to make provision for backward people like the Tribes and for backward areas like the Tribal areas. The communal problem had been one of the knottiest problems which the country has had before it for a pretty long time. The Second Round Table Conference which was attended by Mahatma Gandhi failed because the communal problem could not be solved. The subsequent history of the country is too recent to require narration here; but we know this that as a result, the country has had to be divided and we have lost two big portions in the north-east and north-west.

Another problem of great magnitude was the problem of the Indian States. When the British came to India, they did not conquer the country as a whole or at one stroke. They got bits of it from time to time. The bits which came into their direct possession and control came to be known as British India, but a considerable portion remained under the rule and control of the Indian Princes. The British thought at the time that it was not necessary or profitable for them to take direct control of those territories, and they allowed the old Rulers to continue subject to their suzerainty. But they entered into various kinds of treaties and engagements with them. We had something near six hundred States covering more than one-third of the territory of India and one-fourth of the population of the country. They varied in size from small tiny principalities to big States like Mysore, Hyderabad, Kashmir, etc. When the British decided to leave this country, they transferred power to us; but at the same time, they also declared that all the treaties and engagements they had with the Princes had lapsed. The paramountcy which they had so long exercised and by which they could keep the Princes in order also lapsed. The Indian Government was them faced with the problem of tackling these States which had different traditions of rule, some of them having some form of popular representation in Assemblies and some having no semblance of anything like that, and governing completely autocratically.

As a result of the declaration that the treaties with the Princes and Paramountcy had lapsed, it became open to any Prince or any combination of Princes to assume independence and even to enter into negotiations with any foreign power and thus become islands of independent territory within the country. There were undoubtedly geographical and other compulsions which made it physically impossible for most of them to go against the Government of India but constitutionally it had become possible. The Constituent Assembly, therefore, had at the very beginning of its labours, to enter into negotiations with them to bring their representatives into the Assembly so that a Constitution might be framed in consultation with them. The first efforts were successful and some of them did join this Assembly at an early stage but others hesitated. It is not necessary to pry into the secrets of what was happening in those days behind the scenes. It will be sufficient to state that by August 1947 when the Indian Independence Act came into force, almost all of them with two notable exceptions, Kashmir in the north and Hyderabad in the South, had acceded to India. Kashmir soon after followed the example of others and acceded. There were standstill agreements with all of them including Hyderabad which continued the status quo. As time passed, it became apparent that it was not possible at any rate for the smaller States to maintain their separate independence existence and then a process of integration with India started. In course of time not only have all the smaller States coalesced and become integrated with some province or other of India but some of the larger ones also have joined. Many of the States have formed Unions of their own and such Unions have become part of the Indian Union. It must be said to the credit of the Princes and the people of the States no less than to the credit of the States Ministry under the wise and far-sighted guidance of Sardar Vallabhbhai Patel that by the time we have been able to pass this Constitution, the States are now more or less in the same position as the Provinces and it has become possible to describe all of them including the Indian States and the Provinces as States in the Constitution. The announcement which has been made just now by Sardar Vallabhbhai Patel makes the position very clear, and now there is no difference between the States, as understood before and the provinces in the New Constitution.

It has undoubtedly taken us three years to complete this work, but when we consider the work that has been accomplished and the number of days that we have spent in framing this Constitution, the details of which were given by the Honourable Dr. B.R. Ambedkar, yesterday, we have no reason to be sorry for the time spent.

It has enabled the apparently intractable problem of the States and the communal problem to be solved. What had proved insoluble at the Round Table Conference and had resulted in the division of the country has been solved with the consent of all parties concerned, and again under the wise guidance of Honourable Sardar Vallabhbhai Patel.

At first we were able to get rid of separate electorates which had poisoned our political life for so many years, but reservation of seats for the communities which enjoyed separate electorates before had to be conceded, although on the basis of their population and not as had been done in the Act of 1919 and the Act of 1935 of giving additional representation on account of the so-called historical and other superiority claimed by some of the communities. It has become possible only because the Constitution was not passed earlier that even reservation of seats has been given up by the communities concerned and so our Constitution does not provide for reservation of seats on communal basis, but for reservation only in favour of two classes of people in our population, namely, the depressed classes who are Hindus and the tribal people, on account of their backwardness in education and in other respects. I, therefore, see no reason to be apologetic about the delay.

The cost too which the Assembly has had to incur during its three year's existence is not too high when you take into consideration the factors going to constitute it. I understand that the expenses up to the 22nd of November come to ₹63,96,729/-.

The method which the Constituent Assembly adopted in connection with the Constitution was first to lay down its 'terms of reference' as it were in the form of an Objective Resolution which was moved by Pandit Jawaharlal Nehru in as inspiring speech and which constitutes now the Preamble to our Constitution. It then proceeded to appoint a number of committees to deal with different aspects of the Constitutional problem. Dr. Ambedkar mentioned the names of these Committees. Several of these had as their Chairman either Pandit Jawaharlal Nehru or Sardar Patel to whom thus goes the credit for the fundamentals of our Constitution. I have only to add that they all worked in a business-like manner and produced reports which were considered by the Assembly and their recommendations were adopted as the basis on which the draft of the Constitution had to be prepared. This was done by Mr. B.N. Rau, who brought to bear on his task a detailed knowledge of Constitutions of other countries and an extensive knowledge of the conditions of this country as well as his own administrative experience. The Assembly then appointed the Drafting Committee which worked on the original draft prepared by Mr. B.N. Rau and produced the Draft Constitution which was considered by the Assembly at great length at the second reading stage. As Dr. Ambedkar pointed out, there were not less than 7,635 amendments of which 2,473 amendments were moved. I am mentioning this only to show that it was not only the Members of the Drafting Committee who were giving their close attention to the Constitution, but other Members were vigilant and scrutinizing the Draft in all its details. No wonder, that we had to consider not only each article in the Draft, but, practically, every sentence and, sometimes, every word in every article. It may interest honourable members to know that the public were taking great interest in its proceedings and I have discovered that no less than 53,000 visitors were admitted to the Visitors gallery during the period when the Constitution has been under consideration. In the result, the Draft Constitution has increased in size, and by the time it has been passed, it has come to have 395 articles and 8 schedules, instead of the 243 articles and 13 schedules of the original Draft of Mr. B.N. Rau. I do not attach much importance to the complaint which is sometimes made that it has become too bulky. If the provisions have been well thought out, the bulk need not disturb the equanimity of our mind.

We have now to consider the salient features of the Constitution. The first question which arises and which has been mooted is as to the category to which this Constitution belongs. Personally, I do not attach any importance to the label which may be attached to it – whether you call it Federal Constitution or Unitary Constitution or by any other name. It makes no difference so long as the Constitution serves our purpose. We are not bound to have a Constitution which completely and fully falls in line with known categories of Constitutions in the world. We have to take certain facts of history in our own country and the Constitution has not to an inconsiderable extent been influenced by such realities as facts of history.

You are all aware that until the Round Table Conference of 1930, India was completely a Unitary Government, and the provinces derived whatever power they possessed from the Government of India. It was there for the first time that the question of Federation in a practical form arose which would include not only the provinces but also the many States that were in existence. The Constitution of 1935 provided for a Federation in which both the provinces of India and the States were asked to join. But the federal part of it could not be brought into operation, because terms on which the Princes could agree to join it could not be settled in spite of prolonged negotiation. And, when the war broke out, that part of the Constitution had practically to be abrogated.

In the present Constitution, it has been possible not only to bring in practically all the States which fell within our geographical limits, but to integrate the largest majority of them in India, and the Constitution as it stands practically makes no difference so far as the administration and the distribution of powers among the various organs of the State are concerned between what were the Provinces and what were Indian States before. They are all now more or less on the same footing and, as time passes, whatever little distinction still exists is bound to disappear. Therefore, so far as labelling is concerned, we need not be troubled by it.

Well, the first and the most obvious fact which will attract any observer is the fact that we are going to have a Republic. India knew republics in the past olden days, but that was 2,000 years ago or more and those republics were small republics. We never had anything like the Republic which we are going to have now, although there were empires in those days as well as during the Mughal period which covered very large parts of the country. The President of the Republic will be an elected President. We never have had an elected Head of the State which covered such a large area of India. And it is for the first time that it becomes open to the humblest and the lowliest citizens of the country to deserve and become the President or the Head of this big State which counts among the biggest States of the world today. This is not a small matter. But, because we have an elected President, some of the problems which are of a very difficult nature have arisen. We have provided for the election of the President. We have provided for an elected legislature which is going to have supreme authority. In America, the legislature and the President are both elected and, they both have more or less equal powers – each in its or his own sphere, the President in the executive sphere and the legislature in the legislative sphere.

We considered whether we should adopt the American model or the British model where we have a hereditary king who is the fountain of all honour and power, but who does not actually enjoy any power. All the power rests in the Legislature to which the Ministers are responsible. We have had to reconcile the position of an elected President with an elected Legislature and, in doing so, we have adopted more or less the position of the British Monarch for the President. This may or may not be satisfactory. Some people think too much power has been given to the President, others think that the President, being an elected President, should have even more powers than are given to him.

If you look at it from the point of view of the electorate which elects the Parliament and which elects the President, you will find that practically the entire adult population of the country joins in electing this Parliament and it is not only the Members of the Parliament of India but also the Members of the Legislative Assemblies of the States who join in electing the President. It, thus, comes about that, while the Parliament and Legislative Assemblies are elected by the adult population of the country as a whole, the President is elected by representatives who represent the entire population twice over, once as representatives of the States and again as their representatives in the Central Parliament of the country. But although the President is elected by the same electorate as the Central and State Legislatures, it is as well that his position is that of a Constitutional President.

Then we come to the Ministers. They are of course responsible to the Legislature and tender advice to the President who is bound to act according to that advice. Although there are no specific provisions, so far as I know, in the Constitution itself making it binding on the President to accept the advice of his Ministers, it is hoped that the convention under which in England the King acts always on the advice of his Ministers will be established in this country also and, the president, not so much on account of the written word in the Constitution, but as the result of this very healthy convention, will become a Constitutional President in all matters.

The Central Legislature consists of two Houses known as the House of People and the Council of States which both together constitute the Parliament of India. In the Provinces, or States as they are now called, we shall have a Legislative Assembly in all of them except those which are mentioned in Parts C and D of Schedule I, but every one of them will not have a Second Chamber. Some of the provinces, whose representatives felt that a Second Chamber is required for them, have been provided with a Second Chamber. But there is a provision in the Constitution that if a province does not want such a Second Chamber to continue or if a province which has not got one wants to establish one, the wish has to be expressed through the Legislature by a majority of two-thirds of the Members voting and by a majority of the total number of Members in the Legislative Assembly. So, even while providing some of the States with Second Chambers, we have provided also for their easy removal or for their easy establishment by making this kind of amendment of the Constitution not a Constitutional Amendment, but a matter of ordinary parliamentary legislation.

We have provided for adult suffrage by which the legislative assemblies in the provinces and the House of the People in the Centre will be elected. It is a very big step that we have taken. It is big not only because our present electorate is a very much smaller electorate and based very largely on property qualification, but it is also big because it involves tremendous numbers. Our population now is something like 320 millions if not more and we have found from experience gained during the enrolment of voters that has been going on in the provinces that 50 percent roughly representing the adult population. And on that basis we shall have not less than 160 million voters on our rolls. The work of organising election by such vast numbers is of tremendous magnitude and there is no other country where election on such a large scale has ever yet been held.

I will just mention to you some facts in this connection. The legislative assemblies in the provinces, it is roughly calculated, will have more than 3,800 members who will have to be elected in as many constituencies or perhaps a few less. Then there will be something like 500 members for the House of the People and about 220 Members for the Council of States. We shall thus have to provide for the election of more than 4,500 members and the country will have to be divided into something like 4,000 constituencies or so. I was the other day, as a matter of amusement, calculating what our electoral roll will look like. If you print 40 names on a page of foolscap size, we shall require something like 20 lakhs of sheets of foolscap size to print all the names of the voters, and if you combine the whole thing in one volume, the thickness of the volume will be something like 200 yards. That alone gives us some idea of the vastness of the task and the work involved in finalising the rolls, delimiting Constituencies, fixing polling stations and making other arrangements which will have to be done between now and the winter of 1950-51 when it is hoped the elections may be held.

Some people have doubted the wisdom of adult franchise. Personally, although I look upon it as an experiment the result of which no one will be able to forecast today, I am not dismayed by it. I am a man of the village and although I have had to live in cities for a pretty long time, on account of my work, my roots are still there. I, therefore, know the village people who will constitute the bulk of this vast electorate. In my opinion, our people possess intelligence and commonsense. They also have a culture which the sophisticated people of today many not appreciate, but which is solid. They are not literate and do not possess the mechanical skill of reading and writing. But, I have no doubt in my mind that they are able to take measure of their own interest and also of the interests of the country at large if things are explained to them. In fact, in some respects, I consider them to be even more intelligent than many a worker in a factory, who loses his individuality and becomes more or less a part of the machine which he has to work. I have, therefore, no doubt in my mind that if things are explained to them, they will not only be able to pick up the technique of election, but will be able to cast their votes in an intelligent manner and I have, therefore, no misgivings about the future, on their account. I cannot say the same thing about the other people who may try to influence them by slogans and by placing before them beautiful pictures of impracticable programmes. Nevertheless, I think their sturdy commonsense will enable them to see things in the right perspective. We can, therefore, reasonably hope that we shall have legislatures composed of members who shall have their feet on the ground and who will take a realistic view of things.

Although provision has been made for a second chamber in the Parliament and for second chambers in some of the States, it is the popular House which is supreme. In all financial and money matters, the supremacy of the popular House is laid down in so many words. But even in regard to other matters where the Upper Chamber may be said to have equal powers for initiating and passing laws, the supremacy of the popular House is assured. So far as Parliament is concerned, if a difference arises between the two Chambers, a joint session may be held, but the Constitution provides that the number of Members of the Council of States shall not be more than 50 percent of the Members of the House of the People. Therefore, even in the case of a joint session, the supremacy of the House of the People is maintained, unless the majority in that very House is a small one which will be just a case in which its supremacy should not prevail. In the case of provincial legislatures, the decision of the Lower House, prevails if it is taken a second time. The Upper Chamber therefore can only delay the passage of Bills for a time, but cannot prevent it. The President or the Governor, as the case may be, will have to give his assent to any legislation, but that will be only on the advice of his Ministry which is responsible ultimately to the popular House. Thus, it is the will of the people as expressed by their representatives in the popular Chamber that will finally determine all matters. The second Chamber and the President or the Governor can only direct reconsideration and can only cause some delay, but if the popular Chamber is determined, it will have its way under the Constitution. The Government therefore of the country as a whole, both in the Centre and in the Provinces, will rest on the will of the people which will be expressed from day to day through their representatives in the legislatures and, occasionally directly by them at the time of the general elections.

We have provided in the Constitution for a judiciary which will be independent. It is difficult to suggest anything more to make the Supreme Court and the High Courts independent of the influence of the Executive. There is an attempt made in the Constitution to make even the lower judiciary independent of any outside or extraneous influence. One of our articles makes it easy for the State Governments to introduce separation of Executive from judicial functions and placing the magistracy which deals with criminal cases on similar footing as Civil Courts. I can only express the hope that this long overdue reform will soon be introduced in the States.

Our Constitution has devised certain independent agencies to deal with particular matters. Thus, it has provided for Public Service Commission both for the Union and for the States and placed such Commission on an independent footing so that they may discharge their duties without being influenced by the Executive. One of the things against which we have to guard is that there should be no room as far as it is humanly possible for jobbery, nepotism and favouritism. I think the provisions which we have introduced into our Constitution will be very helpful in this direction.

Another independent authority is the Comptroller and Auditor-General who will watch our finances and see to it that no part of the revenues of India or of any of the States is used for purposes and on items without due authority and whose duty it will be otherwise to keep our accounts in order. When we consider that our Governments will have to deal with hundreds of crores, it becomes clear how important and vital this Department will be. We have provided another important authority, i.e., the Election Commissioner whose function will be to conduct and supervise the elections to the Legislatures and to take all other necessary action and connection with them. One of the dangers which we have to face arises out of any corruption which parties, candidates or the Government in power may practise. We have had no experience of democratic elections for a long time except during the last few years and now that we have got real power, the danger of corruption is not only imaginary. It is, therefore, as well that our Constitution guards against this danger and makes provision for an honest and straightforward election by the voters. In the case of the Legislature, the High Courts, the Public Services Commission, the Comptroller and Auditor-General and the Election Commissioner, the Staff which will assist them in their work has also been placed under their control and in most of these cases their appointment, promotion and discipline vest in the particular institution to which they belong thus giving additional safeguards about their independence.

The Constitution has given in two Schedules, namely Schedules V and VI, special provisions for administration and control of Scheduled Areas and Scheduled Tribes. In the case of the Tribes and Tribal Areas in States other than Assam, the Tribes will be able to influence the administration through the Tribes Advisory Council. In the case of the Tribes and Tribal Areas in Assam, they are given larger powers through their district Councils and Autonomous Regional Councils. There is, further provision for a Minister in the State Ministries to be in charge of the welfare of the Tribes and the Scheduled Castes and a Commission will also report about the way in which the areas are administered. It was necessary to make this provision on account of the backwardness of the Tribes which require protection and also because their own way of solving their own problems and carrying on their Tribal life. These provisions have given them considerable satisfaction as the provision for the welfare and protection of the Scheduled Castes has given satisfaction to them.

The Constitution has gone into great details regarding the distribution of power and functions between the Union and the States in all aspects of their administrative and other activities. It has been said by some that the powers given to the Centre are too many and too extensive and the States have been deprived of power which should really belong to them in their own fields. I do not wish to pass any judgement on this criticism and can only say that we cannot be too cautious about our future, particularly when we remember the history of this country extending over many centuries. But, such powers as have been given to the Centre to act within the sphere of the States relate only to emergencies, whether political or financial and economic, and I do not anticipate that there will be any tendency on the part of the Centre to grab more power than is necessary for good administration of the country as a whole. In any case the Central Legislature consists of representatives from the States and unless they are convinced of their over-riding necessity, they are not likely to consent to the use of any such powers by the Central executive as against the States whose people they represent. I do not attach much importance to the complaint that residuary powers have been vested in the Union. Powers have been very meticulously and elaborately defined and demarcated in the three lists of Schedule Seven, and the residue whatever it may be, is not likely to cover any large field, and, therefore, the vesting of such residuary powers does not mean any very serious derogation in fact from the power which ought to belong to the States.

One of the problems which the Constituent Assembly took considerable time in solving relates to the language for official purposes of the country. There is a natural desire that the we should have our own language, and in spite of the difficulties on account of the multiplicity of languages prevalent in the country, we have been able to adopt Hindi which is the language that is understood by the largest number of people in the country as our official language. I look upon this as a decision of very great importance when we consider that in a small country like Switzerland, they have no less than three official languages and in South Africa two official languages. It shows a spirit of accommodation and a determination to organise the country as one nation that those whose language is not Hindi have voluntarily accepted it as the official language. (Cheers). There is no question of imposition now. English during the period of British rule, Persian during the period of the Muslim Empire were Court and official languages. Although people have studies them and have acquired proficiency in them, nobody can claim that they were voluntarily adopted by the people of the country at large. Now, for the first time in our history, we have accepted one language which will be the language to be used all over the country for all official purposes, and let me hope that it will develop into a national language in which all will feel equal pride while each area will be not only free, but also encouraged to develop its own peculiar language in which its culture and its traditions are enshrined. The use of English during the period of transition was considered inevitable for practical reasons and no one need be despondent over this decision, which has been dictated purely by practical considerations. It is the duty of the country as a whole now and especially of those whose language is Hindi to so shape and develop it as to make it the language in which the composite culture of India can find its expression adequately and nobly.

Another important feature of our Constitution is that it enables amendments to be made without much difficulty. Even the constitutional amendments are not as difficult as in the case of some other countries, but many of the provisions in the Constitution are capable of being amended by the Parliament by ordinary acts and do not require the procedure laid down for constitutional amendments to be followed. There was a provision at one time which proposed that amendments should be made easy for the first five years after the Constitution comes into force, but such a provision has become unnecessary on account of the numerous exceptions which have been made in the Constitution itself for amendments without the procedure laid down for constitutional amendments. On the whole, therefore, we have been able to draft a Constitution which I trust will serve the country well.

There is a special provision in our Directive Principles to which I attach great importance. We have not provided for the good of our people only but have laid down in our directive principles that our State shall endeavour to promote material peace and security, maintain just and honourable relations between nations, foster respects for international law and treaty obligations and encourage settlement of international disputes by arbitration. In a world torn with conflicts, in a world which even after the devastation of two world wars is still depending on armaments to establish peace and goodwill, we are destined to play a great part, if we prove true to the teachings of the Father of the Nation and give effect to this directive principle in our Constitution. Would to God that he would give us the wisdom and the strength to pursuance this path in spite of the difficulties which beset us and the atmosphere which may well choke us. Let us have faith in ourselves and in the teachings of the Master whose portrait hangs over my head and we shall fulfil the hopes and prove true to the best interests of not only our country but of the world at large.

I do not propose to deal with the criticism which relate mostly to the articles in the part dealing with Fundamental Rights by which absolute rights are curtailed and the articles dealing with Emergency Powers. Other members have dealt with these objections at great length. All that I need state at this stage is that the present conditions of the country and tendencies which are apparent have necessitated these provisions which are also based on the experience of other countries which have had to enforce them through judicial decisions, even when they were not provided for in the Constitution.

There are only two regrets which I must share with the honourable members. I would have liked to have some qualifications laid down for members of the Legislatures. It is anomalous that we should insist upon high qualifications for those who administer or help in administering the law but none for those who made it except that they are elected. A law giver requires intellectual equipment but, even more than that capacity to take a balanced view of things to act independently and above all to be true to those fundamental things of life – in one word – to have character. It is not possible to devise any yardstick for measuring the moral qualities of a man and so long as that is not possible, our Constitution will remain defective. The other regret is that we have not been able to draw up our first Constitution of a free Bharat in an Indian language. The difficulties in both cases were practical and proved insurmountable. But, that does not make the regret any the less poignant.

We have prepared a democratic Constitution. But successful working of democratic institutions requires in those who have to work them willingness to respect the view points of others, capacity for compromise and accommodation. Many things which cannot be written in a Constitution are done by conventions. Let me hope that we shall show those capacities and develop those conventions. The way in which we have been able to draw this Constitution without taking recourse to voting and to divisions in Lobbies strengthens that hope.

Whatever the Constitution may or may not provide, the welfare of the country will depend upon the way in which the country is administered. That will depend upon the men who administer it. It is a trite saying that a country can have only the Government it deserves. Our Constitution has provision in it which appear to some to be objectionable from one point or another. We must admit that the defects are inherent in the situation in the country and the people at large. If the people who are elected are capable and men of character and integrity, they would be able to make the best even of a defective Constitution. If they are lacking in these, the Constitution cannot help the country. After all, a Constitution like a machine is a lifeless thing. It acquires life because of the men who control it and operate it, and India needs today nothing more than a set of honest men who will have the interest of the country before them. There is a fissiparous tendency arising out of various elements in our life. We have communal differences, caste differences, language differences, provincial differences and so forth. It requires men of strong character, men of vision, men who will not sacrifice the interests of the country at large for the sake of smaller groups and areas and who will rise over the prejudices which are born of these differences. We can only hope that the country will throw up such men in abundance. I can say this from the experience of the struggle that we have had during the period of the freedom movement that new occasions throw up new men, not once but almost on every occasion when all leading men in the Congress were clapped into prison suddenly without having the time to leave instructions to others and even to make plans for carrying on their campaigns, people arose from amongst the masses who were able to continue and conduct the campaigns with intelligence, with initiative, with capacity for organisation which nobody suspected they possessed.

I have no doubt that when the country needs men of character, they will be coming up and the masses will throw them up. Let not those who have served in the past therefore rest on their oars, saying that they have done their part and now has come the time for them to enjoy the fruits of their labours. No such time comes to anyone who is really earnest about his work. In India today, I feel that the work that confronts us is even more difficult than the work which we had when we were engaged in the struggle. We did not have then any conflicting claims to reconcile, no loaves and fishes to distribute, no powers to share. We have all these now, and the temptations are really great. Would to God that we shall have the wisdom and the strength to rise above them, and to serve the country which we have succeeded in liberating.

Mahatma Gandhi laid stress on the purity of the methods which had to be pursued for attaining our ends. Let us not forget that this teaching has eternal value and was not intended only for the period of stress and struggle, but has as much authority and value today as it ever had before. We have a tendency to blame others for everything that goes wrong and not to introspect and try to see if we have any share in it or not. It is very much easier to scan one's own actions and motives if one is inclined to do so than to appraise correctly the actions and motives of others. I shall only hope that all those whose good fortune it may be to work this Constitution in future will remember that it was a unique victory which we achieved by the unique method taught to us by the Father of the Nation, and it is up to us to preserve and protect the independence that we have won and to make it really bear fruit for the man in the street. Let us launch on this new enterprise of running our Independent Republic with confidence, with truth and non-violence and above all with heart within and God over head.

Before I close, I must express my thanks to all the Members of this august Assembly from whom I have received not only courtesy but, if I may say so, also their respect and affection. Sitting in the Chair and watching the proceedings from day to day. I have realised as nobody else could have, with what zeal and devotion the members of the Drafting Committee and especially its Chairman, Dr. Ambedkar in spite of his indifferent health, have worked. (Cheers). We could never make a decision which was or could be ever so right as when we put him on the Drafting Committee and made him its Chairman. He has not only justified his selection but has added luster to the work which he has done. In this connection, it would be invidious to make any distinction as among the other members of the Committee. I know they have all worked with the same zeal and devotion as its Chairman, and they deserve the thanks of the country.

I must convey, if you will permit me, my own thanks as well as the thanks of the house to our Constitutional Adviser, Shri B.N. Rau, who worked honorarily all the time that he was here, assisting the Assembly not only with his knowledge and erudition but also enabled the other Members to perform their duties with thoroughness and intelligence by supplying them with the material on which they could work. In this he was assisted by his band and research workers and other members of the staff who worked with zeal and devotion. Tribute has been paid justly to Shri S.N. Mukerjee who has proved of such invaluable help to the Drafting Committee.

Coming to the staff of the Secretariat of the Constituent Assembly I must first mention and thank the Secretary, Mr. H.V.R. Yengar, who organised the Secretariat as an efficient working body. Although latterly when the work began to proceed with more or less clock-work regularity, it was possible for us to relieve him of part of his duties to take up other work, but he has never lost touch with our Secretariat or with the work of the Constituent Assembly.

The members of the staff have worked with efficiency and with devotion under our Deputy Secretary, Shri Jugal Kishore Khanna. It is not always possible to see their work which is done removed from the gaze of the Members of this Assembly, but I am sure the tribute which Member after Members has paid to their efficiency and devotion to work is thoroughly deserved. Our Reports have done their work in a way which will give credit to them and which has helped in the preservation of a record of the proceedings of the Assembly which have been long and taxing. I must mention the translators as also the Translation Committee under the Chairmanship of Honourable Shri G.S. Gupta who have had a hard job in finding Hindi equivalents for English terms used in the Constitution. They are just now engaged in helping a Committee of Linguistic Experts in evolving a vocabulary which will be acceptable to all other languages as equivalents to English words used in the Constitution and in law. The Watch and Ward officers, and the Police and last though not least the Marshall have all performed their duties to our satisfaction. (Cheers). I should not forget the peons and even the humbler people. They have all done their best. It is necessary for me to say all this because with the completion of the work of Constitution-framing, most of them who have been working on a temporary basis, will be out of employment unless they could be absorbed in other Departments and Ministries. I do hope that it will be possible to absorb them (hear, hear) as they have considerable experience and are willing and efficient set of workers. All deserve my thanks as I have received courtesy, co-operation and loyal service from all (Prolonged Cheers).

Source: *http://164.100.47.194/Loksabha/Debates/Result_Nw_15.aspx?dbsl=505*

□□□